THE LONG GRAVEL ROAD

A Country Boy's Odyssey

A Clay County Illinois Story

Darold Herdes

Carlsbad, California

2022

Copyright 2023

All rights are reserved. No part of this book may be used or reproduced in any manner without written permission except in the case of brief quotes used in reviews or articles.

All statements of fact, opinion, or analysis expressed are those of the author and do reflect the official positions or views of the U.S. Government. Nothing in the contents should be construed as asserting or implying U.S. Government as asserting or implying authentication of information or endorsement of the author's views. This material has been reviewed by the CIA to prevent the disclosure of classified information.

ISBN: 979-8-9870163-0-5

Library of Congress: 2022918877

Edited by Self-Publishing Services
selfpublishingservices@gmail.com

For

Avery

Sydney

Finley

Piper

Esme

Stella

Maple

TABLE OF CONTENTS

Introduction *1*

PART ONE
THE FIRST THIRTY YEARS: 1940–1970 3

Chapter 1
Early Years *7*

Chapter 2
Neighborhood *15*

Chapter 3
School Days: First to Eighth Grades *31*

Chapter 4
Family *51*

Chapter 5
The Dredge Ditch *63*

Chapter 6
Lathrop Church *79*

Chapter 7
Mom and Dad *85*

Chapter 8
High School Years *93*

Chapter 9
College Days *109*

Chapter 10
Teaching High School *147*

Chapter 11
Graduate School *163*

Chapter 12
Alaska...175

Chapter 13
Gap Year..185

Chapter 14
Marjorie Lynn Burke..189

Chapter 15
Family Events..197

PART TWO
THE NEXT THIRTY YEARS:1970–2000
PEOPLE AND PLACES 201

Chapter 16
Chicago..203

Chapter 17
Indianapolis..221

Chapter 18
Minneapolis..237

Chapter 19
Washington to Bonn...255

Chapter 20
Washington to Munich...269

Chapter 21
Dallas to Colorado Springs..285

PART THREE
1967–1997
MY WINDOW ON WORLD EVENTS **295**

Chapter 22
Perspective on the 1960s and 1970s 297

Chapter 23
Training 305

Chapter 24
Domestic Deployments 315

Chapter 25
The 1980s 329

Chapter 26
Bonn, Germany 333

Chapter 27
Headquarters 343

Chapter 28
In Europe Again 347

Chapter 29
The Decade of the 1990s 351

Chapter 30
Dallas 355

Chapter 31
Colorado Springs 361

PART FOUR
2000–202?
THE GOLDEN YEARS 375

   Chapter 32
   Perspective on the Decades from 2000 to 2020 377

   Chapter 33
   Family 381

   Chapter 34
   Neighborhoods 395

   Chapter 35
   Reunions and Birthdays 403

   Chapter 36
   Activities 409

   Chapter 37
   Sports 417

   Chapter 38
   Travel 429

   Chapter 39
   Omega 439

Epilogue 444

Introduction

Most of my life occurred during the last half of the twentieth century, a period my grandchildren will learn about as history. I wrote this story to give them a more personalized account of that time as I experienced it. I grew up on a small Midwestern farm in the aftermath of the Great Depression and World War II, a time and place much different in so many ways when compared to happenings in their lives. Most striking is how technology and the expansion of knowledge have profoundly impacted how they are developing their own experiences. However, relationships with family and friends remain fundamentally the most important dimension to their experiences, as they did mine. Since I was an American history teacher early in my career, the story will have references to the broader context of events that took place over these past decades.

The approach I have taken with this narrative is to divide the story into four segments. Part One deals with the first thirty years of my life and describes in some detail memories of my childhood and early adult years. Those experiences are quite in contrast to what I see taking place in my grandchildren's lives. Part Two recounts my recollections of the people, places, and events that occurred through the progression of my life from ages thirty to sixty. These memories are largely shaped by my work, which required living in eight different cities. Uprooting and going from one place to another caused a lot of disruption. The downside for me was the pain my family sometimes experienced. The upside was the many opportunities for meeting new people and learning new things. It was a time of enrichment and proved the adage that learning is a lifetime undertaking.

My career in the Central Intelligence Agency is considered in Part Three. In Part Four, I focus on life after age sixty and my time in retirement. Retirement is sometimes referred to as the golden years, and that is an apt description for at least the first twenty-plus years I have thus far experienced. The gold part is having a covey of seven grandchildren.

As this story reveals, the thing about the gravel road: it goes both ways.

Part One

THE FIRST THIRTY YEARS: 1940–1970

World War II was the central event impacting the United States and the world for the first half of the 1940s. Threatened by totalitarian regimes in Germany, Italy, and Japan, the US joined the embattled Western democracies to defeat the Axis alliance after Japan bombed the US Navy base at Pearl Harbor, Hawaii, on December 7, 1941. Almost four years of massive military engagements followed before the US-led coalition defeated the German and Japanese forces in mid-1945.

Over the next five years, the US transitioned from a wartime economy to a focus on pent-up demand for consumer and capital goods. A positive development on the international front was the formation of the United Nations in 1946. Unfortunately, the Cold War emerging between the Union of Soviet Socialist Republics (USSR) and the United States soon overshadowed the effort for international cooperation. It led to a decades-long confrontation that divided much of the world between East and West. President Harry Truman presided over these issues until America's wartime general Dwight Eisenhower was elected president in 1952.

The 1950s through the 1960s was a time of extraordinary economic growth and prosperity aided by technological advances and leadership by the Greatest Generation. College education grew in importance, advances were made in civil rights for African Americans, and demands grew for equality for women. President John F. Kennedy was elected to replace Eisenhower in 1960, but his positive start ended tragically with his assassination in 1963. His vice president, Lyndon Johnson, was elected to the presidency in 1964.

Meanwhile, the Cold War remained the dominant issue in foreign relations. In addition to the arms race, and especially the growing arsenals of nuclear weapons, the Soviets launched Sputnik, the world's first satellite, in the mid-1950s. This raised concerns that the US was behind in advanced technologies, so major funding was allocated for the US space program and the development of more sophisticated intercontinental ballistic missiles. The conflict with the USSR reached a crisis point in the early 1960s when the Soviets attempted to place nuclear weapons in Cuba and built the Berlin Wall.

Johnson's achievements on the domestic front with the Great Society program and the Civil Rights Act were overshadowed by the war in Vietnam, also a by-product of the Cold War. Richard Nixon was elected president in 1968 on the heels of the assassinations of Civil Rights leader Martin Luther King and presidential candidate Robert Kennedy. The end of the 1960s was a tumultuous time in the US when widespread demonstrations, riots, and demands for social change challenged societal norms and the political order. My twin brother and I were born in 1940 at the very start of this dramatic period in American history.

Chapter 1

EARLY YEARS

The car lurched sideways and slid into the ditch. Dad, who rarely expressed any emotion, let out a line of cuss words. Mom remained silent. My twin brother, Garold, and I sat in the back seat of the car and looked at each other as the rain poured down. Dad put the car into gear, alternating between low and reverse, trying to rock the car out of the ditch, but soon it was up to its axles in the mud. Dad left us sitting in the car while he walked the half mile back to our house. He harnessed his

Dad with Prince and Charlie

My war ration book

team of farm horses and brought a log chain back to attach to the car. He hitched the horses to the car while Mom got behind the wheel. The powerful horses easily pulled us back onto the road. Dad got thoroughly soaked, leading his team of matched sorrel shires, Prince and Charlie, back to the house.

By this time, any thought of continuing our trip to Clay City to do the weekly trading had vanished. Everyone was frustrated for different reasons. Dad had not been too happy about going in the first place. Mom had looked forward to getting out of the house and bringing home needed supplies. Garold and I were always up for going to town, where we might get a treat. Our favorites were candy bars like Snickers, Milky Way, PayDay, or a Baby Ruth, which cost a nickel.

The year was 1945, and World War II was coming to an end, but the economy was still under wartime restrictions. Many items were rationed, like coffee, gasoline, tires, and sugar. Sugar came primarily from the Philippines, and the Japanese had cut off imports after their invasion. Ration

Wedding photo of Mom and Dad

stamps and cash were required for the purchase of these restricted products. Individuals, as well as families, were given ration books. My brother and I both were issued our own ration books. When making the trip to town, Mom could use our stamps as well as her own and Dad's. Shopping was called trading because many farm families traded money they had received from selling eggs and cream for supplies. Some general stores would have scales set up at a rear entrance to receive the farm products, and the credit was then used to pay for supplies at the front of the store.

Mom and Dad were married in 1933. After almost giving up on having kids, Mom finally got pregnant. We were born on June 5, 1940. She didn't know she would have twins until after Garold came out and the

Garold and Darold at six months old

doctor told her she wasn't finished yet. Minutes later, I appeared. I was somewhat blue and was described as "puny" by Mom's friend who was helping with the delivery. That could explain many things.

Dr. Johnny Shore drove out to the farm from Sailor Springs for the delivery. A neighbor drove to town to awaken him since we didn't have a telephone. Mom's friend Vida Frutiger was there to help, as was Blanche Koehler, the neighborhood midwife. Vida's husband, Everett, stayed in the living room with Dad. Vida and Everett were important people in our lives then and throughout our growing up years.

Having twins in those days, before fertility drugs, was quite unusual. Friends and neighbors came from all around to check us out. Mom kept a list of the people who came to visit, and it had over one hundred people on it. She also made a list of rhyming names for twins, which I saw later and wondered how we had ended up with what we got. I figured we had unusual names because Mom and Dad were dumbfounded to find

1943

they had two babies. My other theory is that their names, Denby and Floy, were not exactly common, either. But we were it, and Mom and Dad had no more kids.

Garold and I are fraternal twins instead of identical, and we were different in appearance. As we grew up, I was generally taller and skinnier. Garold was sturdier and more muscular. But Mom made our clothes and dressed us alike. One of my earliest memories is being awake in the small bed with Garold when we were probably about three years old. We still slept in Mom and Dad's bedroom and were put to bed by seven p.m. with the door to the adjoining living room was left ajar. I could hear the voices of people visiting and cried to get up. That got me nowhere.

1945

Sometime after that, we were moved to the house's second bedroom, where we had a double bed. Above the bed in a large, old, gilded frame was a calendar picture of two horses, one black and the other white. Both horses were standing on their hind legs, their eyes wide in fright, with a lightning bolt glaring behind them. My brother and I never did like that picture. After Mom died, Garold took the picture out of the frame and found what became a family treasure. There were two identical charcoal drawings of Mom's grandparents on her mom's side, Richard and Catherine Bryant. They were married after Richard came home from the Civil War. The drawings were made from the couple's wedding picture. Photographic paper in that day tended to disintegrate, so enterprising artists

Charcoal of my maternal great-grandparents, Richard and Catherine Bryant

during the 1890s traveled the countryside and preserved family likenesses with drawings of the old photographs.

Chapter 2

NEIGHBORHOOD

Clay City, Illinois, was a small farming town of around twelve hundred people located in the southeastern part of the state. Clay City was the primary shopping town for people living in Pixley and Clay City Townships on Clay County's east side. The town's high school drew students from this area as well.

US Route 50, a coast-to-coast highway, came through Clay City and formed part of Main Street. The interstate traffic created some local business, and combined with shopping by the farming community, kept the town bustling. In the early 1950s, however, US Route 50 was widened and rebuilt to bypass many towns, including Clay City. The reduced traffic adversely impacted some of the town's businesses, although

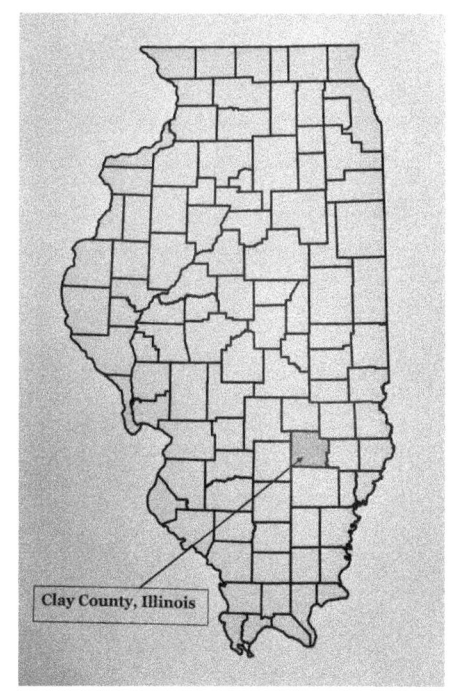

Clay County, Illinois

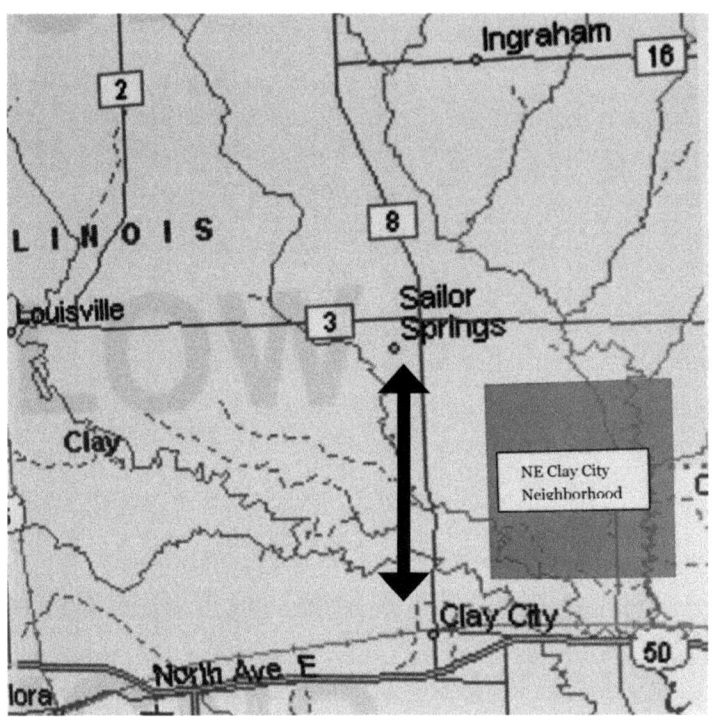

Clay City, located in Clay County
on the Highway 50 bypass

the town would continue to prosper for another decade because of the county's oil boom.

Our neighborhood in Clay County was located northeast of Clay City and southeast of Sailor Springs. The highway going north from Clay City to Sailor Springs, a distance of about five miles, formed the western boundary of our neighborhood. Only one lane of the road was paved. Going north, the left lane was made of concrete and was called the slab. The right side was gravel. To avoid the gravel and potholes on the right side, drivers going north would use the left slab until they saw a car approaching, at which time they would swerve to the right lane.

Car crossing old raised highway bridge

On the way to Sailor Springs, two roads went to the east of the slab into our farm neighborhood. We typically used the first turnoff. However, we had to use the second turnoff another mile up the road if there were heavy rains. This was necessary because the Little Muddy Creek crossed the first road shortly after the turnoff and flooded the low-lying bottom ground after heavy rains. Our farm was located a mile after crossing the bridge over Little Muddy Creek. The Little Muddy Creek is a tributary to the Little Wabash River. The Little Wabash was the main drainage basin in Clay County and ran diagonally from the northwest to the southeast. The slab that went to Sailor Springs crossed over the Little Wabash River about a mile north of Clay City.

Clay City was built on what amounted to a swamp. The land north of town up to the Little Wabash regularly flooded. Almost every spring, the river's floodwaters reached the edge of town. A half-mile long bridge was built along part of the raised highway before getting to the river. The kids on our school bus got quite familiar with it after it got so rickety that it was condemned. We had to get off the bus and walk across the bridge, where we waited for the bus. The new concrete bridge that replaced the old bridge became the perfect drag strip for coming generations.

The Home Place (house is on the right, in the trees)

Our farm was five miles away from both Clay City and Sailor Springs, but our address was RFD 1 (rural free delivery), Clay City, Illinois. Our granddad Herdes owned the farm, and Dad rented the farm from him. He paid the customary rent in the form of one-third of the crops. We were called tenant farmers, although we would have been called sharecroppers in some parts of the country.

There were approximately fifty operating farms in our area, with an average size of 150 acres. The farms were a step above subsistence farms, with some cash sales of livestock and grain crops, but a lot of the acreage was used for pasture and grain crops for feeding animals. Our farm was divided by a road running north and south such that 80 acres were on the east side of the road and 40 acres were on the west. The house and farm buildings were on the east side. The farm fields and lots around the buildings were usually fenced with woven wire topped by a couple of strands of barbed wire to deter the horses and cattle from venturing out where the grass looked greener. Fences went around the yard, the garden, the chicken yard, the barn lot, and the feedlot.

All that fencing meant that winter was repair time and time to cut out the brush along the fence rows. These jobs were almost as unpleasant as daily chores as far as I was concerned, and they took up many weekends when we were home from school.

When my brother and I were six, Dad decided we needed to be doing more chores. Although we gathered eggs from the chicken house each evening, we started feeding and watering them. In addition to the chickens, we raised cattle and hogs, plus a team of workhorses. Some farmers also raised sheep and goats. The hardest job for Garold and me was milking cows. Neither of us liked it. We could hardly get our hands around the teats, and the cows tended to get annoyed and tried to step on us. This got better as we got older, but it remained an unpleasant chore. The only fun was teaching our barn cats to sit on their back legs and drink from the streams of milk we aimed at them.

Garold and I accompanied Mom when she visited Vida to exchange help with one project or another, but we usually stayed outside to explore. Garold and I got to feed lambs in the spring, when we visited Everett and Vida's farm. On one such occasion we went out to one of Everett's barns that had an enclosed hog pen on the side. We hopped over the wood fence and into the pen to get inside the barn. This proved a big mistake, as a huge, old, 350-pound sow came out of the barn, making loud and angry grunts. She must have thought we were going to harm her little pigs as she lunged toward us at full speed. Garold was quicker than I was in getting to the fence. Running as fast as I could, with that sow's breath almost on my heels, I jumped up and caught the top board under my chest and tumbled over. We both knew it had been a close call and vowed never to tell anyone.

On another occasion, Garold and I were in bed when loud noises outside our house awakened us. We looked out our north-facing window to see our barn on fire. Neighbors were gathering, and later, the fire en-

Feeding the lambs

gine from the Clay City volunteer fire department pulled in. We rushed out to watch, but Mom very sternly ordered us back to bed despite our protests. We finally got back to sleep under the photo of the two horses rearing up on their back legs. The following day, we went outside to look, but all that was left of the barn was a heap of smoking ashes. Fortunately, Dad had heard the fire early enough to get the animals out, but some farm equipment had been destroyed. The cause of the fire was spontaneous combustion from hay that was still too green when it had been put up in the barn loft.

The fire happened in the fall of 1947. Somehow, Dad managed to get through the winter without the barn. The following summer, Grandad hired a carpenter named Paul Erwin to build a new barn. Dad, Granddad, and Dad's brother, Uncle Earl, made up the crew. Garold and I had a lot to watch, but, finally, a job came along that we could do. When it was time to put a floor above the lower level to create the loft, our job was to nail the floorboards to the crossbeams. Taskmaster Paul was patient with us, despite the fact that we bent several nails. After a few blood blisters under our fingernails, we got pretty efficient at wielding hammers.

The layout of the interior of the barn was standard for the time. It had a raised walkway down the center and a ladder going up to the loft. On one side were stalls for the horses and an enclosure in the back for pigs. On the other side were stalls for the cows and a pen for their calves. Both sides had wood mangers for feeding the animals grain and hay from the loft. Using a rope tied to the rafters, we had a great time swinging back and forth like Tarzan before dropping onto the soft hay. An extension on the side of the barn was constructed as an equipment shed.

Some years later, when the barn's exterior paint began to deteriorate, I took on the job of repainting. I was pretty good at it since, by then, I had spent a summer working for a contractor painting farm buildings and installing lightning rods. The barn's peak was forty feet high, and I still got the shakes when balancing a paint can and brushing on the paint while standing at the top end of a ladder. Painting the house was a piece of cake after tackling the barn project.

One downside to growing up on a farm was the lack of playmates. Fortunately, Garold and I had each other, but we were excited when Berlin Frank came home from the war and moved his family in with his parents, Sam and Katy, who lived just down the road from us. Berlin and

New barn at the Home Place

his wife, Mary, had three boys: Johnny, Donny, and David. Johnny, the oldest, was our age. When they lived with their grandparents during the summer, we often got together with them and our dogs. One day our male terrier, who had come to our house after being dumped along the road, decided to mate with the Franks' black cocker spaniel. Not knowing what was going on with this spectacle, we tried to separate them. It didn't keep the spaniel from having a good-sized litter a few months later.

Three other boys lived on farms not too far away, although two were quite a bit older. Carrol Lee Frutiger, whose mom and dad were Vida and Everett, was eight years older; Bill Mitchell lived on the farm adjoining ours to the north and was four years older; Jimmy Brown lived a little farther up the road and was our age. One thing the three of them had in common was that they all owned ponies. My brother and I ached to have one as well and put up quite a fuss. It was a lingering disappointment long after Dad nixed the idea.

We came closest to getting a horse to ride when one of the workhorses had a colt. He had beautiful coloring with a white circular pat-

Our colt

tern around his middle. When he was ready to break for riding, a black summer thunderstorm came through the area, and he was struck and killed by lightning. That was a crushing event and ended our hope of becoming cowboys. In those days, dead horses and cattle were picked up by a company that sent out a truck to take the bodies to a rendering plant. So our horse was made into dog food, tallow, and other products. It is a process we would now call recycling.

Farm chores were constant, and like all the farm activities, they were closely tied to the seasons. Chores dealing with the livestock had to be done every day, year-round. Take chickens, for example, which were mostly in our Mom's bailiwick. Every April, the big event was buying two hundred female chicks (or pullets) and one hundred chicks that were a random mixture. The females were raised to lay eggs, and the males from the mix made delicious fried chicken.

Since it was still too cool for baby chicks to survive, they huddled under a metal covering in the brooder house. They got water from a watering device that dripped into bowls from quart jars that were turned upside down. It was quite a trick for Garold or me to fill the jars with water and then flip them over. The feed for the chickens was a mixture of corn from our fields that we took to the feed mill in Clay City. The corn was ground into cornmeal and was then mixed with protein and vitamin supplements.

After eight weeks into the summer, the roosters got big enough to butcher. The old hens were sold when the pullets were ready to start laying eggs in the fall. We then had to catch the young chickens at night when they were sleeping and relocate them from their brooder house to the much larger hen house. One night, we forgot to shut the door on the hen house. A fox got in and killed more chickens than he could possibly eat.

Cleaning chickens for eating was a nasty undertaking. While some folks chopped the heads off the roosters with a hatchet, our method was to wring their necks. After a few swinging circles holding the chicken by his head, a quick jerk would separate the head from its body. I eventually got the hang of it, but Garold was content to stand back and watch. Once beheaded, the body would flop around, headless, on the ground for quite a few minutes before giving up. Mom would heat water in a black kettle in the chicken yard to scald the dead, headless chickens, which made pulling off their feathers easier.

The reward for all of this unpleasantness, however, was worth it. Except maybe for the Épicure in Paris, my mom's summer Sunday dinner (noon meal) was the best. We feasted on fried chicken, mashed potatoes with milk gravy, corn on the cob, garden-fresh green beans, slices of red tomato as big around as a cantaloupe, hot rolls with homemade butter and strawberry jam, and especially, a cherry or apple pie hot out of the oven.

My mom's dad (Cyrus Stanley) had a family tradition of giving each of his thirteen kids one of his registered Milking Shorthorn cows when they married. More on this story later, but the result was that we even-

Mom and I cleaning chickens

tually had our own small herd of about thirty cows. The cows provided milk for drinking and making cream, butter, and cottage cheese. Their calves were sold to the St. Louis stockyards to add to the farm's income.

We used a hand-cranked cream separator contraption to separate the cream from the milk. Garold and I took turns cranking so that the whirling metal discs in the machine separated the cream that went out a spout and into a crock. The skimmed milk went out a larger spout and into a bucket. Mom used some of the cream for making butter and baking. Most of the cream was sold at the Saturday market.

Another ongoing chore was taking care of the pigs. Leftover milk was used to supplement their feed. During the winter, the young pigs reached market weight and were sold. Dad hired a neighbor with a truck that took them to the stockyards. The primary buyers of animals at the stockyards were the Armour and Swift companies, which were the country's two largest meat processors. The sale of cream and eggs also provided a source of cash income.

Raising crops was a significant seasonal activity. After World War II, most farmers transitioned quickly to using tractors rather than horses for fieldwork. Dad had an old John Deere tractor from the mid-1930s with steel wheels on the rear. Buying all new implements to replace those pulled by horses was an expensive proposition. Dad (and most other farmers in our area) jerry-rigged some of the old horse-drawn tools to enable them to be used with the tractor. Mostly this involved cutting off the wooden tongue on the implement that went up between the horses. So our horse-drawn planters, mowing machines, wagons, and other equipment continued to be in use.

Dad still preferred to use the horses for some jobs, especially for pulling the corn planter. The horses were also necessary for shucking corn. Shucking corn by hand required the horses to pull a wagon down the corn rows while Dad walked and hand-shucked the corn ears from the stocks. The horses would stop, start, and turn when Dad would give voice commands.

One Thanksgiving weekend, when we were about seven or eight, the corn was still standing in the fields because of a very rainy fall. Garold and I walked along, shucking one row while Dad took three. The far side of the wagon had a high board rack so that when we threw the ear of corn, it had a better chance of getting into the wagon bed instead of sailing over. Burned in my memory is how cold and tired Garold and I got while walking down those muddy corn rows with light snow coming down. It would be several more years before Dad had enough money saved to buy a corn picker.

The house on our farm had four rooms, plus a small kitchen on the back. A front porch wrapped around the living room, and the two bedrooms were on each side of the living room. The dining room extended to the back and connected to the kitchen. Gables above each room

Dad's farm horses

on the exterior made the house look more prominent from the outside than it was on the inside.

There was no electricity, telephone, indoor plumbing, or running water in the house. There was a wood-burning stove in the living room for heating in the winter, and Mom's wood-burning cookstove heated the back of the house. For water, we relied on a well in the front yard. We carried it into the house, one bucket at a time, using a three-gallon bucket that was heavy to carry when we were little. We kept the water bucket on a small table located in the kitchen. The table was where we cleaned up. Mom would have to stoke the wood-burning stove and use a pan or teakettle to heat the water on the stove for hot water. One day, the water began to taste bad, so Dad and Uncle Earl took the pump off the well and found a dead rabbit floating in the water. There was probably a connection between the unsettling discovery and the more frequent trips we took to the outhouse, which was inconveniently located behind the chicken house.

We were very excited when electricity finally came to our neighborhood in 1948. Although a New Deal program enacted during the Great

Front of the house at the Home Place

Depression had created the Rural Electrification Administration to bring electricity to rural America, World War II had disrupted the program before it could reach our neck of the woods. When electricity did arrive, Clay County set up the Clay Electric Cooperative Inc. to organize and operate the local electric company; users were members of the co-op. When electrical lines were strung along rural roads to reach farmhouses, most houses were wired with a ceiling light in each room and one electrical outlet. Now, instead of doing our homework at night with light from a kerosene lamp, we were able to prolong our eyesight with that light bulb hanging from the ceiling. I never minded the kerosene lamps after reading that Abraham Lincoln had read with light from a fireplace.

It was cool to have an outside electric light mounted on a pole to light up the yard and barn lot. With money in short supply, we weren't able to get new appliances. So Mom still used her old washing machine that operated with a gasoline engine. Instead of getting a new electric stove for her kitchen, Dad bought her a stove that still burned wood or coal. Moreover, we still didn't get indoor plumbing.

Everett and Vida's house that burned

An issue caused by wood-burning stoves was house fires. Within a couple of years, two of our neighbors' houses burned to the ground. One belonged to Everett and Vida, and the second was the Mitchell residence on the farm next to ours. Fortunately, no one was injured in the fires, and afterward, neighbors all pitched in to help after these tragedies. The Mitchells lived in one of the abandoned one-room schoolhouses until they could rebuild. Everett and Vida's house that burned was unusual because Everett had built an electrical system for their house using a bank of batteries.

Christmastime at our house was as festive as Mom could make it. Our Christmas tree was usually made from the branch of a cedar tree that grew in our yard. Mom made many of the ornaments, including strings of popcorn and small stuffed figures. We always looked forward to Christmas morning to open gifts. Vida Frutiger always had gifts for us. Often, we would get only one toy that we had to share. We eventually got a bike, but we had to take turns riding it since there was only one. During the winter, Mom would often make one of our favorite treats: popcorn balls. Each spring, she would plant a couple of rows of popcorn in the garden for our wintertime treat. She used molasses to make the popcorn, and our fingers, stick together.

Chapter 3

SCHOOL DAYS: FIRST TO EIGHTH GRADES

The long years of the Great Depression in the 1930s made for some very lean years for small farmers. The lack of progress was apparent on many fronts. Like the road that passed in front of our house, most of the county farm roads were dirt roads. This changed for us in 1946, when one-room schools were closing and farm kids were being bussed to town. The county required that roads for the bus routes be graveled.

The gravel was hauled by dump trucks, and a big yellow road grader operated by the township road commissioner spread it over the roadbed. My brother and I spent long hours sifting through the gravel in front of our house, looking for what we called Indian beads. They were actually small pieces of petrified tree limbs that typically were about one inch long and one-quarter inch in diameter. Other treasures in the gravel were pieces of white quartz.

We briefly went to a one-room school before being bussed into Clay City, where Garold and I started first grade at the Clay City elementary school. The one-room school was named Burcham School after the farmer who had donated the acre lot for the building. With no preschool or kindergarten at that time, we weren't scheduled to start until the fall at

Burcham School

the age of six. But, in the spring of 1946, Garold and I were sent to Burcham so the school could legally remain open. It seemed that a family had moved out of the neighborhood, leaving only three students at the school when a minimum of five was required. To enable the other kids to finish the school year, we joined the three neighbor kids from down the road. Mary, Shirley, and Richard Frank were the youngest of the ten Frank siblings who lived on the farm adjacent to ours. Their Mom, Katy, was the teacher. Garold and I walked to their house and joined them on the mile-and-a-half walk to the school. The Frank girls were favorites of our mom. She would bake cookies for them when they knocked on our door for a visit.

Our schoolhouse had one large room, but a small cloakroom was on each side of the front door, one for boys and the other for girls. Before classes began, we put our coats, muddy boots, and lunch buckets in the cloakroom. The desks were connected together and had hard wooden seats. Each desktop had a hole at the top for the ink well, although we were using wooden lead pencils by this time. Dad sharpened ours at home with his pocketknife. One day, Katy scolded me for playing around and dropping the glass ink bottle, which I then put carefully back in the ink well.

A big potbellied stove in the back of the room burned coal to heat the room. Initially, the school fathers would chop a wood supply for the school, but a small concrete coal bin was built against the school wall to store coal for the stove just before the start of World War II. Our water came from a well with a hand pump behind the building. On the back corner of the lot was the outhouse, which was used by both girls and boys.

One-room schools faced with declining enrollments were consolidated with schools in neighboring towns. Before World War II, there were over one hundred one-room schools scattered throughout Clay County. Four one-room schools were in our neighborhood, but three were closed by 1946. The remaining school was the Snyder School, and it had enough enrollment to stay open until 1950. The Snyder School was named after my great-great-granddad Samuel Snyder, who donated the land. It was also where my dad and his brother and sisters went to school. Neighbor kids living a quarter mile to the north of our house were in a different township, and there were enough of them for the one-room Snyder School to remain open for an additional four years.

In the fall of 1946, Garold and I started first grade at the Clay City Elementary School. Mom packed our lunches in paper sacks, and we got on and off the bus in front of the house. The bus was for high school kids, but we rode it because no other grade-school kids were left in the Burcham school district. The bus ride added an hour to the school day. Too, it wasn't always a pleasant ride. The bumpy gravel roads made reading on

Clay City Elementary School

the bus impossible. We always tried to hurry past one high school bully who liked to hit or pinch us when we walked by his seat.

Clay City Elementary looked so big and felt overwhelming at first. There were four classrooms on the lower level for grades one through four, and four on the second level for the upper grades. Each classroom usually had over thirty kids with a single teacher. In addition to the eight teachers, other school personnel included the principal, secretary, physical education teacher, a band instructor, a janitor, and the school bus drivers. For our first two years at the school, the principal was Albert Craig. For our remaining time, the principal was his twin brother, Calvert. Both ran the school with firm hands. There were no nurses, counselors, librarians, or aids at that time.

Our first-grade teacher was Mrs. Fern Hunley. She was a strict but excellent teacher. Since Mom had taught us the alphabet and numbers, we adapted fairly quickly to learning. Our first-grade class had thirty-five kids, and twenty-two of us were still together for eighth-grade graduation.

I hadn't thought too much about being a twin until we started school in Clay City. Although we weren't identical, Mom always dressed us the same. Mom was an excellent seamstress and made most of our clothes until we started first grade. Then we started school with brand-new overalls

First-grade class (Garold and I in first row, in new overalls)

from JCPenney and the store's underwear brand (which I continued to buy for another seventy years). As twins, we slept in the same bed, played with the same toys, had the same playmates, ate the same things, and were always together. The first time we had a photo taken individually was for our school pictures. One day at recess, one of the school bullies started pushing me around, but with good timing, Garold showed up, and the kid backed off.

Second grade seemed much more challenging than first grade. Our teacher in second grade was Mrs. Blackledge. She was a demanding teacher and maintained strict order. My brother struggled more than I did, and one day in class, he was having trouble with some concepts and began to cry. He sat across from me, and I tried to help him but had a helpless feeling that I couldn't shake. Mrs. Blackledge's favorite punishment, short of sending a miscreant to the principal's office, was having the misbehaving kid sit out in the hallway on a little red chair for an hour. I received that punishment only once, but I felt humiliated when the principal walking the hallways came by and saw me sitting there.

Corduroy suits made by Mom

Sometimes we would have an all-school assembly in the gymnasium where the bleachers could seat all three hundred students. It might involve school matters or entertainment, like a juggler or a dog show—and one time, a little man shot trick basketball free throws from all angles and never missed. During such an assembly when Garold and I were in the second grade, a big snowstorm started and the high school dismissed classes. The high school bus came to the front of the grade school to pick us up, so the principal announced to the assembly that kids riding the northbound bus had to leave. At first, my brother and I weren't sure he was referring to us, but we got the message and trudged across the gym floor wearing our rubber overshoes. When the bus driver drove north of town toward Sailor Springs, he stopped the bus at the turnoff road that

My report card from first grade

went the three miles to our house. He said the snow was too deep to make it down the turnoff road and that we should get out. We had a moment of panic because we were the only kids to get off. It was almost dark, and the driving snow had accumulated to over a foot, and it was freezing.

With no option and no telephone at our house, we took off walking. It was a two-mile walk going east to reach the right-hand turn that led south to our farm. Before we reached the end of the two-mile road, we looked across the farm fields to the south and could see a light in the window at our house. By this time we were so cold and tired that we decided to leave the road and take a shortcut by walking across the fields to get home. We soon realized it probably wasn't such a good idea to leave the road. Walking across the first field was doubly hard because snow covered up the downed corn stocks that kept tripping us. Our seven-year-old legs weren't long enough to step over the snow-covered stalks. We finally got across the field and reached the fence on our farm. The fence was

Our house in the winter

topped with a string of barbed wire that wouldn't let go of our jackets. Our hands and fingers were so cold that we had a heck of a time getting ourselves loose.

Finally, we got to the house where Mom let us in, trying not to show us how worried she was. The good part was that the chores were already done, but my fingers remembered the cold for a very long time. Although it was a scary experience that stayed with me for years, everyone in our generation seemed to have a story about how they had to walk uphill both ways to get to school. We never got—nor expected—any sympathy.

Our experiences during the third and fourth grades were much better. Our third and fourth-grade teachers, Mrs. Wheatley and Mrs. Hortin, were excellent. Mrs. Wheatley had a practice of having kids who excelled in reading help the slower ones by reading to them. The boy I assisted was painfully slow, and all I could think of was avoiding his bad breath.

We were beginning to form friendships and develop some discernment about social differences during this time. We became aware that there was a difference between town kids and us kids from the country. I had no awareness at first that we might be considered poor, and indeed

Left: Mrs. Wheatley, third grade
Right: Mrs. Hortin, fourth grade

we didn't have it as bad as some in our class. But riding the school bus, wearing overalls, and carrying our lunches with homemade bread and jelly sandwiches instead of sliced white bread seemed to set us apart, especially later when we couldn't stay after school for sports.

Probably most telling was that the town boys who played together year-round always picked us last when choosing teams to play softball during recess. But one thing I became aware of was that I was considered smart because I made good grades. This made up to some degree for feeling inferior, but those feelings never really went away.

Before we started our fifth-grade school year, we moved from the Home Place to a new farm we called the Ringy Place (more on that later). It was a much longer bus ride from the new home to school. Our teacher was Clarence Workman, our first male teacher, who happened to be our uncle. His wife, Aunt Luella, was Mom's sister and one of the thirteen Stanley siblings. Not only was Clarence our uncle, but he was also an excellent teacher. Clarence and Luella Workman lived on a farm close to Ingraham, Illinois, near where they had grown up. When Clarence started teaching in Clay City, they came up with a clever plan to reduce his long commute. They bought a small twen-

Top left: Uncle Clarence Workman,
Top right: Mrs. Gould, sixth-grade teacher
Bottom left: Mr Craig, principal
Bottom right: Mr. Long, eighth-grade teacher

ty-acre farm on the west edge of Clay City on Fifth Street (just down the street from the house we own now in Clay City). The Workman family moved into their home in town at the beginning of the school year.

Their home became a haven for Garold and me. We could stay all night with them during the school year. It was especially cool because they had a TV. We also got to spend time with our cousin Keith, who was two years older. Our job was to help him do his farm chores. When the Workmans made their annual relocation in September, they would bring down some animals, including milk cows. We escaped our long bus ride when we stayed with them, but not the chores. Mostly we stayed with Clarence and Luella when we played in the band at basketball games. There was no separate bus for after-school activities, and our location at the end of the road eliminated hitchhiking as an option. While this lack of transportation kept us from playing sports, which meant missing out on playing basketball, staying at the Workmans offered a chance to at least participate in the band's activities outside of the school day.

Our sixth grade teacher was Mrs. Gould, the only female teacher at the upper level. The principal, Mr. Craig, taught arithmetic that was, at least for that year, my favorite subject. Mr. Fehrenbacher, who taught seventh grade, may have been the best teacher of all. He was excellent at being able to reach kids of differing abilities. In eighth grade, the basketball coach, Mr. Long, was our teacher. He was subject to good and bad days but overall did OK. If he judged that class behavior on a given day was good, he would end the school day by reading a chapter from Mark Twain's *Tom Sawyer* and *Huckleberry Finn*. The class looked forward to this because he would use a hilarious voice and accent for each character. His renditions would not be politically correct in this epoch, but he was very entertaining.

During seventh grade, the school principal, Mr. Craig, appointed me the school patrol boy. My job was to act as a crossing guard to keep kids from crossing a busy intersection. I wore a white belt with a cross-shoulder strap and a badge. It was supposed to be an honor, and the perk was getting out of class five minutes early to be at my post. I didn't find it all that honorable when some of the older boys ignored my instructions, especially when a woman once reported me to Mr. Craig. However, at the end of the year, he took me to a multicounty picnic for all the patrol boys in the region. It never struck me that there were no girls as crossing guards and that what we were doing would become paying jobs decades later.

We were still carrying our sack lunches to school during these years as there was no school lunch program. During eighth grade, my friend Myron Dunigan would invite me to go to the pool hall over the lunch hour. He always beat me at pool and would pay the dime for the game, even though losers were supposed to pay. Though not the best of students, Myron was popular and a good athlete. He was naturally strong, and

Myron Dunigan

no one in the class dared pick on him. Tragically, Myron and one of his brothers were killed in a car/train accident the summer after we graduated from high school.

A couple of years before becoming fifth graders, the Clay City grade school and high school principals jointly hired a band director named Jack Gengler to create bands in both schools. Mr. Gengler was a master musician and developed very successful and competitive bands at both schools. His instrument was the trumpet, which he played in a jazz band. On one occasion, the high school principal, Vergil Shafer, told me that he had hired Gengler because he was interested in more than just music and was an all-around guy. Indeed, Mr. Gengler had passed on the opportunity to play minor league baseball after college. He was also a St. Louis Cardinals fan, which was almost a requirement in southern Illinois.

Garold and I started our interest in the band by persuading Mom and Dad to take us to an introductory evening event for kids. The big decision was choosing an instrument and then coming up with the money to pay for it. We both wanted to play the trumpet, so the school loaned us one to try. At our first lesson, Mr. Gengler decided that I should play the baritone horn and not the trumpet. Since the school provided some instruments, including the baritone horn, Dad relented and bought a trumpet for Garold.

Mr. Gengler was a stern taskmaster. He took it upon himself to give individual lessons weekly to all band members. At first, I dreaded these encounters because he used his baton not only for tapping the beat on the music stand. As I became more proficient, I enjoyed being part of the band. Being in the band led to

In my band uniform

opportunities that got us involved in school. The band played at home basketball games and for a couple of concerts during the school year. The major deal for the band, however, was the annual band contests held each spring. The first round was the district contest, which was generally hosted at an area high school. If the band received a first-place ranking, it was eligible to continue to the state contest. The Clay City bands usually received "first superior" status at both the district and state competitions. The contests also featured solo competitions on most instruments, so I started entering these contests with my baritone horn in seventh grade. After a second-place start in seventh grade, I received first-place medals at the district and state contests each year from eighth grade through my senior year in high school. While I was somewhat musically inclined because of my Stanley genes, I practiced a lot. I never got over anxiety when I was asked to play solos for graduations and community events.

A big deal for me during eighth grade was being selected to play my horn in the 1954 All-State Grade School Band. Three of us in the band from Clay City were chosen for the honor. My fellow band mem-

Illinois State High School Band, 1954

bers from Clay City were Trevor Bissey and Sue Ann Sunday, who were seventh graders and were more talented than my eighth-grade classmates. Sue Ann was the best and went on to a career in music. Mr. Gengler didn't drive, so our principal, Mr. Craig, drove us to our initial practice and concert at the University of Illinois in Champaign. The next event for the band, however, was an eye-opening experience. The band was invited to play before the National Association for Music Education Conference in Chicago. At thirteen, I had hardly been out of the county, so the trip to Chicago was one to remember. The band was hosted outside Chicago in Plainfield, located about forty miles southeast of downtown. We stayed with host families in Plainfield and practiced at the Plainfield school. I didn't have a suitcase, but Mom found a small black tin suitcase for the trip that cost three dollars at the Sears, Roebuck and Company store in Olney.

On the day of the concert, we got up very early for the trip from Plainfield to downtown Chicago. This was before interstate highways and expressways, so it was a long two-hour bus ride on local highways and

The Chicago Theater

streets. I had a window seat and sat the whole time staring at the passing sights. After a few miles of cornfields, we got into the industrial area with factories spewing smoke. Coming up through the south Side of Chicago, we drove through the slum areas that made a lasting impression on me and put a different perspective on living on a tenant farm.

Arriving downtown, we drove through the famous Chicago Loop. Watching the tall buildings and the people kept me glued to the window. Our destination was the huge Conrad Hilton Hotel on Michigan Avenue, where the music educators had their convention. We walked into the venue for the concert. It was a grand ballroom, and I was blown away by the place's grandeur, with its plush carpeting and chandeliers. Our band set up on the enormous stage, and looking out at the audience of several hundred, I had a case of butterflies in my stomach. The concert was nonetheless deemed a success.

Mr. Gengler attended the conference for the day, so Mr. Craig took Sue Ann, Trevor, and me into downtown Chicago. The highlight was attending a movie at the Chicago Theater. I had no clue at the time, but the Chicago Theater on State Street was the first of the lavish palace theaters that had been built in the early 1950s. It was almost as overwhelming as the Hilton ballroom. There was a large semicircular stage in front of huge, dark-red curtains that hid the movie screen. Prior to the film's start, it was common for the theater to have pre-show entertainment. On our day at the theater, a comedian walked onto the stage for a monologue. Then we were given cardboard glasses to see the movie that was a 3D film. This was a new deal for me, but 3D pictures had a popularity phase in the early 1950s. We saw *Murders in the Rue Morgue*, set in Paris. I found it hard to follow, and I am not sure it was entirely age-appropriate!

Sunday's Ice Cream Parlor, located on Main Street in Clay City, was the town hangout for kids of all ages. Oris Sunday and his wife operated the restaurant. Oris had lost one of his legs during the war, so standing on his wooden leg for hours each day caused him a lot of pain. One of his daughters, Linda, was in our class. Garold was lucky enough to have her as a girlfriend. Some kids with more spending money would walk uptown to Sunday's for a hamburger at lunch on school days. But it was most popular for teenagers on Saturday nights after the movie was over at the Clayton Theater, three doors down. Garold and I each got a quarter as our allowance on Saturday nights and usually went to the movies. Admission to the movies for kids was nine cents, but the cost went up to fifteen cents by the early 1950s. We still had a dime left for either an ice cream cone or a small cherry Coke at Sunday's, but not enough for the fifteen-cent milkshake.

Sunday's Ice Cream Parlor, circa 1955

Before the main feature at the movies, there was a newsreel, a cartoon, and previews. Since we didn't have television, the newsreels were fascinating to us. Many of the first ones we saw had footage of the war ending in Europe and Japan, which brought the impact of the war more vividly into our lives. Our favorite movies were Westerns with cowboy heroes like Gene Autry, Roy Rogers, Tom Mix, Randolph Scott, and Lash LaRue. A high point for Clay City and the Clayton Theater was when Roy Rogers came to town early in his career and appeared on the stage before one of his movies.

The only vacation our family ever took was a trip to the Smoky Mountains when Garold and I were thirteen. We made the trip with a neighboring family, Tommy and Vida May Brown, and their eight-year-old daughter, Shirley. Tommy drove his 1949 Plymouth, and somehow all seven of us and our clothing squeezed into the car. Garold and I made a game of identifying the makes of the cars we met on the drive. Most of our meals were roadside picnics after Mom and Vida May went shopping for groceries. In addition to the Smokies, we visited Lookout

Mountain Park and the adjacent Civil War battlefield In Chattanooga, Tennessee. This was my first encounter with segregation, and I was upset when I was reproached for drinking out of a water fountain with a sign above it that read "Colored." The trip, however, made me want to travel to see more of the country.

Eighth-grade graduation in 1954 was a big deal for us. The ceremony was held in the grade-school gym, and our class sang the song "I Believe," a popular inspirational song during the 1950s. When it came time for awards to be handed out, I received the band award. In addition to a medal, I was given a new suitcase. Apparently, my tin one didn't measure up. I was also selected for the American Legion award. The faculty nominated a boy and a girl for the award, based on six character qualities: courage, honor, leadership, patriotism, scholarship, and service. I think I was lucky to be in a small class.

Cowboy star Roy Rogers appeared at the Clayton The

Roy Rogers in Clay City

Our class went to St. Louis for an outing at the Forest Park Highlands amusement park. The amusement park was adjacent to the St. Louis Zoo and a major city park that had been the site of the 1904 Olympics. The main attraction at the amusement park was the Comet, a large wooden roller coaster. It may have been the only time I voluntarily set myself up for a scare and then willingly did it again.

Top: Our eighth-grade graduation photo
Bottom: eighth-grade report card

The first time Garold and I had been to St. Louis was when Everett and Vida had taken us there a few years earlier. When driving into St. Louis from Illinois, we crossed over the Mississippi on the Eads Bridge, the oldest bridge that crossed the Mississippi River from Illinois to St. Louis. After crossing the bridge, we saw the congestion of shanties and corrugated tin dwellings of the St. Louis slums. The depth of poverty seemed particularly stark when contrasted to the opulent houses that lined Forest Park Avenue a few miles to the west

Chapter 4

FAMILY

One of my earliest memories is that of my Mom and Dad gathered around our battery-powered radio. Without electricity at that time, an old battery-powered radio enabled Mom and Dad to listen to President Franklin D. Roosevelt's fireside chats along with war news reports from reporter Lowell Thomas. The radio had a lot of static, so it had to be turned off when there was a storm. Listening to the radio during the war years was especially important because Mom had three brothers in the military, and two were deployed in the Pacific. She was a loyal sister and wrote frequent letters to them. Their responses were written on stationery provided by the military and were censored to protect military secrets. Mom was overjoyed when Japan surrendered and her brothers returned home safely.

The Stanley Family

Our social lives mostly revolved around family visits and church. Mom's parents, Cyrus and Sally Stanley, had thirteen children. She was number nine in the lineup of four girls and nine boys. Their progeny meant that Garold and I had thirty-two first cousins on the Stanley side of the family. The Stanleys were close-knit and got together each year for April birthdays, June strawberries and ice cream, the annual family re-

The thirteen Stanley siblings (at Grandma's funeral)

union in August, and Thanksgiving and Christmas. The family gatherings were held at Granddad and Grandma's house while they were living, and later at siblings' homes on a rotating basis. Fifty or sixty usually attended to enjoy a potluck meal and at least twenty-five desserts.

Most of the older cousins were boys, and we fell into two groups. The older cluster of nine hung out together. We didn't have much to do with them. The second group of five included Garold and me, along with Jerry Stanley (son of Jay and Mary Stanley), who was our age. The other two were Jerry's brother Larry, and Keith Workman (son of Clarence and Luella Workman). Jerry was just two months younger than Garold and me, but Larry and Keith were two years older. This grouping gave us a ready-made set of playmates for our growing-up years. Our cluster of five guys would spend afternoons exploring old houses, wooded areas, and

Stanley cousins, 1945
Front row: Larry, Darold, Garold, Keith, and Jerry

stream beds until we were old enough to drive. The next group to come along included two boys and eight girls.

After summer dinner gatherings, we often would have weeklong visits with a cousin. Jerry's house was a favorite place because he had three older brothers. When we were about ten years old, one of our favorite activities was to play with farm equipment toys. Somehow, we discovered that lids for canning vegetables made with lead were easy to melt. So we "borrowed" some of Aunt Mary's canning lids for our project. Making a fire in the chicken yard with no grass, we would heat the lids in an old coffee can until the lead turned into a silvery liquid. We made molds in the dirt and poured in the molten lead to make implements to pull behind our toy tractors. The making of the toys was fun, except for many burned fingers. This playtime activity might have struck a chord with Garold, who later developed an extensive collection of farm toys, many of which he restored.

Both Grandma and Granddad Stanley died not too long after the war ended, with Grandma going first. She died in 1947 from a stroke

The Stanley family with grand champion cow

when we were seven. Granddad died when we were nine. When Grandma died, she was "laid out" in her coffin in the living room of their house, as was the custom, for friends and neighbors to pay respects. She was the first dead person I had seen, and it was a bit scary going into the room where she was laid out. Granddad was sitting in his chair, rocking back and forth and muttering over and over to God that he was a sinner.

Granddad Stanley was a fascinating character in many ways. He was quite a successful farmer and was the subject of several newspaper and magazine articles. As I discussed in my book about Cyrus and Sally Stanley, dated 2010, one newspaper even gave him the title of the "Miracle Man." In 1924 he won the Illinois Corn Growers Association's award for the highest corn yield per acre using a seed he developed. He also received a lot of trophies and awards for his prize herd of Milking Shorthorn cattle. He got the breed started in southern Illinois when he persuaded a couple of his friends to join him in importing breeding stock from England. He was active in the breeder's national association and took his show cattle to major livestock exhibitions in San Francisco, Fort Worth, and Chicago. He was most proud of his cow that won the grand champion trophy at the Chicago Exhibition.

Our baby buggy from Grandpa

The last time I saw Granddad Stanley was when he came to our house early one morning looking for his foxhounds. He died a few months later from a heart attack. Grandpa had first-class dogs, and he and his friends would take their hounds out hunting at night. They didn't use horses to hunt foxes, like in the movies, but they would walk or listen for the dogs from their cars. The idea wasn't to capture or kill the fox but to enjoy listening to the dogs' different howls (hound music) as they found a scent, followed the trail, and cornered the fox in his den. They could distinguish the dogs by their sounds. Sometimes the dogs didn't come back to the car, which was why Granddad was at our house the next day looking for his dog. Unfortunately, I never felt a close connection with Grandpa. I suppose it was because we lived farther away than most of the grandkids. However, Grandpa did buy Garold and me our first set of wheels: a baby buggy!

Stanley family band (my Mom, Floy, holding neck of banjo)

Grandpa and Grandma Stanley lived and raised their family near the small town of Ingraham, Illinois. Many of Mom's brothers had farms in the immediate area, but Mom moved out of the neighborhood when she married Dad. Dad met her in Sailor Springs, which was about five miles south of Ingraham. Mom played the banjo in the Stanley family band, and they often played for church socials, square dances, and ice cream gatherings in the surrounding small communities, including Sailor Springs. Granddad led the band with his excellent fiddle playing. Somehow Dad got up the nerve to introduce himself to Mom after one of the concerts. He didn't mind riding his horse ten miles from his family's farm to court her.

The Herdes Family

The Herdes family got its start in Clay County when a German immigrant, Joseph Herdes, moved there just before the Civil War. As I discussed in my book about the Herdes family, dated 2019, Joseph died at age thirty-five, shortly after he got out of the army, from a disease he had contracted when he was deployed with the Union Army in Tennessee.

Joseph had one son named James Monroe, who was four when his dad died. James Monroe went on to have three sons who carried on the name. One of these boys was my granddad, Charles Herdes, who went by his nickname, Chart. He and my grandma Ruby had four children: two boys—Earl and our dad, Denby—and two girls—Sadie and Imogene. The family remained tightly connected as well, and we had many gatherings. Earl's farm was a half-mile from Granddad and Grandma's place, and our farm was only about two miles away. There were seven Herdes family farms in the area.

Grandma Herdes was an only child. The fact that Grandma was illegitimate was never talked about in the family, and I never learned who her father might have been. When she was nine, her mother, Emma Byrne, married Thomas Johnson. Thomas's first wife had died during childbirth, so Grandma had both half and stepbrothers and sisters when her mom and Thomas had additional children.

Two of Grandma's favorites in her expanded family were her half-sister Margaret and her sister-in-law, Ethel. When Garold and I came along, Margaret was divorced and lived in San Francisco, where she wrote children's books. Ethel was married

Tombstone of Joseph Herdes

Dad, Earl, Grandpa Chart, Grandma Ruby, and Sadie (Imogene in front)

to Grandma's brother Truman Johnson, who was in World War I. When the war ended, he became a cop in New York City, where he met Ethel. Margaret and Ethel were great friends, even though they lived on different coasts. When Uncle Truman died, they would travel by train to meet each other back in Illinois, where they stayed with Grandma. Garold and I, along with our Herdes cousins, always looked forward to the visits by our great-aunts Margaret and Ethel. They were interesting, fun, and loved to tell us stories. Later in my travels, I visited Margaret in San Francisco and Ethel in Brooklyn.

We also liked to stay all night with Granddad and Grandma Herdes. Grandma made us treats and let us drink coffee spiked with a lot of cream and sugar. We got together with the extended Herdes family often. Our cousins numbered two boys and nine girls, so we didn't have the favorable ratio of boys and girls that we had with the Stanleys.

Great-aunts Ethel and Margaret

Granddad Herdes, Uncle Earl, and Dad worked together on many farm projects. When Garold and I were about five years old, Dad and Granddad were helping Uncle Earl dig a well. Typically, you could hit the water table at around fifteen to twenty feet down, so they would take turns digging the well with shovels while using a tile spade to keep the sides of the well smooth for bricking. They rigged up a tripod and a pulley to pull the dirt bucket up when they got down several feet. Granddad was handling the rigging when he somehow got his thumb caught in the pulley. It was smashed entirely off. Dad and Earl drove him to the closest hospital, but that was twenty-five miles away in Olney, Illinois. At this time, limbs could not be reattached, so Granddad had no right thumb from then on. Afterward, when Granddad was driving his Ford Model A, his manner of doing the customary wave to oncoming drivers was to lift the four fingers on his right hand.

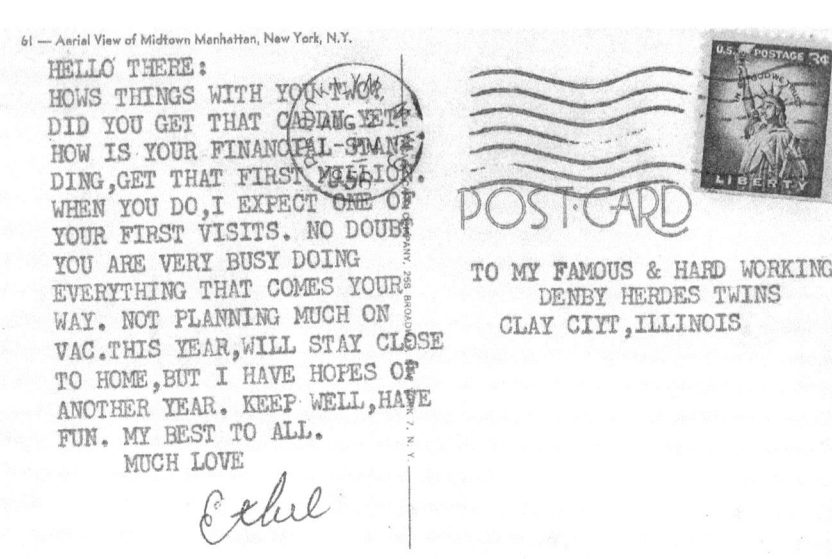

Note address: Mailed by Aunt Ethel from New York City, 1958

Most of the meat we consumed came from the animals we raised on the farm. Chickens and hogs were the primary sources. As we did with chickens, we butchered our hogs, usually three pigs each year, weighing about 250 pounds each. Dad, Uncle Earl, and Granddad worked together on each farm at butchering time. Mom, Aunt Lelia, and Grandma cut up and packaged the meat. Earl brought his rifle to shoot the pigs, a job I inherited when we were in high school. After draining the blood, the pig was doused in a kettle of scalding water to loosen the hair on the pig's hide so it could be easily removed with scrapers. The carcass was hung on a tripod and cut in half for the meat to cool. It was an all-day project done in the winter or spring months.

Before we finally had refrigeration, the shoulders and hams were cured by rubbing salt and spices into the meat. This was Dad's job. He then wrapped the large cuts in newspaper, placed them in a gunnysack, and then hung them in the smokehouse. The pig's outer layer of fat next

Butchering day

to the skin was cut into small chunks and put in a large, black kettle to boil down into a liquid fat. The fat was poured into lard cans, where it solidified before use in cooking throughout the coming year, a kind of homemade Crisco. When the liquid was poured out of the kettle, the remaining pieces of skin were called cracklins. They were similar to pork rinds, only with more fat.

On one occasion, I visited Jimmy Brown when his family was doing their butchering. I was about ten and had walked to their house. Jimmy and I had a contest to see who could eat the most cracklins. I don't know who won, but I had a very long walk home, and not even a Sears catalog page for toilet paper.

Many cuts of meat were hard to preserve, so they were eaten right away. These included some of the organs, like the heart, liver, and sweetbreads. One of the first things to be eaten was the brains, which looked

Herdes cousins

to me like scrambled eggs when served. I never cared too much for eating the tongue, but the biggest treat were the pork chops. Mom fried them, and we chewed them until everything was gone from the bone. Aunt Lelia was in charge of packaging the sausage. The lesser cuts were cut into small pieces and ground with a hand grinder, a job for Garold and me. Lelia would clean the pig's intestines to use as casings for the sausage meat that was blended with spices. Typically, the cuts of meat that couldn't be preserved were divided among the three families at the end of the day.

Although the Stanley and Herdes families were very different from each other, Garold and I learned the importance of our extended families during our growing-up years. Much of our social lives involved family gatherings. Holidays, birthdays, and weddings brought us together, as did the sad occasions when a relative was sick or died.

Chapter 5

THE DREDGE DITCH

1950 was an eventful year for our family. Until then, Dad had rented the farm where we lived from his dad, Grandpa Herdes. Garold and I called that farm the Home Place because we were born there. The farm where Grandpa rented and lived was owned by Lawrence Rengier, who lived in the Chicago area where he was an electrician for a Borden's ice cream plant. When we were ten, Grandpa Herdes decided he wanted to live on his farm that he was renting to Dad, and so it was time for Dad to purchase his own farm.

This created a lot of excitement for Garold and me. Dad and Mom visited two farms that were for sale. Both were much closer to Clay City than the Home Place. Garold and I would have been happy with either, because living closer meant we would have a better chance of staying after school for sports. After much deliberation, Dad decided to buy a sixty-acre farm located southeast of Clay City. We were exuberant about the change, and the family spent some time working on the property to get it ready to move in. Before the big day could arrive, Dad inexplicably got cold feet and sold it for the same price he had paid for it. We wouldn't be moving closer to school after all.

Rengier Place: Our second farmhouse

Instead, we ended up switching places with Grandpa Herdes, and Dad rented the farm from Lawrence Regnier. Ironically, it was the same place where Dad had grown up.

We exchanged farms with Granddad in the spring of 1951 in time for the new crop season. The sharecropping arrangement remained the same as at the Home Place, only the landlord changed from Granddad to Lawrence Rengier. Lawrence got one third of the crop as rent, and Dad got 2/3s.

Although disappointed by moving even farther away from school, Garold and I were initially OK about living on the Rengier place because of its size. The house was two stories tall with four bedrooms. It had been built around the turn of the century in the I-house architecture style common for farm houses in the Midwest during that time. The front of the house had two rooms below and two above. Centered at the back of

Rengier farmhouse in the winter

the two front rooms were the dining room and, beyond that, the kitchen, with rooms above on the second floor for a total of eight rooms.

Once again, however, there was no indoor plumbing or running water. Worse, the well for drinking water was about one hundred yards away from the house and down a hill. We had to carry five-gallon buckets of water up the hill for drinking and cooking. For some relief in hauling water, the house had a cistern in the cellar. The cellar was mainly used to store potatoes and glass jars of fruits and vegetables that Mom had canned throughout the summer. The cellar had a dirt floor and was accessed by steps outside the house. About a quarter of the cellar was occupied by the cistern, a brick tank about eight-feet square. The cistern was filled by rainwater coming down gutters from the house roof. The trick for improving the water quality, at least a little, was letting the initial rainwater clean the roof's surface before putting the downspout into the cistern. The cistern was just below the kitchen so that water could be pumped up to a sink with a small hand pump. This was a great advantage for the cleaning and washing Mom did. We were deterred from drinking the water, especially after I lifted one of the boards that covered the cistern one day and saw a mouse floating in the water.

Although there were four bedrooms on the second floor, Garold and I continued to sleep in the same bed for the entire time we lived in the house—partly because we were twins and had always slept together, and partly for warmth in winter. Cold winter nights were problematic with no insulation in the walls and loose windows in our bedroom. On more than one snowy morning, we awoke to a dusting of snow on the pile of comforters we were hiding under. Summers were even worse for sleeping. It got so hot upstairs that we would drag a blanket downstairs to sleep in an open doorway, hoping the whining mosquitoes wouldn't come through the screen door. Being in the bigger house also made getting to the outhouse more complicated at night. We had to go down the narrow steps from the second floor before running out of the house to the backyard.

As far as Garold and I were concerned, the big perk of our new location was a fairly large stream that ran through the property, only about a quarter-mile down the hill from the house. The stream bed was a man-made drainage ditch that had been dug about forty years earlier to drain the low-lying swamplands that extended along a twelve-mile stretch parallel to the Big Muddy Creek.

The stream is locally referred to as the Drudge Ditch. Farther upstream from the Rengier place, the Big Muddy Creek was inadvertently channeled by erosion into the Dredge Ditch not long after it was dug. This resulted in a lot more water coming down the ditch than was originally intended, and the twelve-foot-wide ditch washed out to a width of over one hundred feet.

The Dredge Ditch became our playground. At first, we made hideouts to protect against invading Indians. Later we were content looking for arrowheads dating from one of the Illini tribes that had lived in the area before settlers came around 1820. The Dredge Ditch had what we called a deep hole, where the water stayed deep enough even during

The Dredge Ditch

drought conditions for swimming and fishing. Swimming in the less than clear water carried somewhat of a risk, especially if we mistook the head of a water moccasin for that of a turtle. I would set a trotline in the deep hole for catching catfish during the summer. When heavy summer rains came, the ditch would overflow its banks and flood several acres at the bottom of our hill. The water was usually quite warm and perfect for learning to swim, though I never became much of a fan of being in the water.

The large, wooded areas bordering the ditch made hunting squirrels in the fall a favorite undertaking. Later, when in high school, I ran a trapline to catch small fur-bearing animals. Probably the most fun was running down to the ditch to play when we had family gatherings. Our cousins always liked to go exploring and looking for adventures.

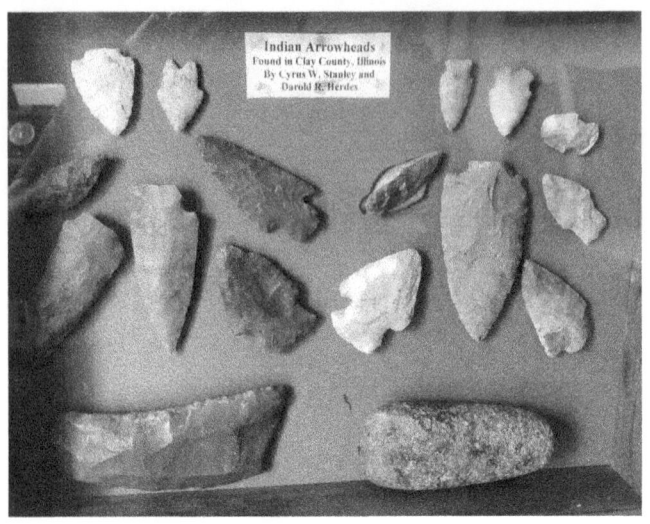

My Indian arrowhead collection

The Rengier place was located at the end of a mile-long gravel road. The road extended eastward from our farm into the next county, but it had closed some years before we lived there because of the high cost of maintaining two bridges. Several decades earlier, Clay County had been divided to form a new county called Richland. The boundary between the two counties was the Big Muddy Creek, about a mile east of our farm. It seemed neither county wanted to maintain the bridges, so eventually, the road terminated at our farm.

We had a long lane from the gravel road that went up a small hill to our homestead. There was, however, another house on the road before it dead-ended at our lane. The Frutiger family owned this house and the surrounding eighty acres of farmland. Vida's parents, Bill and Ollie Clinton, lived there for a short time after our move. Garold and I visited daily when dropping off their mail. For some reason that was never clear to me, the mailboxes for us and the Clintons were located a half-mile up the gravel road instead of at our houses. Garold and I walked to the boxes to

Left: Helen and Carol Lee Frutiger
Right: Proud ushers

retrieve the mail, and on the return, we would drop off the mail and visit with Bill and Ollie. Bill regaled us with stories about his life, all the while working on his chewing tobacco. Ollie would get us drinks and quietly listen to Bill's stories for the hundredth time, occasionally interrupting to correct some of his exaggerations.

Bill and Ollie lived in the house only a few years before moving into town. Later, we had new neighbors when Carol Lee Frutiger got married after returning home from a tour in the army. He and his wife, Helen, worked hard to remodel the house so they could move in after their wedding. Garold and I proudly served as ushers for their ceremony. Sadly, they were in the house only two weeks before it caught fire and burned to the ground. The tragedy was compounded because their belongings, including their wedding gifts, were destroyed.

While neither Garold nor I ever really liked farm chores, we had an unspoken sense that we were part of the family operation where everyone did their share. Most appealing, especially for my brother, was getting to drive the tractor to do the farm work. Before moving to the Rengier farm, Dad had an old-model John Deere "B" from the mid-1930s. When rubber tires became available again after the war, Dad removed the lugged steel wheels on the tractor's rear and replaced them with rubber tires. The two-cylinder motor had to be started with a hand crank, which neither of us could turn fast enough to start the engine.

Trading the old 1930s tractor for a new 1951 "B" John Deere was a big deal. The cost of the new tractor was $1,100. Instead of using the converted horse-drawn implements, Dad gradually started to buy more implements for the new tractor. One day, when Garold was driving the new tractor, he didn't slow down enough to turn around the corner to enter our lane at the bottom of the hill. He hit a corner fence post and damaged the steering column on the front end. Dad took it surprisingly well, and it didn't keep Garold from wanting to continue driving.

Since we were getting big enough to do more work, Dad also bought a smaller used tractor, a John Deere "H." It was so small that it could not pull as much as a team of horses. Although not totally worthless, the tractor was eventually sold, and Dad got us a used John Deere "A" tractor with more horsepower than the newer "B." With two tractors and two sons as drivers, Dad rented some additional acreage to farm.

One summer evening, not long after our eleventh birthday, a neighboring farmer named William Spencer came to our house. Mr. Spencer, the area's 4-H leader, came to ask us to join the club. Dad again said no, but after a lot of complaining, he finally relented. We started our first 4-H project by persuading Dad to give us each a calf to raise and show at the annual Clay County Fair in Flora, Illinois. Showing cattle requires a lot of work, including getting the animals to lead with a halter. Neither of us had a very good-quality calf, but we continued to show even if we never got a blue ribbon.

My Milking Shorthorn heifer at Clay County Fair, 1953

Our membership in 4-H lasted for several years, and later I served as president of the club. We both attended 4-H camps in southern Illinois for a week in summer, and later we added other 4-H activities to the cattle raising and showing.

The summer following eighth grade, I went to a 4-H forestry camp in northern Illinois. The camp was held at the White Pines State Forest, one of the very few locations where virgin white pine trees were preserved in the state. My obligation after the camp was to write an article about the experience for the local paper. Based on my camp experience, I decided I wanted to be a forest ranger. Too, the idea of being a farmer was rapidly losing its appeal.

Garold and I were fortunate to have pretty good health during our growing-up years, although I was (and still am) prone to a lot of upper respiratory issues. Two doctors served our community. Dr. Johnny Shore in Sailor Springs was the doctor who delivered us. At one point, Dr. Shore wanted to take out my tonsils that were always getting infected. Mom

and Dad decided not to do it. The upside was not having surgery then, but the downside was having to get them out later as an adult.

The second doctor for our community was Dr. Henderson, who had his office in Clay City. He lived in the town's largest house that was an area landmark. His home had been built by an early resident of Clay City shortly after the Civil War. Dr. Henderson gave me my first shots of penicillin for my recurring tonsillitis. Penicillin was a new drug that was first mass-produced in 1943 during the war years.

Dr. Henderson also came to the Clay City elementary school to give us newly available vaccine shots for diphtheria, tetanus, and pertussis (whooping cough). Vaccines were not yet available for measles, mumps, or chicken pox, so both Garold and I suffered through these diseases without any long-term adverse consequences that we knew about. The big scare for everyone during the 1950s was polio. While Dr. Jonas Salk, fortunately, developed the vaccine to protect against polio in 1955, I didn't get the shot until I was in college.

One evening, when we were six, our family had a gathering at the Charley Brown Memorial Park in nearby Flora (named not after the Charles Schulz comic strip character but a prominent local farmer whose wife donated the site for the park after his death). One of the cool things in the park was a sliding board that at the time seemed very high. My brother and I decided we would try it. When I got to the top, I made the mistake of looking down at what seemed to be at least ten feet. I toppled over and landed on my head. With a big bump rising and not being very responsive, Mom and Dad decided to take me to see Dr. Henderson in Clay City. He got up and opened his office to check me out. He gave me two aspirin and sent us home. This incident and a few others, like breathing fumes out of the gas storage barrels and playing with mercury when we broke thermometers, undoubtedly hindered my brain development.

When we were about thirteen, Mom took us to the bank in Clay City where we each opened a savings account with the $60 we each had saved over the years. After a couple of years, we had saved about $300. Interest earned was meager at $0.98 a month.

Finding ways to earn money was a problem until we could drive. One way I devised to earn money was to clean eggs for a premium of three cents per dozen. Egg prices for farmers in the mid-1950s were about thirty-eight cents a dozen, but large eggs that had been cleaned could be given an A rating and sold for the premium. I persuaded Mom to give me the three cents premium if I gathered, cleaned, and crated the eggs. A crate of eggs held thirty dozen, so when we had two crates to sell, I could make $1.80. The downside of this moneymaking adventure was sitting in our dank cellar after school and using a damp cloth to clean the chicken shit off of the eggs. I grew to have a strong disdain for chickens with their pea-sized brains and the tendency for an old hen sitting on a nest to peck my hands when I tried to remove her eggs.

During the winter, we only heated two rooms in the big house. The kitchen had Mom's large cooking stove that burned wood. The dining room served as our family room because it was a comfortable place to hang out during the evenings. It was heated by a wood/coal-burning stove called a Warm Morning with a metal jacket around the firebox. Both stoves ran out of fuel during the night, so Dad's first job in the morning was to rekindle the fires. The stove pipe from the stove in the dining room went up through the ceiling and into our bedroom. When Garold and I awoke on cold winter mornings, the first thing we would do after crawling from under the covers was to stand around the warm stove pipe to put on our clothes.

Adjoining one of our farm fields was a large, wooded area. In addition to being a good place for squirrel hunting in the fall, it was our source of fuel. During Christmas vacations, Garold and I accompanied Dad to the woods to cut down trees and trim the logs for firewood. Dad was an expert at wielding an axe. Garold and I were put on each end of a crosscut saw that we pulled back and forth to saw down the trees and to saw the logs into shorter lengths. In snowy, cold weather, one might call our work "character building." One of our evening chores was chopping the firewood into smaller pieces and carrying the pieces from the woodpile to the back porch. With no TV, we spent evenings listening to the radio and playing a few games, like Monopoly and a board game called Carrom. I usually stayed up later than the others to read before climbing the stairs to our cold bedroom.

In the winter months, we hurried to get our chores done after school to listen to our favorite radio shows like *Sergeant Preston of the Yukon*, *Dragnet*, *Sky King*, and *The Lone Ranger*. On Saturday night, the family listened to *National Barn Dance*, a program broadcast by WLS in Chicago. *National Barn Dance* was a combination of humor and country/

Western music, and some of the popular stars appearing on the show were George Gobel, Gene Autry, Rex Allen, and Lulu Belle and Scotty.

The radio was Mom's primary source of entertainment during the day, and one of her favorite shows was Art Linkletter's long-running radio show called *House Party*. Sears, Roebuck and Company started the WLS station in the 1920s to advertise their products to rural Americans. After a few years, Sears sold their WLS station to a popular farm magazine called *Prairie Farmer*, also based in Chicago.

Sears, along with Montgomery Ward, started as mail-order catalog companies in Chicago. Sears catalogs, called "wish books," listed almost every product imaginable. Sears provided a lifeline to families in rural areas who were often far from major shopping opportunities. (They were the Amazon of their day.) It was even possible to buy a house from Sears, Roebuck and Company. The catalogs were about three inches thick and were generally tattered by the time they were replaced the following year. Old copies were recycled to the backyard outhouse, where the slick pages made for a poor-quality toilet paper. When their moms weren't looking, boys (including Garold and I) pored over the bra and underwear photos in the women's clothing section.

The two shopping destinations for our neighborhood were Clay City and Sailor Springs, but Clay City was preferred because it was larger and had more stores. Sailor Springs, however, had a more colorful early history at the turn of the nineteenth century. The town had several artesian springs with water many believed had healing properties. It had a strong sulfur smell and, in my opinion, had a horrible taste.

When taking the waters became a health fad around the turn of the century, Sailor Springs became a resort that attracted wealthy people from St. Louis and Chicago. A large hotel called the Glendale was built, along with many amenities, including a man-made lake. The springs on the park-like setting were covered with large decorative gazebos. The resort declined when the popularity of "taking the waters" faded away. The final knell came when the hotel burned in the 1920s, but the resort grounds continued as a local park for several years after World War II.

We liked going to the "spring grounds" for picnics and to play around the still-standing gazebos covering the flowing springs. The most fun was laying a handkerchief over the bubbling water to catch the gas. It formed an air pocket under the hankie and made a loud *poof* when one lit a match to the gas.

Going to Sailor Springs on Saturday nights, not unlike what Mom and Dad had done when they were kids, was when we would sell cream and eggs at the Levitt General Store before shopping. The Levitt family were early settlers and landowners in the township, and Russell Levitt was the store's proprietor. Near the front was a large glass case displaying candy, so that was where Garold and I hung out. In the summer months, the town store owners sponsored free outdoor movies. A projector was set up on a vacant lot next to the old bank building, and people sat on the grass to watch the scratchy film being projected on the side of the building.

Dad would take broken metal parts to the blacksmith in Sailor Springs to fix during the farming season. The blacksmith's shed was small but full of old tools on the walls surrounding his forge, anvil, and water barrel. The place had a strong acrid smell of coal dust and smoke. After a local farmer and welder, Walter Crackel, opened a welding shop with his sons in Clay City, the old blacksmith shop in Sailor Springs closed.

Clay County oil well

Clay City was our preferred town, in part because we could see our friends from school there, plus there was the theater. The village of Clay City got its start in 1854 before the Civil War as a stop on the Baltimore and Ohio Railroad. Tourists going to the Sailor Springs resort got off the train in Clay City. Later, freight trains loaded cars at the grain elevator in Clay City, which the Duff family farm store operated.

An oil boom centered south of Clay City in the 1930s was the most historic event for the town. Hundreds of oil workers descended on the town, with many coming from oil fields in Texas and Oklahoma. The Pure Oil Company obtained most of the oil leases and built a complex about three miles south of town that included housing for their engineers and managers. The boom lasted for nearly twenty years. Dozens of oil field production and supply companies set up shop in Clay City, providing many jobs and bringing prosperity to the community.

Dad worked on a drilling rig during World War II, and both Garold and I worked on oil service rigs after high school. There were many positive impacts for the community as a result of big oil, in addition to the influx of money and jobs. Many new kids arrived to attend the elementary and high schools and added variety to all the school activities, including sports. A linguistics professor at the University of Illinois studied speech patterns around the state. After the influx of migrants from Texas and Oklahoma, he found that a new accent was formed in our area when the new arrivals' Southern drawls mixed with the locals' river-bottom brogue.

Chapter 6

LATHROP CHURCH

One of the constants in our lives was the Sunday morning ritual of going to the Lathrop Methodist Church. The church had a congregation of about forty people, mainly from the neighborhood. Early on, Methodist ministers in rural America might serve more than one congregation as circuit riders, so the congregations were referred to as charges of the minister because he was charged with providing pastoral care. Lathrop was a charge of the Clay City Methodist Church, and the minister

Lathrop Methodist Church

Grace Lutz with our Sunday school class

drove out each Sunday morning to deliver his sermon. After the sermon, the congregation broke up into three Sunday school groups for children, young adults, and adults.

Grace Lutz, the children's teacher, also taught school and lived on a farm on the Dredge Ditch about a mile north of our farm. There were usually six to ten of us in her class. She was a large, energetic woman. Aside from having us memorize Bible verses each week, she was very creative. Her daughter was a missionary in Mexico, so once she had a party for us complete with a piñata and a game for learning a few Spanish words. In the fall, we had wiener roasts and hayrides at their farm, and in the winter, she took us bowling. The three boys in the class were Garold, Jimmy Brown, and me.

We were ten years old when Mrs. Lutz decided that the three boys could form a trio and sing on the radio. The local radio station (WVLN) was in Olney, a big city to us, with a population of about ten thousand. Grace arranged for us to be on a Saturday morning program for kids. Our performance didn't get us any more bookings, maybe because our friend Jimmy couldn't carry a tune.

Young adult Sunday school class

In high school, our Sunday school teacher was Vida Frutiger. She would take us to monthly MYF (Methodist Youth Fellowship) meetings to join kids from other churches. Garold and I also attended a couple of weeklong MYF camps.

Lathrop Church members formed a tight-knit community, and Sunday was a time for catching up on the neighborhood news. The women had a club called Lathrop Circle, and they met at one another's homes once each month. Mom was an active member, and the group continued to meet after the congregation moved to the main church in Clay City. The church sponsored a fall chowder for a fundraising event for a couple of years. Chowder, in the local parlance, was basically a soup picnic. Everett and Vida hosted the gathering in their woods, and people flocked from all over. The men of the church got together early on the day of the chowder to build fires under large, black kettles set on tripods to cook the stew. Vegetables for the chowder came from the gardens of church fam-

Cooking the chowder

ilies who also provided the meat, usually chicken and pork. At the more popular chowder held annually on Elm River, south of Clay City, squirrel hunters would provide the chowder meat.

Many Methodist churches in the Bible Belt still held annual revival meetings into the 1950s. A guest minister would come to the church for one or two weeks of nightly church services. Many preachers had an evangelical fervor and sought to convert nonbelievers into the fold. Garold and I were about thirteen when we joined Dad during the altar call at the end of a sermon and went down to the front of the church. The hymn "Just As I Am" was soulfully sung by the congregation as we knelt at the altar. The preacher leaned over to lead us to conversion. It was quite a psychological experience and, in retrospect, it set us up for some very conflicting situations when we got into high school.

Mom was a devoted Christian all of her life and had her Bible by her reading lamp for study almost every day. However, she never put any pressure on Dad or her somewhat wayward sons to study the Bible or live a more religious life. My early church experiences did, however, give me a lasting ethical foundation for dealing with life issues.

Although not connected to the church officially, the neighborhood cemetery was located on the same forty-acre farm field. The Smith Cemetery was named after the farmer and church member who had donated the land. For several decades, Everett Frutiger—and later, his son Carrol Lee—volunteered as managers, known as sextons, for the cemetery. When someone died, Everett would recruit members from the church to dig the grave. Garold and I would occasionally go with Dad to watch when he helped dig a grave, which could be an ordeal when the ground was frozen in winter. Later in high school, I mowed the grass during two summers for a good wage of a dollar an hour. The mower had big wheels and a motor that turned the circular blades, but it still required pushing. The blades had no cover guard, and it was a delicate process to trim around the stones without cutting a chunk out of the corners.

I learned a lot about the neighborhood families from taking care of the monuments, including the four generations of the Herdes family buried there. Much is made of rural and small-town values such as family, hard work, traditions, commitment, simplicity, pride, support, teamwork, nature, and God. While never articulated directly, these principles were how we lived our daily lives.

Ruby and Charles Herdes's tombstone, Smith Cemetery, Clay County

Chapter 7

Mom and Dad

The summer of 1951 was a troublesome time in our household. Dad became increasingly disoriented and talked to himself constantly. One morning, he disappeared and finally ended up at his brother Earl's house. Earl, Aunt Lelia, and Mom took Dad to the hospital in Olney. After a two-day stay, the doctor arranged his admission to the state mental hospital in Alton, Illinois. Alton was located on the Mississippi River just north of St. Louis and about a hundred miles west of Clay City.

The Alton State Hospital was one of over a dozen mental institutions built around the state in the 1920s for housing the mentally ill, although in the vernacular at the time, they were called insane asylums. The Alton complex was built to house a thousand patients, but over two thousand were in the facility when Dad was admitted. Antipsychotic drugs would not be developed until the early 1950s. Instead, the treatment for mental illness starting in the 1940s was electro-convulsive therapy or shock treatments. Lobotomies were also in vogue, but fortunately, Dad only got the shock treatments.

Dad was in Alton for over two months, from late July until October 9, 1951. Every couple of weeks, on a Sunday, Mom would take us to see him in Alton. We were joined by either Everett and Vida or Mom's sister Clora and her husband, Harmon. Mom packed a picnic, and Dad was

Alton State Hospital

allowed to leave the building and join us on the hospital grounds. Dad seemed normal to Garold and me, but after the shock treatments, he lost his short-term memory for a time.

He was supposed to remain in Alton for six months, but he announced that he had checked himself out during one of our visits. He came home after three months and resumed a somewhat normal life, but it took some time for the fuzziness of his memory—and likely, the trauma of the shock treatments—to wear off. He remained troubled until his death many years later.

When Dad was at Alton, Garold and I started sixth grade. Fortunately, neighbors pitched in with their time and equipment to harvest our fall crops. When we got home from school, however, Garold and I tackled all of the evening chores we'd earlier split between Dad and us. We also brought in the cattle from the pasture for milking, and fed and watered the hogs, chickens, and horses.

One evening, I changed out of my school clothes, not relishing doing the chores. When I walked out to the barn lot, I saw that Dad's two workhorses had broken the fence and were in Uncle Earl's cornfield. I think that was the last time I cried for another twenty years. But the only option was to suck it up and move on, so I did.

At school, kids were curious about what was wrong with our dad. At that time, the way mental illness was discussed was to say a person had had a nervous breakdown. So that was how we tried to explain what was going on. This seemed to work, and we had no teasing about his being crazy or off his rocker.

In later years, after Dad died, I pondered what kind of illness Dad had and how he had been diagnosed. By this time, the Alton State Hospital had morphed into an outpatient mental health center. I learned that patients' files had been transferred to an archive at the state capital in Springfield. Because of new privacy laws, I had to hire a lawyer to get a court order appointing me executor of his estate before the state would release his records. This finally came about in 2004, and I received his file containing three reports by two different psychologists.

The reports were very revealing, with some observations that seemed accurate. Since psychology as a therapeutic practice was still somewhat new in the early 1950s, the terminology for his diagnosis was confusing. In one instance, a psychologist described Dad as a manic depressive. Two psychiatrist friends reviewed the reports and concluded that he was more likely to have been very clinically depressed. Throughout the reports, terms such as nervous, anxious, extremely agitated, guilt-ridden, self-deprecatory, and self-absorbed were used to describe his condition. He was also concerned about what people might think of him and repressed his aggressive feelings.

There were two observations in the reports that helped clarify what had been going on. The first was that, while Dad had held deep-seated feelings of inadequacy and low self-esteem since childhood, he had been tipped over the edge earlier in the year when he had bought a farm and then turned around and sold it three weeks later. Because his dad and mom wanted him to move off their farm and buy his own, he thought they didn't love him and that he was being rejected.

The second involved purchasing and reselling the new farm we never occupied. When Dad couldn't handle the pressure of spending $9,000 to buy the sixty-acre farm, he sold it, only to become guilt-ridden about his decision. Mom was disappointed, too, since the inheritance from her dad had allowed them to buy the farm. Dad joined the church at this time because he thought God could help him keep the devil from telling him what to do.

The more personal note that got my attention was that he told the psychologist he thought I had an illness just like his. Well, that could also explain a lot. Dad also said that he expected Garold and me to work long hours, and that he was ruining us by not working us hard enough. It rings true in retrospect and is consistent with his approach to life, which was barren of any hobbies, including sports. Another thing that became clear to me as I worked through what had happened to Dad was that everyone in a household with a mentally ill person is impacted somehow. I was no exception.

Mom was the glue that held our family together and the rock of our family who sustained my well-being. I suppose many boys would like to confer sainthood on their moms, but I think my mom was deserving of such a designation. I developed a strong sense of loyalty to her, which probably kept me from becoming too rebellious as a teenager. Mom never got a daughter, but she always seemed pleased to get two for one with her twins.

Coming from a family where Mom was number nine of thirteen children, everyone had a role in supporting Granddad's large farming operation. Although only five foot three inches tall, Mom had extraordinary stamina. Like Dad, Mom only went to school through the eighth grade. She wanted to go to high school, but her dad didn't think girls needed further education. An excellent seamstress, she made most of her clothes, as well as mine and Garold's until we started school. She used a classic foot-powered Singer sewing machine. She made sure we were dressed and ready for church each Sunday. She was also a passionate quilter and pursued this craft all her life. One of her volunteer activities was serving as a leader for the local girls 4-H club.

Our subsistence farm with few amenities meant long days. Mom usually got up with Dad at four thirty in the morning. Monday was laundry day, quite an undertaking before we had electricity. She carried water from the well to a large, black kettle for heating before putting it into the washing machine. She made soap using lye and the lard from butchering. The clothes were hung to dry on a line with clothespins. Tuesday was ironing day, and she ironed by using triangular flat irons that were heated on the wood stovetop.

Most of Mom's work was determined by the seasons, especially growing and preserving fruits and vegetables and preparing meals. Gardening was a big activity for the whole family, and none of us escaped the long hours of planting, hoeing, and harvesting various vegetables during the summer and fall. Before refrigeration, Mom had a huge task in canning our fruits and vegetables. We stored potatoes from a large patch in a bin in the cellar. When cherries, peaches, grapes, and apples ripened over the summer, Mom would often get together with her sisters to "put up" the fruit for the coming winter.

While Mom was shy and reserved, she loved being with her family and friends. Despite her workload and Dad's reservations, she was a determined and dedicated member of her clubs. This included the Lathrop Circle (the women's group from our country church), the garden club, and the Home Bureau, all of which met monthly. Her garden club met at members' homes and was probably her favorite. She had dozens of flower varieties that she grew from seeds or bulbs, which she exchanged with

Mom (far left, back row)
with sisters Mary, Clora, and Luella

other members. Since we didn't have a phone, family members or neighbors would often drop by with no notice. The tradition at our house was that Mom would first give the women a tour of her gardens.

Most important to Mom, however, was her membership in the Home Bureau. The Home Bureau was a county organization for farm women, somewhat parallel to the Farm Bureau. The University of Illinois Extension Service provided a Home Adviser to each county to advise farm women and provide classes and demonstrations on a wide variety of subjects related to home economics. Mom got many ideas from the monthly classes dealing with nutrition, finances, home decorating, and arts and crafts. She had a local reputation for her cake-baking skills and won ribbons at the county fair. She made a lot of angel food and chiffon cakes for weddings and anniversaries. Although she had limited formal

Stanley Christmas at our house, 1955

education, after forty years of Home Bureau work, she likely had the equivalent of an associate's degree in home economics.

At the end of the gravel road, our big house had one advantage for Mom. There was room for her to host the Stanley family's annual Christmas gatherings. She and her sisters continued getting together for fun and work throughout their lives.

One thing my mom and I shared was an interest in music. She had learned to play the banjo and guitar when she was younger and played in the Stanley family band. She taught me a few chords on her old guitar, and I started to play on my own. I lamented that Garold wasn't interested, for I envisioned us becoming an act like the Everly Brothers. Without lessons, I never got very proficient but kept playing anyway. I learned a few Stephen Foster songs on the harmonica, as well. For a 4-H competition, I bought a contraption that fit around my neck to hold the harmonica while accompanying myself on the guitar. The judges at the contest weren't impressed, but it didn't dampen my enthusiasm for music.

In high school, I began to define myself as the opposite of Dad. He could not overcome his demons to extend any support to us. My brother, however, had a better relationship with him as they shared an affinity for farming. Mom was helpful to us by being a good listener and finding understated ways of showing her love, like being supportive of our choices. Neither Mom nor Dad ever uttered the words "I love you" in my memory.

The Depression era and the belt-tightening required during World War II had profoundly impacted my folks' generation. The lessons of frugality and delayed gratification influenced my brother and me for most of our lives. The other lesson was that work came first before play, which often meant there was no time left for play. I don't think I ever recovered from this perception of priorities. Much later, I came to regard it as an affliction rather than a virtue.

Chapter 8

HIGH SCHOOL YEARS

In the fall of 1954, Garold and I started our freshman year at Clay City High School. It was a rough beginning because, soon after we began school, Mom became ill. We were told she was having female problems, and finally, she was taken to the Richland Memorial Hospital in Olney, where she had a hysterectomy. She was in the hospital for two weeks, and the bill for her stay was $293 plus $205 for the surgery. We had no health insurance in those days, and health-care costs seemed reasonable, except that our annual farm income was not much over $2,000.

Mom's sisters rightly judged that she would not be able to recuperate if she came home directly from the hospital. They took care of her in their homes for two additional weeks so she could rest and not be tempted to jump back into work. We survived on casseroles that had been dropped off by our neighbors. Much like mine today, Dad's cooking skills were limited mainly to what he could fry in a skillet. In addition, 1954 was a challenging year financially because of a severe drought that adversely affected crop yields. Average farm income was less than $3,000 in a good year, and we made far less than that in southern Illinois.

Our beginning at Clay City High School seemed like a giant transition. During the first week, freshmen had to wear beanies and obey orders from upper-class members. The hazing that went on seemed pret-

Clay City High School

ty scary at the time when some of the upper-class guys got too physical. Garold and I enrolled in the same classes that included math, English, science, agriculture, physical education, and band. Without guidance on what courses to take, I only learned later that taking math instead of algebra was a mistake. Not having taken algebra as a freshman meant later not being able to take calculus or trigonometry.

For the most part, we had good teachers, especially our female teachers. In those years, women who went to college tended to become teachers or nurses. Many were extraordinarily bright, and in a different time, they could have gone into a variety of professions and positions of leadership. My favorite subjects were English and American history; Garold preferred shop and agriculture.

Agriculture was a four program, and Garold pursued that route while I only took it for one year. By this time, Garold was set on becoming a farmer, but I had decided that farming was not for me. As freshmen, we joined the Future Farmers of America (FFA) and participated in several competitions with other schools. Judging livestock was a major event. Teams from competing schools would judge cattle, sheep, hogs, and chickens. There were other contests, including soil judging and identifying noxious weeds. Garold and I were picked for the school team that went to the state contest at the University of Illinois in Champaign. Despite hating chickens, my best performance was on the chicken judging team. The best part of the trip to Champaign was seeing the university campus and touring the agriculture and engineering colleges. Near the campus was a Steak 'n Shake restaurant, one of the first fast-food chains. I thought my hamburger and milkshake lunch was the best.

Back in Clay City, the FFA had an annual pest control contest. Points were given for the different kinds of pests that were eliminated. At that time, many birds and creatures were considered problems for farmers, and the number of points for each was determined by how difficult they were to collect. So a mouse tail was worth five points, as was the head of a sparrow. Pigeon heads were ten points, but a hawk's head or a foxtail was worth fifty points. Garold and I went to many of our neighbors at night and climbed into their barn lofts with flashlights to collect pigeon and sparrow heads. We thought we were doing pretty well, but Raymond Hentischer, an upperclassman, blew away the competition. He collected specimens year-round and put his mixture of mice tails and bird heads in tin buckets that he stored in his mother's freezer. When he brought in his collection for counting, the sight of the coagulated mess thawing in his buckets was not recommended before lunch.

Our agriculture teacher, Mr. Loren Petty, invited some of us to take on a summer job detasseling corn for the Pioneer Seed Corn Company in Champaign, Illinois. The detasseling period lasted only a few weeks, and the job required walking up and down the rows of corn to remove immature pollen-producing tassels. The removals were required to produce hybrid seeds to create higher yields and provide disease and insect resistance. The summer after our freshman year, five of us crowded into Mr. Petty's station wagon to ride to Champaign, each carrying a blanket and a toothbrush. No room or board was provided, so we decided to camp at a park called Lake of the Woods. The twelve-hour days started at six o'clock in the morning when the dew was still heavy on the corn leaves that scratched our sunburned arms. The heat and humidity came close to being unbearable. Many teenagers considered it their worst job; for me, it was a step up from cleaning out chicken houses or cleaning eggs. And it paid eighty cents an hour.

In the evenings, we congregated at our lake campsite, usually eating baloney sandwiches, but one evening we decided to have frog legs. Giant bullfrogs were croaking at us from the lakeshore, and we were able to spear them with sharpened sticks. We went to bed hungry after the blackened exterior and the raw interior had tested our carnivore instincts.

One of the five involved in the detasseling work was Myron Taylor. Myron was the only Black kid in our school (and probably the whole county). He was fun to be around, and we later got to know him better on the track team, where he and Garold ran relays together. Despite acceptance from his classmates, Myron received a lot of harassment outside of school. He quit after his junior year and joined the navy.

During our freshman year, the high school opened a new cafeteria for serving hot lunches. Many of us still ate our sack lunches sitting on the gym bleachers. In our sophomore year, Mom gave us her quarter collection for buying lunch in the cafeteria. The lunches cost a quarter, but a government program provided milk free to school lunch programs thanks to the surplus of milk. We could buy an extra glass for a penny. Sometimes, between classes, a small group of us would hurry to the cafeteria and drink a couple of glasses of chocolate milk. The cook was Marie Weiler, a very warm and kind lady, who often gave us milk for free. We continued to ride the school bus, and I carried the big case with my baritone horn for practicing at home. To reduce the noise annoyance for the rest of the household, I practiced my horn in the front room of the house that was not heated during the winter. Mr. Gengler gave me more complex music to practice, and he helped me prepare for the annual music contests.

Our class size doubled when we started high school. There were only three high schools in the county: Clay City, Flora, and Louisville. The Clay City high school district encompassed three smaller villages with only elementary schools. Kids of high school age were bussed to Clay City High School from the north of town in Pixley Township and the villages of Sailor Springs, Ingraham, and Wendelin. They added a new mix to the student body, especially those from Wendelin, which was a German Catholic settlement. These kids were generally smarter and, unfortunately, subjected to a certain bias by those with Protestant backgrounds. Kids from a couple of rural grade schools south of Clay City in oil country also joined us.

One of the friendships Garold and I developed was with an unusual fellow from south of town whose name was Hugh Lynn. Hugh was a pear-shaped kid weighing over two hundred pounds and wearing glasses. He was interested in doing things like our ancestors, such as trapping, fishing with nets, using old-style tools, and playing a fiddle. We occasionally stayed all night with one another for outdoor outings.

Hugh Lynn, 1954

Hugh gave me a book on trapping that I read until almost all the pages were worn. We searched for places to set traps and carved stretchers for animal skins out of old door panels. Each fall, we boiled our steel traps in water with walnut hulls to take away any scents before setting them in water and land pathways. Hugh was much more successful than I was, but I dutifully got up early each morning before school to check on my traps.

It was invigorating to walk in the frosty air at daylight, anticipating what I might find. All I had for a gun was a single-shot .22 rifle that had belonged to Dad's sister Imogene. It was a challenge hunting squirrels with it, but it was sufficient for killing animals that had been ensnared in a trap. My major success was capturing two wild mink. The fur buyer paid twenty dollars each for them, but raccoon and muskrats only brought between two and five dollars. I found skinning the animals before mounting them on a stretcher a bit distasteful, and on an hourly basis, the wages for trapping were meager.

Hugh dropped out of high school after two years. He was a good student, but he had been bullied and teased so much because of his weight and looks that he gave up. Later, in 1959, Hugh joined a group from Michigan called the Fifty-Niners who went to Alaska to homestead. Since one had to be 21 years of age to receive 160 acres of federal land to homestead, Hugh returned from Alaska after a short time to live on his granddad's farm. Hugh was a recognizable figure around the area with his full beard and his attire consisting of bib overalls. He raised sorghum cane and traditional crops on his farm. He bought an old processing mill to boil down the cane into molasses that he bottled in gallon jugs and sold. The old-time sawmill he operated to saw lumber for neighboring farmers was more profitable. We kept in touch over the years, and at my brother's funeral, he implored me to visit him. I was on a tight schedule but made the time to see Hugh. We had a good visit, and he showed me the large scar on his back where he had had cancer surgery the prior year. Six months later, he died after refusing to have any further treatment. I was sure glad that I had taken the time to see him.

Getting a driver's license and a car was a big deal in our lives. It would give us the chance to get off the farm independently. It was a blow for Garold and me when Illinois changed the age for getting a driver's license from fifteen to sixteen when we were fourteen. We would have to wait another year before we could enjoy all the opportunities driving would open up for us. Meanwhile, we saved as much money as we could.

The week after we turned sixteen, we got our driver's licenses and went car shopping. We found a used car that had been previously owned by a farmer; it cost us $300. We each withdrew $150 from our bank savings accounts to make the purchase. The black 1949 Chevy was not in the best shape, but we made it our own. We added silver stars on each fender skirt, a green-winged duck as the hood ornament, and an AM radio. One advantage was filling up with gas from the gas storage tank used for the farm tractors. We learned how to do most of the maintenance, including oil changes and tune-ups.

Owning a car allowed us to start dating. We usually had double dates and long drives if the girls lived on farms in different neighborhoods. Often, we would meet our friends in Clay City on Saturday nights and drive to either of the two larger nearby towns of Olney and Flora. Sometimes, we joined the parade of cars dragging main streets, usually from the Dog and Suds on one end to the Dairy Queen on the other. A new quarter-mile-long bridge over the wetlands just north of Clay City made a perfect drag strip. One night, Garold put our 1949 Chevy up against Jimmy Brown's 1950 Ford and came out on the short end. When Garold tried to speed shift from first to second gear, the rear axle broke. This took a toll on our budget and ended our racing careers.

Garold and I mostly had the same friends, which was a plus since we only had one car. One group we met up with had a bit of a wild side, although none of us started drinking while in high school. We did, however, shoot out all the streetlights in Sailor Springs one night. On Hal-

Our first car, 1949 Chevy

loween, we drove around the countryside turning over outhouses. One farmer heard us and came out of his house with a shotgun. We escaped by scattering in his farm fields in the dark.

The Clay City constable, Perry Long, always parked his Pontiac on the main street, monitoring our driving speeds. On occasion, he would give chase as we drove up the highway toward Sailor Springs. After a band practice one night, he stopped me when I was driving home. He thought I was speeding. I showed him my horn case and gave him my sob story. I was lucky he didn't give me a ticket. His wife, Clara, was our senior-year English teacher, and she was as stern as he was. By our senior year, we each had steady girlfriends. We persuaded Mom and Dad to let us use their car on Saturday nights, so we didn't have to double date. Dad had a 1954 Chevy that was a step up from our 1949 model. Garold and I took turns taking Dad's car.

Garold was dating Elaine Wolfe, a junior, whom he later married. My girlfriend was Janet Schack. She and I had a lot in common. Many

Dad and Mom's 1954 Chevy

of our friends played in the band, and we had known each other since grade school. Our relationship didn't extend beyond high school, but we remained friends, especially since we both went to the same college.

During our high school years, Garold and I were big enough to do farm work for neighbors after we finished our farm work helping Dad. Generally, we got lunch and five dollars a day for driving a tractor and putting up baled hay. Allis Chalmers came out with a hay baler in the early 1950s that was relatively inexpensive. The baler didn't have to stop when it kicked out bales that were round. These round bales were harder for us to handle than traditional square ones. It was a toss-up as to what job was harder: walking beside a wagon picking up the bales and lifting them to the guy stacking them on the wagon, or being on the other end in a hot, dusty barn stacking bales as they came off the elevator.

Another job that was soon to fade away as farming techniques changed was shocking redtop. Redtop was a grass whose seeds were used primarily to plant pastureland. Machines called binders cut the redtop and tied the grass stems into bundles that were then kicked out and onto the ground. Our job was to set four bundles together in a shock, with one bundle spread on top as a cap to repel moisture. Later, the bundles were picked up for threshing. When farmers no longer needed horses, and when many no longer raised cattle, the demand for redtop dropped dramatically. These jobs helped us earn enough money to eventually buy our car.

After our junior year in high school, Garold and I followed different paths. Because he was good at mechanics and handling machinery, one of our uncles, Donald Blair, married to Mom's sister Mary, hired him on his farm for the summer. I was hired by my Uncle Nelson during the summers of 1957 and 1958 to show cattle on the fair circuit. Two of Mom's brothers, Nelson and Fletcher, continued Granddad Stanley's tradition of showing their Milking Shorthorn cattle at the county fairs in southern Illinois. The cattle show entries were made under the name "Stanley Brothers," but Nelson was the principal. Cattle showmen were mainly on the fair circuits to advertise their brands and sell breeding stock at higher than market prices. The Stanley Brothers also showed to make money from the cash awards. Part of the tradition was that the Stanley cousins were hired as herdsmen to help care for and show the cattle.

I was on the fair circuit with Nelson for eight weeks, ending in late August at the state fair in Springfield, Illinois. The job required long hours, starting at daybreak by bringing the cattle in from tie-outs to the tents where fairgoers could view them during the day. The tie-outs were located in a grassy area where we led the cattle out and tied them to fences at night where it was cooler than in the tents. We then cleaned out the stalls and laid down clean straw for the next day. After leading them back to the tent before breakfast, my jobs included feeding, watering, milking, then cleaning and brushing to make them pretty for fair visitors. Each weekend we would load the cattle in a large truck and move on to the next fair.

Our herd of Milking Shorthorn cattle

Show day was the high point each week at the fair. Uncle Fletcher would join Nelson and me for the day. Fletcher was called Red, and Nelson was known as Curly. They had been showing their cattle for over thirty years and were well-known and popular among other cattle breeders on the fair circuit. The show herd included about twenty head of cattle and had cows and bulls of different ages. Several show entries were made showing the cattle individually or in mixed groups. The brothers did most of the showing while I stayed in the tent, primping the cattle for the show ring. I would wash, brush, and trim their hair; trim and oil their horns and hoofs; and put on their show halters.

I took a lot of teasing during the first summer, but I also learned a lot from my uncle Nelson. Nelson would tell me I had a grasshopper ass because I was so skinny. He was a very frugal guy and rolled his cigarettes in a ritual that was fun to watch. He was a World War II veteran but never talked much about it, even though he had had to remain in the army for five years. He was stationed in the Philippines and served as a tank mechanic during the island-hopping campaign.

The second summer I worked with the show cattle, Nelson often left me on my own. I had over twenty head in the show herd at the Edwards

Stanley Brothers' champion bull

County Fair. The scariest animal in the herd was a large bull that weighed over two thousand pounds. Only a ring in his nose made him manageable in the show ring and for getting him in and out of the truck at moving time. During the summer, one of the cows had twin baby bulls. I entered the babies in the show class for pairs of bull calves, and they placed because there were so few entries in that class. Nelson wasn't too happy with me for taking the initiative to show the calves, even though the calves won prize money. It seemed they had to be registered with the Milking Shorthorn Society before they could be officially shown.

    I was paid fifty dollars a week on the fair circuit. This seemed like a good wage, but I had to buy my meals. There were no McDonald's or Subways, so we went to local cafés, some of which we called greasy spoons. I tried to get by on spending just a dollar a day, so I ate better when family members would often bring us picnic meals. I slept on an army cot in the tent behind the cattle. It was easy making friends with the other herdsmen on the circuit. In the evenings, when we finally finished our work, we would shower under a hose, dress in clean clothes, and walk the midway carnivals to people-watch. We tried to find a girl in every port but not with much success.

Nelson would figure out how much I was owed at the end of the summer after deducting what he gave me each week for expenses. My earnings for the two summers were enough to pay half of my first year's college expenses. One major expenditure I made during my senior year was to buy a television for the family that cost $400. Dad reimbursed me in the fall after the bean harvest when he had more cash.

In our junior year, having obtained our driver's licenses and a car, Garold and I could finally go out for a sport, but we were limited to track and field. It was too late to pick up the skills for other varsity sports. Since I was skinny, the track coach thought I should run the mile, but that was a disappointment for both of us. Finally, he was content to have me run the 440 and the mile relay. I also competed in the high jump and the high hurdles. Our school didn't have hurdles to practice on, so I jumped over our farm fences. That didn't go so well. Once I got caught on a barbed wire and cut my leg near a sensitive spot. I still bear the scar today. I was mediocre at track, but I did place in the 440 event at the conference meet.

Garold, however, became a track star. He was still shorter than I, but he was stocky, muscular, and fast. He ran all the dashes, including the 50-yard, 100-yard, 220, and relays. I think he still holds the school record in the 220. He also competed in the broad jump and low hurdles and did especially well in the pole vault.

Playing in the band was an important activity for me throughout high school. Mr. Gengler's success in creating winning concert bands at contests was enticing to me and others. Over 25 percent of the student body played in the band. The band received first-place awards at the district and state contests during my four years in high school. I matched the medals playing baritone solos.

One of the highlights of my junior year was being selected to play in a regional band to back up a concert by Rafael Méndez, a Mexican virtuoso on the trumpet. Méndez toured the United States giving public concerts using student bands. Most people came to hear him play one of his classics, "Flight of the Bumblebee." There were approximately three hundred students in the school and only fifteen faculty members. We had no foreign language offerings, no school nurse, no counselors, and no vocal or drama classes. The coaches taught academic subjects, but they were usually better at coaching.

Track star on right

School activities were important to me, and making good grades helped me obtain some recognition. I was on the student council all four years, president of the band, biology club, and the sophomore class, and coeditor of the yearbook. Being a bigger duck in a smaller pond was easier since our class started high school with only sixty-two students. Forty-eight of us graduated from high school, ten of us went to college, and twenty had started first grade together. Several girls married their high school sweethearts shortly after graduation.

At graduation, I was co-valedictorian and received the band award and the American Legion medal. The class voted that I was most likely to succeed, most popular, and hardest working. In my view, hardest working was the most accurate; others were smarter than I. Mr. Shafer, our principal, gave us this message: "Plan to make a contribution, however small or great it may be, to the welfare of the greatest nation in history, your country. Do not be a drifter."

Top: Garold and Darold, high school graduation
Bottom: My senior year report card

Chapter 9

COLLEGE DAYS

Our high school senior year was a time of hard decisions. Garold and I, like all of our classmates, had to set the course for what would come next in our lives. Garold already knew he wanted to be a farmer, get married, and have kids. I knew I wanted to go to college but was without a real mentor or another source of guidance. The closest role models for me were our teachers. My favorite teacher was Mr. Brandon, who taught American history and coached basketball and track. I didn't feel comfortable focusing on math and science, so I considered music and social studies. I later discovered that majoring in history was the right choice for me.

Paying for college seemed a bit daunting. Fortunately, the state gave out tuition scholarships for state universities. I applied and, presumably because of my grades, received one that would cover the $450 annual tuition at a state school. With the money I had saved from summer jobs, I figured I could at least get through one year of college.

Where to attend college was the next question. I had visited the University of Illinois, but I was intimidated by the size of the place. I had also visited the campus at Eastern Illinois University (EIU) in Charleston a couple of times for a science fair competition and a jazz concert with Mr. Gengler. EIU also had the benefit of being somewhat closer to

Garold and I connected but
going separate ways

Clay City. Too, there were only two thousand students at Eastern versus twenty thousand at the University of Illinois.

It turned out I was the only one in our class to go to EIU. Many of my classmates continuing to college decided to attend Southern Illinois University in Carbondale. After completing work on the summer fair circuit, I drove the 1949 Chevy up to Charleston to find a place to live. Garold kindly gave me his share of our car, and he upgraded to a newer Chevy.

Finding a place to live was also a challenge. The dorm rates seemed too expensive, so I looked for a room off campus. A couple, who had a two-story house two blocks from the campus, rented out their three upstairs bedrooms. Three guys had one room while there were two in the others. The seven of us shared a small bathroom. Mrs. Dede clearly wore the pants in the family, and she yelled at us if there was any noise after ten o'clock at night. She managed the rental, and I later learned it was not a

Old Main at Eastern Illinois University

good idea to get on her bad side. I signed up for one of the rooms for five dollars a week.

I was impressed by the university's campus that had an imposing building at the entrance. It was the first structure built on the campus when the university was founded in 1895 and was called Old Main. Old Main was patterned after a castle and stood at the front of the campus that expanded through a quad to the library.

Freshman Year: 1958–59

First-year students arrived on campus a few days early for orientation and class registration. I drove up with some clothes and went to my rooming house at 915 Ninth Street, the Dede residence. I met my roommate, Dallas Puckett, for the first time. Dallas was from another southern Illinois town where his dad was the superintendent of schools. He was an OK kid but not much of an example. He only wanted to play pinball machines, so he flunked out before the first year was over.

Two other freshmen lived in one bedroom, and three upperclassmen shared the large bedroom. One of the freshmen, Barry Wilber, and I became friends as time went on. I would let him borrow my car once a week to take out his girlfriend, and he paid me a dollar for gas. Barry played on both the varsity basketball and tennis teams. He patiently tried to teach me to play tennis, and I learned a lot from being around him with his higher level of sophistication.

On my application to EIU, I had checked the box to study in the Social Sciences Department, which covered history, geography, political science, economics, and sociology. By taking courses in these subjects and the classes for education majors, I could graduate with a teaching degree and theoretically be qualified to teach all of them. The Department assigned advisors, so I went to see mine, who turned out to be Dr. Glenn Seymour, head of the department.

EIU had hired Dr. Seymour in 1929. He gave me an outline for what courses I should take, but I rarely saw him afterward. Dr. Seymour was a short fellow with a booming voice. He was also a Stephen A. Douglas scholar and had written a well-received Douglas biography.

After obtaining a list of required classes, I went to a converted gym where the registrar had set up tables for students to register. The place had a zoo-like atmosphere, with everyone running around trying to get the classes they wanted before they were filled. The good news was that the class sizes were small, usually around thirty students, and almost all the professors had a PhD. I carried paper cards to various tables to sign up for the classes Dr. Seymour had recommended. I discovered that freshmen were at a disadvantage for picking the suitable courses since selecting the right professor was as important as choosing the right class.

During my first week, I was walking across the campus week when I was joined by a friendly fellow who introduced himself as John Huffman from Olney, Illinois. He asked me questions and made me feel comfortable about being on campus. I soon learned he was president of the student body. I later ran for that office, unsuccessfully.

Left: Dr. Seymour
Right: Dr. Syndergaard

EIU followed a quarter system rather than a semester system, so every twelve weeks we had final exams. At midterm, I took my first test in geography. The professor was Chinese and very detail-oriented; the questions were short answers. I finished before anyone else, so I took my time handing it in. When we got the test back, I had received a D, even though I hadn't missed any questions. It turned out there had been a backside to the questions sheet. The professor looked at me skeptically when I appealed and gave me no sympathy. I managed to turn the page on the following tests and got an A for the course. My science course was biology, and Dr. Leonard Duncan, an excellent professor, almost made a science major out of me. But I stayed with my decision to study the social sciences.

The fall of 1958 was the centennial of the famous Lincoln-Douglas debates. Abraham Lincoln and Stephen A. Douglas had had several debates around Illinois as part of their campaigns for the US Senate. Charleston had been one of the debate locations. There was no questioning the names given to the two men's dorms on the campus: Lincoln Hall and Douglas Hall. Charles Coleman, a Lincoln scholar and EIU faculty member, wrote a play about the debate for presentation during homecoming weekend. Dr. Seymour played the role of Stephen Douglas, and Dr. Rex Syndergaard played the role of Lincoln. Dr. Syndergaard, a tall, good-looking man and a Russian history scholar, would become my favorite professor. The play was a highlight for me during the homecoming weekend.

Mr. Gengler had encouraged me to play in the concert band when I went to college. He followed up by sending a recommendation to Dr. George Westcott, the EIU band director. The school provided me with a horn, and I joined the baritone section with three other players. I met some talented students and quickly concluded that I had made the right decision not to major in music.

Our road trips to play concerts were fun, and I enjoyed playing in the band. Most of the band members were music majors, which meant their absences for missed classes during the concert tours were excused. Since I was not a music major, I got absences marked against me in the classes I missed. That, and the time squeeze created by my cafeteria job, led me to abandon playing in the band the following year. Ironically, one of the band's biggest concerts during my year with the band was playing in a concert with none other than Rafael Méndez! I ended up with two of his autographs.

Managing my finances to remain at school was going to be tricky. To make sure I could cover my expenses, I took a job in the school cafeteria. I was assigned to wash dishes and became acquainted with Clay Dungy. Clay, an African American, and I took turns so that one of us was not stuck with the hated job of washing the giant bowls used to mix dough every day. A new student union was under construction, which would house a new cafeteria the following year. The campus cafeteria during my

Expenses	1958-
1st Quater	3rd Quater
meals 135	meals 115
rent 65	rent 70
tuition 15	tuition 15
mis 5	mis 10
watch 40	clothes 10
clothes 50	220
310	
	Total '58-'59
2nd Quater	meals 370
meals 120	rent 195
rent 60	tuition 50
tuition 20	mis 20
mis 5	watch 40
cloth 10	clothes 70
215	745

My tally of expenses from 1958

freshman year was in an old Quonset hut that had been built during the war years.

I ate most meals at the cafeteria. I could usually get by paying thirty cents each for my noon and evening meals, including a piece of pie. On mornings I would stop in at one of the private eating joints around the campus for a glass of milk and a donut. At the end of each week, I wrote down my expenses and made a tally at the end of each quarter, and later for the year. My first year at EIU cost $750.

By the end of the school year I had made several observations about going to college. First, even though college was much harder academically than high school, I could be successful. I was not the smartest, but I learned how to study, and I knew how to work hard. In the first quarter I received three B's and one A. I got three A's and one B in the last quarter, but my annual grades improved over the next three years. Second, I figured that I could get through financially if I found decent summer jobs. But perhaps most revealing was the third thing I learned: my social situation required some changes.

EIU had several students from the Chicago area, but it was still a more regional university drawing most of its students from within a seventy-five-mile radius. Many students commuted, and others were known as suitcasers who went home on weekends. Kids who stayed at school and had the most fun were in fraternities and sororities. Freshmen boys were at a distinct disadvantage because upperclassmen dated the best-looking girls. It seemed especially rude at the time that Illinois law allowed girls to drink at eighteen, but boys had to be twenty-one. All of this led me to believe I would benefit from joining a fraternity when I returned to campus in the fall.

I also realized that it would be good to know how to dance if headway was to be made socially. Early on at EIU, I was inspired at Ike's, one of the campus hangouts. The dance floor jumped with kids doing the jitterbug to "Rockin' Robin." Two years of physical education were required at EIU, and each class lasted one quarter. One of the classes was ballroom dancing. Thanks to Glenn Miller's "A String of Pearls," I became proficient at the jitterbug.

Summer, 1959

On the way home for the summer, my old 1949 Chevy gave out. I walked to a nearby farmhouse and, thanks to the kindness of strangers, was able to call Garold to rescue me. He towed me home with his pickup. I then went to Uncle Harmon's Chevy dealer in Flora and traded for a black 1951 Chevy. My high school pal, Jim Weiler, had previously owned the car.

I spent a couple of weeks at the beginning of the summer helping Dad get the crops planted, then I found job at a small oil field company in Olney. I was a tool dresser on a double-drum service rig equipped to

My black 1951 Chevy

install pumps on newly drilled oil wells and service existing wells. The two-man crew consisted of the drill operator, Ed Steele, and me.

This summer job was quite an education on several fronts. An oil well promoter from Clay City named Bob Billingsley hired us to reclaim an old oil field lease in the southwest corner of Kentucky. Ed drove the big truck-mounted rig, and I followed in the company pickup. We passed small tobacco farms and went into the hills of southwest Kentucky near Mammoth Cave National Park. When we came to a narrow one-lane bridge over a creek, Ed stopped his truck. We walked onto the bridge, contemplating whether we could cross. Ed decided to give it a try while I watched the bridge groan and sink at least two feet as he made it across with the heavy rig.

The tiny town of Hardyville near the oil lease had a gas station and general store. We bunked with an older couple whose farmhouse was a few miles outside the town. The lady of the house fixed our meals and our sack lunches. Her cooking made it seem that she must have had a dozen varieties of beans in her garden. Beans, grits, fried okra, and fried pork kept Ed and me supplied with ample calories.

During our frustrating weeks on the old oil lease, a bright spot was going to the general store. The proprietor usually had an ongoing conversation with the guys sitting around the old potbellied stove, trying to spit their tobacco juice into coffee cans. The owner had a very pretty, young daughter who was a high school cheerleader. Ed allowed me to take the pickup so that Mary Rose could show me around the Ozarks.

Ed and I headed out early each morning to the oil lease, stuffed on pancakes, ham, and grits. The abandoned wells still had the pumps mounted, and we first hooked up our rig to a well located on a hillside. The slope was so steep that we had to jack the truck's front end up about six feet to level the rig.

Our experience with this well was one we were to repeat. The wells were very shallow and only 800–1,000 feet deep. We had to remove the pump jack from the wellhead and pull the sucker rods connected to the pump at the bottom of the well. Each of the thirty-foot rods had to be pulled up one at a time. My job was to clamp each rod when pulled to the top of the hole, disconnect it from the remaining rods in the hole with a quick snap using pipe wrenches, then grab the loose end and carry it out and away from the well head as Ed lowered the cable holding the top end of the rod. I put on several miles running those rods out and stacking them.

We soon encountered the reality of what we were dealing with. The bottom of the hole was filled with old, broken cable and other junk. Our on-site boss was called the producer. He was a seasoned former driller from Oklahoma who had a good time teasing me about being a college kid and tested my ability to do the work. It took a while to get his respect, but I learned a lot from him about the oil business and smoking unfiltered Marlboros.

The site boss had to drive a hundred miles to rent fishing tools so that we could attempt pulling up the debris. Those fishing tools also got stuck down in the hole. After a few weeks, it was apparent that the old wells were beyond rescue. It had been very dubious in the first place whether there would be any remaining oil, and we were learned later that we had been dealing with a hoax.

The promoter, Bob Billingsley, had known the lease was kaput, but he had schemed to sell more than 100 percent of the shares in the project. For this scam to work, the well (or wells) had to be dry, and the investors who had fallen for his bill of goods had to write off their losses. Bob made his 10 percent regardless, and this—and subsequent shenanigans—landed him in prison. However, the summer job paid $1.10 an hour and helped me bankroll another year at EIU.

The summer of 1959 was the last time Garold and I lived together at home. Garold had plans to get married the following spring. Before heading to EIU in the fall for my second year, we were invited to a party. Our high school buddy Roger Franklin was dating a lovely girl who had been a year behind us in school, Sandra Clark. Sandra had two cousins who were visiting her from northern Illinois, so she had a backyard party to introduce them to her friends. Somehow, the younger sister, Phyllis Townsend, and I hit it off well. She was a high school senior in Princeton, Illinois.

Phyllis and I started a letter-writing relationship and made plans to get together. She took a bus down to Charleston to join me for EIU's homecoming in the fall. Over the Christmas vacation, I drove my 1951 Chevy two hundred miles on two-lane roads to visit her in Princeton. Her family was very welcoming and arranged for me to stay with an elderly cou-

Phyllis Townsend

ple who lived nearby. The old man loved telling me stories about his experiences working as a teamster driving a six-horse team pulling a threshing machine. During the 1920s, he had been part of a large harvesting crew that had started the wheat harvest in the Texas Panhandle and moved through the wheat-growing states to end the season in Saskatchewan. Phyllis and I continued our relationship for the next couple of years.

Sophomore Year: 1959–60

The fall of 1959 at EIU got off to a good start. I was promoted to busboy in the new student union cafeteria and felt more focused on my studies. The most dramatic change began when I pledged one of the six men's fraternities on campus, Alpha Kappa Lambda (AKL). The AKL chapter was three years old and the newest fraternity on campus. I was impressed by the seniors I met who had formed the group, and that the chapter had the highest grade point average among campus fraternities. Early in the second quarter, my pledge classmates and I became active members, and I moved into the fraternity house.

The AKL fraternity house was a three-story Victorian located eight blocks from campus. We were assigned second-floor rooms for our stuff, and the third-floor attic was converted to a dorm full of bunk beds. A charming and sophisticated older woman, Katherine Marvel, who was quickly dubbed Captain Marvel, was hired as the housemother. Her presence and etiquette lessons made for a more dignified atmosphere. Meal service included a ritual sit-down dinner that started with a prayer and ended with group singing. Several members majored in music, so there were some fine harmonies.

I moved into the fraternity house just as the first quarter grades came out and members posted their report cards. I received all A's and immediately seemed to have an elevated status. I had been a member for only a few weeks when the fraternity chapter elected new officers for the

In front of the fraternity house at EIU

coming year. The seniors and charter members huddled and nominated me for president. This group of mentors included the current president Larry Pattison, Lou Crane, Cal Stockman, Tom Drury, Harvey Hurst, and Howard Unterbrink.

Suddenly, I knew I was in way over my head, especially knowing that this group of my mentors in the fraternity would soon graduate. I was conducting weekly chapter meetings while still trying to learn the ropes. The pressure somewhat dampened the fun of social activities since I had a major role in planning events and dealing with budget issues. But the perks were undeniable. I was on the campus interfraternity council and I had started to meet other students beyond my off-campus housing roommates. Our faculty advisor for the fraternity was none other than Dr. Syndergaard. We invited the EIU president, Dr. Quincy Doudna, to our house for dinner one evening. Dr. Doudna was only the third president of the university since its founding in 1895. He was instrumental in taking the university on a path of growth and excellence. Sitting across from him challenged my limited conversational skills.

The AKL fraternity held a National Conclave every two years. The chapter selected me and two other members, Max Coffee and Joe Daughtery, to represent the fraternity in August 1960. The Conclave would be held in Estes Park, Colorado. I was excited about my first trip West.

The social part of fraternity life exceeded my expectations. The fraternity sponsored an all-school dance, played intramural sports, participated in Greek events, and ended the year with the highlight, our formal dinner dance. One of the Greek events

Dr. Quincy Doudna, president, Eastern Illinois University

was a musical competition. Our chapter had several music majors and musicians, so we put together a full-scale seventeen-piece big band. My baritone didn't fit the instrumentation, but the band rocked with their rendition of Duke Ellington's "Take the A Train." The following year, three of us (with me playing guitar and singing harmony) mimicked The Kingston Trio's "A Worried Man."

Our fraternity's formal dance was held at a country club in nearby Paris, Illinois. Phyllis was by this time a freshman at Illinois State University in Normal, Illinois. I had driven there on a couple of weekends to see her, and she took the bus to Charleston to attend our fraternity formal. The guys all wore tuxes with white jackets, but no one paid attention because the girls took the spotlight with their formal attire and corsages. The proceedings gave me the opportunity to present awards. This included a tribute to member and friend Tom Fowler, and an award of recognition to both the AKL sweetheart and our treasured housemother, Ms. Katherine "Captain" Marvel.

Left: With Phyllis at fraternity formal
Right: Recognizing housemother and chapter sweetheart

My sophomore year ended with grades that were pretty good, all things considered. I managed to finish the year with eleven A's and one B. The B was in an economics class that met at eight o'clock in the morning during the winter quarter and was taught by the droning Dr. Plath.

In the spring of 1960, my brother Garold married his high school sweetheart, Elaine Wolf. I came down to Clay City from EIU for the event. Their wedding was a small family affair, and I was proud to be his best man. By this time, Garold was working in the oil field, but he was getting ready to pursue his dream of farming. Elaine was an administrative assistant at the Clay City Banking Company. They started their married life living in a rental house in Clay City. Ironically, two weeks later, I was the best man in our mutual friend Roger Franklyn's wedding to Sandra Clark.

Garold and Elaine's wedding; Kay Gill on left, and me on right

Summer, 1960

The summer of 1960 presented several challenges. First, I had to find a summer job to finance my junior year in college. I tried without success to find a job in construction. Since Phyllis was going to summer school at Northern Illinois University in DeKalb, Illinois, I applied at the Del Monte pea canning factory in nearby Mendota, Illinois. The Del Monte job only paid ninety cents an hour, but it provided the potential to work a lot of hours.

I arrived at the factory in late June, along with other workers. We were ready to start, but unfortunately, heavy rains set in. The company allowed us to sleep in their barracks without charge until weather conditions improved. We were able to buy our meals in the adjacent company cafeteria. It was a good thing that the meals there were relatively cheap because it turned out that we would be waiting for over three weeks for the weather to clear. The wait took a big bite out of our potential earnings, to say nothing of my cash supply.

There were upsides to the delay. I did get pretty good at playing pinochle. More importantly, the situation allowed more time to drive to DeKalb to see Phyllis. While there, I got to eat at the newly opened McDonald's. Hamburgers cost fifteen cents, as did a milkshake. It sure beat the cafeteria food, and the company was much better.

When the rains finally stopped, I was assigned to a field team for harvesting the peas. Del Monte was not yet using automatic harvesters and still used stationary vining machines to thresh the peas from the vines. The pea vines were mowed down in the field, then a conveyor was used to load the vines into dump trucks. The trucks came to the vining station, where I was assigned to a twenty-man crew.

Two of us worked as a team at each of the ten vining machines lined up parallel in a farm field. One position was the pitcher, and the other was the boxer. We traded jobs after each truckload. The dump truck driver emptied his load on the ground in front of the vining machine. The pitcher's job was to use a pitchfork to lift the tangled vines into the threshing machine. The peas were separated from their pods and filled hoppers along the side of the machine. The boxer was in charge of getting the peck-size boxes filled and stacked for transport to the canning factory in town. Our workstations had lights for night work, and one week I managed to work 110 hours.

One hot afternoon, I was working the pitcher position and had reduced the pea vine pile to one last bundle. When I picked it up, a bewildered skunk ran out, spraying me with his delicate scent. The supervisor had me pile into the back of his pickup truck, and he drove me back to our bunkhouse. The cook at the dining shack gave me a can of tomato

Joe Daughtery and Max Coffee

juice to wash off the scent. It helped somewhat, but my housemates kept their distance for a while.

Our bunkhouse had two rows of bunk beds and a shower and toilet on one end. A water tank fed the shower that was mounted overhead so the sun could heat the water. Most of the crew came from a small, religious school called Harding College in Searcy, Arkansas. When the pea harvest ended, the Searcy boys went home, but I stayed to work more hours in the nearby Del Monte corn canning factory. By that point, my coworkers were mostly bums the company had picked up off the streets of Chicago, so I was ready to leave after a few days to join my fraternity brothers Max and Joe for our trip to Estes Park. Unfortunately, the series of events left my summer savings pretty anemic, which would make financing my third year at EIU problematic.

In late August 1960, the three of us from the AKL fraternity—Max Coffee, Joe Daughtery, and me—packed into Max's tiny Morris Minor British car with no air conditioning and headed out to the then-fash-

Max and me, Rocky Mountain National Park

ionable Stanley Hotel in Estes Park, Colorado, for the AKL Fraternity Conclave.

The three-day conclave was full of activities, seminars, and speeches. I was assigned to a committee to redraft the national fraternity bylaws. The alumni moderator of our panel was an impressive gentleman, an investment banker from Los Angeles. He had been a member of the founding chapter of the fraternity when he was a student at the University of California in Berkeley. As our chapter representative, I accepted the prestigious national award for achievement that included a sizable trophy. Our chapter had just recruited a large pledge class, and apparently, our campus activities were impressive to the selection committee. When Max, Joe, and I left the conference, we drove west through the Rocky Mountain National Park instead of heading back to Charleston. This was the first trip to Colorado for all of us, and I was so impressed with the state and mountains that it became my dream destination.

Junior Year: 1960–1961

During the conclave in Estes Park, I somehow came to the attention of the fraternity's executive director, Lewis (Lou) Bacon. Lou came to the EIU campus not long after the conclave, during the Fall quarter of my junior year, with two propositions. His first proposal was that we build a new fraternity house to accommodate our growing membership. Lou, it seemed, had more than a passing interest in the company that would undertake the project. In any case, we decided to sign the contract after we got the backing of the president of our chapter's board of directors, Vernon Heath. Mr. Heath was the owner and CEO of the Heath Candy Company in nearby Robinson, Illinois.

Lou's second pitch was a two-part proposal to me. The first part was that I visit Richmond University in Virginia to help a struggling group set up a new fraternity. To get to Richmond, Lou sent me tickets to fly a small commercial plane to St. Louis, take an Ozark Airlines flight to Washington, DC, then take another flight to Richmond. This was my first time in an airplane, and six flights on a long weekend was quite an immersion.

The second part of Lou's pitch was that I take a volunteer position as a national chapter representative. His idea was to have a team of undergraduates stationed around the country to provide leadership training to other chapters. So, the following summer in 1961, I flew to Boulder, Colorado, along with six other AKL members from around the country, to participate in a training conference. I was assigned to schools in Illinois and Indiana, including the University of Illinois and Purdue. I thought it was presumptuous that I would talk to these chapter officers about how to run their organiza-

Vernon Heath, president
Heath Candy Company

With Butch Swanstrom

tions. Somehow I managed these undertakings and concluded that I had learned more than I had in many of my classes.

In selecting classes for my junior year, I decided to focus my elective courses on subjects I knew little about. Not having studied a foreign language, I enrolled in German for no reason other than that our family's namesake was from Germany. Later I took classes in music history, philosophy, and art appreciation. Sitting next to me in the German class was Gary "Butch" Swanstrom. Butch was outgoing, funny, and very bright.

Since we were sitting together, Herr Professor Dr. Martin Miess assigned Butch and me to present the daily dialogue in German. Herr Miess was from Austria and had a very formal and proper demeanor, but I think he enjoyed our animated dialogues. Butch had joined the Sigma Pi fraternity, but he would come to the AKL house to practice our German dialogues together. The predictable result after about fifteen minutes was that Butch would drive us in his 1953 Ford to a local bar in downtown Charleston called Chink and Leno's. His view was that we could learn German better while drinking a beer. A Schlitz or a Pabst beer cost twenty-five cents, and the establishment overlooked checking our driving licenses. Over winter break, Butch invited me to go with him to Chicago to visit one of his friends. The Swanstroms lived in a small town called DeLand, not far from Champaign. I drove there, and we took his trustier 1953 Ford to Chicago. I hadn't been there since the eighth-grade band trip, so we decided to meet our friend at the only place I knew, the Conrad Hilton Hotel. Butch parked on a dark side street off Michigan Avenue. We naively left our suitcases in the back seat. We returned to find the rear-door glass broken and all our possessions gone. The good part, in the end, was that Butch and I aced our German course.

The big political event in 1960 was the presidential race between Richard Nixon and John F. Kennedy. On Thursday, November 3, just five days before the election, JFK's brother Bobby came to EIU for a campaign rally. One of our fraternity brothers, David Johnson, was a member of the Young Democrats of America. He was chosen to accompany Bobby from the airport to the campus for his speech in the student union ballroom. Bobby asked for chocolate ice cream as a snack before he spoke. David's claim to fame was that he fetched the ice cream for Bobby Kennedy.

When springtime came in 1961, my term as the fraternity president ended. Harvey Hurst was still living in the house while working on his master's degree. He and others in the house persuaded me to run for president of the student senate. Harvey ran my campaign and helped write my platform speech. My opponents were my old cafeteria colleague Clay Dungy and Barry Wilber, my freshman-year housemate at Maw Dede's. Clay and I were the leading vote-getters with about 90 percent of the votes, but he received four votes more than I did among the thousand cast. After three recounts with Clay, me, and the dean of students present, Clay was declared the winner. Secretly, I felt a sense of relief. Ironically, the person winning the vice-presidential race was Tom Huffman, younger brother of the former president John Huffman whom I had met my first day on campus. As a consolation prize, the dean appointed me to chair the student court and serve on the student union board.

Futile presidential run for student senate

One perk for honor students at Eastern was receiving a pass to study in the library stacks among the books rather than at the large tables in the public area. I had lost mine, so I talked one of my fraternity brothers, Ed Steele, into loaning me his pass. I was sitting at a small table in the stacks and lit up a pipe, forgetting where I was. Unfortunately, the head librarian smelled the smoke. I received one of my worst scoldings but escaped by having to turn in Ed's pass. I was surprised that Ed took it so well when I confessed to him. On another evening, I drove to the library and parked in the lot in the back. The drill was to study in the library until about 9:30 p.m., then go to the ballroom at the student union to dance. It was dark outside, so I decided to drive on a campus sidewalk and bounce off the curb into the lot by the union. I was going along fine until I spotted the campus cop car speeding behind me. I gunned the motor and headed

Duke Ellington band

for the side streets by the campus with my lights out to escape. Quickly turning a corner, I saw the cop car go whizzing by, and I went in the opposite direction. I let my car cool off for a couple of weeks, hidden behind the fraternity house.

One of the great things about campus life was going to football and basketball games and especially musical events. Rock and roll emerged, but traditional musical groups were still making rounds on the college circuit. The Dave Brubeck Quartet, George Shearing, and Roberta Peters were among the groups. I was invited to a backstage reception and enjoyed a friendly conversation with Ms. Peters. I liked the big bands best. These groups included Harry James, Louis Armstrong, Stan Kenton, Ralph Marterie, and Duke Ellington.

My grades suffered somewhat, and I ended the year with four B's and eight A's. The downer during my junior year was that I ran out of money. I ventured to the dean's office to consider my options. A new federal student loan program called the National Defense Education Act (NDEA) had just been enacted. The schools administered the individual loans, so I filled out an application and kept my fingers crossed. I wasn't proud to have to borrow money, but I signed a promissory note for $520. I got an additional loan of $450 the following year. An advantage of the loan program was that 10 percent was deducted for each year that a borrower taught school.

Summer 1961: Yellowstone Park

After a busy junior year, the summer of 1961 came around with no job prospects. To the rescue came Tom Fowler. Tom and I were in the same class and were pledges together at the AKL fraternity. Tom, whose dad was a member of Eastern's faculty, was active on campus and chaired the committee that brought musical groups to perform. At six feet six inches tall, he was a striking figure. The previous summer, Tom had worked in Yellowstone Park and was so excited about the experience that he planned to return. He asked me and another classmate, George "Rupert" Hill, to go with him, so Rupert and I applied for a job and were accepted. We drove out in Tom's 1956 Chevy with an eight-cylinder engine. We were hired by the Yellowstone Park Service Station company, which had six stations in the park. We reported to their offices in Gardiner, Montana, located at the north entrance to the park. The road through the park was open, but ten-foot snowdrifts were piled on each side. We stayed overnight in Gardiner, and the following day we got our assignments, with each of us going to different locations. The unique thing about the night in Gardiner was that I celebrated my twenty-first birthday and drank my first Coors beer. At that time, Coors was only sold in the Northwestern states.

Tom was assigned to the station at Old Faithful, Rupert was at the West Thumb Village, and I ended up at the Fishing Bridge Village station. Fishing Bridge was the bridge over the Yellowstone River at its origin, where it flowed out of Yellowstone Lake. The lake was at an altitude of 7,700 feet, and my new friends and I quickly felt the impact of the altitude after a hike left us out of breath. There were fifteen guys on the service station crew, and we had a bunkhouse near the station. Our meals

Fishing Bridge in Yellowstone Park

were provided at an employee cafeteria where we ate with other workers. Our crew boss was John Wooten, a soft-spoken guy from North Carolina. He divided us into two groups of nine. One group started the early shift at six o'clock in the morning, and the second began at two o'clock in the afternoon with an hour overlap. Each week, the schedule reversed so that we had to get up early only every other week, and we had one day off each week. The station had three lanes of gas pumps, plus a tire room and an outdoor grease rack. Our weekly pay was a paltry fifty dollars for our sixty-hour work week, but we could add a few dollars from our sales bonus and tips.

I had somewhat of an advantage over the others because, growing up on a farm, I was more familiar with mechanics. John gave us tutorials on each job, but I liked the grease rack where tips were more likely. We also had presentations on how to sell auto parts to our customers. The incentive was a 10 percent bonus on sales of tires, windshield wipers, air filters, fan belts, and motor oil additives. In addition to pumping gas and washing windshields, we hurriedly checked out parts that we might replace. Sometimes drivers weren't too happy when we carried around a dirty air filter and tried to persuade them to buy a new one. One of our more pleasant tasks was providing tourist information to the park visitors. We gave

My gang at the service station in Yellowstone Park

out free maps and our "expert" advice on what to see and do in the park. The director of the visitor's center acknowledged that we were a major source of information for park visitors.

Yellowstone Park employed over four thousand college kids to work at the various concessions during the summer. We workers were called "savages," and the nickname for tourists was "dudes." The good thing about the savages was that there were more girls than boys, and workers came from almost every state. I shared my day off at the station with a kid from Iowa, Randy Schlack, who went to an all-boys Catholic school in Iowa called Loras College. Randy had a Mensa-caliber IQ and a hilarious sense of humor, but he was scared of girls and in awe that I wasn't. Each week, we planned excursions on our days off to explore as much of the park and surrounding area as we could. We climbed several of the peaks in the park and luckily teamed up with two adventurous girls who shared our days off.

On one outing, the four of us hitched a ride out of the park's northeast entrance leading over the Beartooth Mountains to Red Lodge, Montana. We shared a buffalo steak in one of the restaurants before trying to hitchhike back to Fishing Bridge. The bitter lesson was that no cars were making the long drive back into the park from Red Lodge in the late afternoon. After a couple of futile hours with our thumbs out, we decided to hitchhike to Cody on the park's east side as darkness set in. We figured we would have a better shot at getting to work on time the next day. A lovely family with two kids picked the four of us up, and Randy and I curled up in the back of the station wagon with their dog. On the way down the Chief Joseph Highway, we used our service station experience to change a flat tire in the dark. The family dropped us off on the main drag in Cody. We didn't have enough money for a hotel, and there was no traffic heading west toward Yellowstone. Luckily, Randy spotted Jimmy Ratliff driving by in his mom's pickup and hailed him to stop. He agreed to take us to a supper club his mom operated that was located on a creek outside Cody.

Jimmy's dad, also named James, and a close buddy fought with Patton's army in France during World War II. The two decided to open a bar and restaurant when the war was over. His buddy was killed, but Jimmy's dad decided to continue their plan. He brought home one of his buddy's boots and had it bronzed. He mounted it on a mantel in the restaurant he named the Bronze Boot Nite Club.

We had met Jimmy when we had gone to the club a couple of times previously. We had gone to celebrate our station buddies' birthdays and order the famous plate-sized steaks. The Bronze Boot had a small band and a dance floor. Jimmy, who was fifteen, played a washtub bass in the band. After Jimmy picked us up in downtown Cody, he drove down a

Hitchhiking after a night at the Bronze Boot

dusty gravel road with Randy and me hanging on in the back. He went over a swinging bridge that crossed the creek, which emanated a strong sulfur odor, to reach the restaurant building where Jimmy and his mom lived on the second floor. His mom got the restaurant following her divorce from Jimmy's dad. We got a few winks of sleep lying on the restaurant floor before getting up at daylight to get back into the park.

A few weeks later, Randy and I and the girls hitchhiked south from Yellowstone Park to Grand Teton National Park. A dozen of us took a thirteen-mile trail ride on horseback around Jenny Lake to the Cascade Trail near the Grand Teton peak. My horse was smaller than the rest and did a bouncy trot to keep up. My butt muscles were sore for days, but the misery didn't erase my memories of the awesome Teton vistas. We stopped at Jackson Lake Lodge, still in its heyday as an elite hotel, a legacy of the Rockefeller family.

Four horsemen in the Tetons

Back at Fishing Bridge, I began spending more time with a young lady from Rhinelander, Wisconsin, Sandy Schauder. Sandy had more energy than three people and supported the party image of the University of Wisconsin, where she went to school. A tradition among the savages was to hold a beauty contest to select Miss Yellowstone Park. I escorted Sandy to the Fishing Bridge pageant, where she was runner-up.

Tom, Rupert, and I stayed in Yellowstone until after Labor Day. It snowed that weekend, but we continued plans for our last outing to climb up Mount Washburn for a final look at the magnificence of the park and the array of wildlife. We then piled into Tom's Chevy for the return trip to EIU. When we drove east out of Cody, Tom opened up the V-8, and we made the first one hundred miles to Sheridan in ninety minutes.

Senior Year: 1961–1962

In the fall of 1961, I returned to EIU for my senior year. We had sold the fraternity house over the summer to finance the construction of the new house. The fraternity brothers scattered for housing, and Barry Guinagh asked me to stay with him at his parent' house across the street from campus. Barry was a year younger, played trombone in the band, was on the swim team, and majored in physics. His father, Dr. Kevin Guinagh, who spoke eight languages, headed the foreign language department at EIU. Dr. Guinagh was a former priest and was considerably older than Barry's Mom, Katherine. To me, Dr. Guinagh was a true intellectual. He usually immersed himself each evening in his study to write, and he had an amazing collection of ancient books dating to the early printing press. On occasion, they would invite me to join them for dinner, and each night around midnight, Barry and I sneaked into the kitchen where his mother always had snacks for us.

With Sandy Schauder at the Miss Yellowstone contest

Following up on our summer in Yellowstone Park, Sandy Schauder invited me to homecoming at the University of Wisconsin. She fixed Barry up with a date, and the two of us drove his parents' new Nash Rambler from Charleston up to Madison, Wisconsin. It was an eye-opening weekend drinking a beer in the student union, attending a Big Ten football game, attempting to sleep on a couch in a wild fraternity house, and hearing Johnny Mathis sing "Chances Are" at the homecoming concert. But the distant relationship with Sandy didn't last.

That fall, I focused on my nonpaying job as an AKL representative and my studies. My favorite class was twentieth-century Russian history, taught by Dr. Syndergaard. Dr. Syndergaard's wife was the daughter of a Russian émigré who had come to the US after the Russian Revolution to escape arrest. He had been the minister of education in the short-lived Kerensky government during the revolution in 1917. Dr. Syndergaard invited his father-in-law to speak to the class about the revolution. His lecture was so impassioned that he brought himself to tears. My second favorite class was twentieth-century diplomacy, taught by Dr. Joel Goldfarb. He was an impressive academic, and I had had him for an American history class as a sophomore. In that course, the final's prescient question was: "The Civil War was an unmitigated disaster. Explain."

During the winter quarter, I moved to Lawrenceville, Illinois, to do my student teaching. My supervisor, Mr. Alan Pierson, was a steady, respected teacher who guided me through the process. One of the highlights was a TV assembly where the students watched astronaut John Glenn make the first manned orbital space flight. I rented a room from an elderly lady whose house was a few blocks from campus. I tiptoed around the kitchen and tried to relax, but the quiet and aloneness were driving me nuts. After a couple of weeks, I was rescued by a fellow student teacher who invited me to move with him to an apartment behind an insurance office. I was also closer to Clay City and could drive home on weekends. While the student teaching seemed to go well, I can't say that it aroused a deep-seated passion for pursuing teaching as a long-term career.

My last quarter at EIU in the spring of 1962 was packed with social, academic, and job-search activities. My courses were first-rate, but at this point, the professors all assigned term papers. I never learned to type, but a couple of lady friends agreed to type them for me. They helped me end the year with eleven A's and one B. The end of the year coincided with the depletion of my bank account. The second tranche of $450 from the

NDEA loan meant that I had a total loan of $970. My obsession with record-keeping and tracking expenses showed that my four years at Eastern had cost $4,050. On the social front, it was fun to be invited to some of the formal sorority dances and attend the AKL formal. Marjorie (Margie) Holland, one of EIU's cheerleaders, was a regular date. We were not destined to have a continuing relationship.

With Margie Holland at her sorority formal

Most of us who were graduating spent a lot of time during the spring quarter focusing on what would come next. I had gone to the University of Illinois to take the graduate record exam (GRE), but I decided against graduate school, not wanting to continue my impoverishment. Next, I looked into the navy's officer candidate program. I backed out when I saw how much training was required in the water. Lou Bacon offered me a full-time position with the national fraternity that I dismissed as a dead-end option. I decided to return to my original intent and look for a teaching position. Most teacher candidates were getting jobs in southern and central Illinois, but the big attractions were teaching positions in the higher-paying Chicago suburban schools. The baby boomer generation was very prolific, so there was an explosion of new schools. I sent applications for the heck of it to schools in Boulder, Colorado, and San Francisco, but they required that I come out for interviews on my dime.

I drove up to two Chicago suburbs to interview for teaching positions at Niles West High School in Skokie and Rich East High School in Park Forest. Niles West was a larger school in a fast-growing community on the North Side of Chicago. Park Forest was a new planned community on the South Side. The Rich East job was considered a plumb position because of the school's pay and progressive reputation. There seemed to be some competition for the position, but I was offered the contract at Rich East for $5,200. In this recommendation letter, I later learned that Dr. Syndergaard said that I was one of the brightest prospects for teaching social studies to come out of the department in years.

In winding up college life, I was elected to the education honorary society called Kappa Delta Pi and served as vice president of the club. Members were invited to an end-of-the-year banquet where the speaker was Dr. Guinagh. He gave a stimulating and humorous presentation on student life in the Middle Ages, one of his many areas of expertise. I was elected to Who's Who among American Colleges and Universities in my junior and senior years. I think it was mostly a scam to sell a fancy directory of our names. I also received the title of Mr. Education, and the yearbook described it as the image of the scholar and the intellectual in pursuit of a four-point average. To me, it proved Lincoln's adage that you could fool some of the people all the time.

At graduation, I was a co-valedictorian. Three of us graduated with high honors and summa cum laude status. There were, however, only about four hundred graduates out of our starting class of eight hundred. Graduation ceremonies were held on the grassy central area of the campus facing the front steps of the stately library. I was proud that four generations of my family were able to come. My granddad and grandma Herdes, Dad and Mom, Garold and Elaine, and their baby son Gregory came. (Later, Greg and his sister, Kim both graduated from EIU.) It was somewhat of a historic event for the family, as I became the first Herdes to receive a college degree.

The four years at EIU were transformational in many ways. My limited worldview expanded, starting with a better sense of history. But courses in art, music, language, literature, sociology, and philosophy challenged me in different ways by letting me know how little I knew. Not growing up with newspapers and dinnertime discussions of politics, I didn't develop a clear political point of view. When Garold and I were in grade school, we asked Mom and Dad whether they were Democrats or Republicans. Mom considered herself a Democrat, like most of the Stanleys. Dad said he was a Republican. The next question was what we should be. Dad said that we should be Republicans while Mom indicated her displeasure. Over time I found myself to be more of an Independent.

Darold Herdes . . . Mr. Education

Mr. Education

Summer, 1962

Since my financial resources were exhausted after graduation, I looked for a summer job. My friend Butch Swanstrom had left EIU after our junior year to study veterinary medicine at the University of Illinois. His hometown of De Land, Illinois, was located a few miles west of the

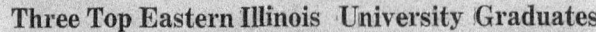

Charleston, Ill.—Darold Herdes of Clay City has his honor chevron adjusted by two other 1962 Eastern Illinois University high honor graduates, Carol Sue Vaught of Lawrenceville, left, and Dena Mae Wilson of Palestine.

The three were the top graduates and all received bachelor of science in education degrees.

Herdes was a social science major. Miss Wilson majored in French. English was the major of Miss Vaught.

university in Champaign. He invited me to spend the summer living at his family's house and work for his dad, a painting contractor. Our crew was made up of Butch, his older brother Steve (Mick), and a teacher who had the summer off. Mostly we painted farm buildings, but another part of the job was installing lightning rods. The first week got me a lot of teasing for holding so hard onto the ladder that water drops came out. Soon, though, I could walk straddling a roof ridge row while carrying a lightning rod or a paint bucket.

The Swanstrom family dynamics were so different from what I had experienced. Their mom, Daisy, was an amazing woman. She taught high school Latin and English and had a master's degree in Latin from the University of Illinois. Dad Barney had finished eighth grade, but he and Daisy had a very compatible relationship. Mick was just home from the army and was ready to return to college. He ended up going to EIU as

With Jim Weiler on the road to Seattle

well. Mick was well-spoken, and even his brother acknowledged that he was a lady's man. We had terrific dinner discussions guided by Daisy, but Barney usually disappeared with a glass of Coke to retrieve his whiskey bottle. I had a lasting friendship with the Swanstroms.

Early in the summer, I had made plans to go to the 1962 World's Fair in Seattle in late August. Jim Weiler (my high school band buddy), Don Tolliver (a fraternity brother), and Don's cousin (Fred Kincaid) made up our crew. All of us were from Clay County with a lot in common as we drove west in Jim's 1957 Chevy. We were all on a budget, and most nights, we slept outside with a blanket and sometimes on a picnic table.

The fair was an eye-opening event. The two gee-whiz technology structures were the monorail and the Space Needle. The international exhibits, plus the city itself, got our full attention. In addition, we took the ferry over to Victoria on Canada's Vancouver Island and had tea at the Empress Hotel. On the way back to Illinois, we stopped in Yellowstone to show the park to my buddies and visit old haunts.

1959 big-fin Chevy

We returned to southern Illinois, and I began preparations for my upcoming move. Uncle Harmon once again took my 1951 Chevy in trade for a 1959 Chevy with big fins. It was the first time I had to get a loan to buy a car, but it was necessary for my upcoming commutes. For the last time, I filled it up at Dad's farm gas tank and headed for Chicago to start a new chapter.

Chapter 10

TEACHING HIGH SCHOOL

New teachers at Rich East High School in Park Forest, Illinois, arrived two days early in the fall of 1962 for orientation. There were around thirty of us, and there was a sense of excitement, although I felt a bit of nervousness. The administrators gave us an overview of the school's history and programs. The school had about twelve hundred students. I found the background on the town of Park Forest very informative. The town was a planned community built for returning World War II veterans. The plan included a large central shopping mall, a full range of housing options, schools, churches, parks, and curving streets. Its location at the end of a commuter train line leading to downtown Chicago was significant for the residents. The homogeneous population in terms of age and education emphasized upward mobility and good schools for their children. The men were employed mainly by large companies in the city. Their image was that of loyal employees more devoted to the company and conformity rather than pursuing individualism. This depiction was the basis for a popular sociological study in the 1950s called *The Organization Man* by William Whyte. Park Forest was the model for his book.

Rich East was considered a progressive school for implementing popular education innovations. The school had a merit system for determining teacher pay, so raises were based on performance evaluations

Rich East High School

rather than seniority. Academic programs were organized into interdisciplinary divisions rather than separate departments. Team teaching was in vogue for some subjects as well. My assignment was to teach three classes in American history to juniors and an economics class to seniors.

American history was taught using the team-teaching method, so I was partnered with a more senior teacher. The advantage of having two teachers in the classroom was exposing students to differing points of view. The two of us would hold debates on controversial issues. The downside of the method was assigning too many students to classes, which numbered around eighty students for each of the three team-teaching classes. It took me quite awhile to get to know their names. I led the American history teaching team and supervised a student teacher by my third year. Throughout this experience I think I learned as much from my students as they did from me.

My economics class was based on the same college textbook I had in college called *Economics* by Paul Samuelson. This class was by far my biggest challenge in terms of my level of knowledge and maturity. Becoming a teacher meant acting like an adult at all times, which wasn't always easy in my early twenties. I also discovered that, despite my education, teaching required a lot of homework—not only for better mastery of the subject matter but also for developing effective classroom presentation and interaction.

During my first year of teaching I learned that Jewish students made up 25 percent of the student body. I read Leon Uris's book, *Exodus*, and was curious about the Jewish diaspora. World War II had ended only seventeen years earlier, and the horrors of the Holocaust were still being divulged. I attended a conference on the Holocaust at the University of Chicago to learn more. Many survivors were in attendance, and their stories made a lasting impression on me—these experiences combined to give me a lifelong appreciation and admiration for the Jewish people.

One of the unexpected perks for single teachers was occasional invitations by parents to join them for family dinners. During my second year, the Gerber family invited my two roommate teachers and me to celebrate a Seder with them. We each had their son, Tom, in class, and his father, Dr. Aron Gerber, was a World War II veteran and a surgeon. It was an interesting evening with stimulating conversation, and while it was my first Seder, it would turn out not to be my last. Ironically, the following year, Dr. Gerber removed my tonsils. Other families who invited us to their homes were equally welcoming. After graduation, four of my favorite students attended Harvard, Brandeis, Northwestern, and the University of Chicago. Three of the four students were Jewish.

One of the highlights of teaching the American history classes was when we studied World War II. With the war having ended less than twenty years earlier, the fathers of most of our students were veterans of the war. We asked the students to bring any of their dads' war memorabilia for a demonstration. We were overwhelmed with the responses. The team-teaching room consisted of three classrooms separated by folding doors that, when opened, created a much larger space. The students brought in a large volume of their fathers' memorabilia, which covered

long tables in front of the extended classroom. Two rooms were dedicated to items from the European Theater and one for the Pacific. The students brought several weapons, including rifles, pistols, bayonets, and knives. Banners displaying swastikas were hung on the walls. It was quite a collection of war memorabilia. The returning GIs carried home more than personal items in their duffel bags.

The students also got involved in other interesting ways for their study of American history. When studying the Civil War, a member of the Civil War Round Table was invited to give a presentation that included a large display of Civil War memorabilia. Each year we took the entire junior class to a downtown Chicago theater to see a film. Two of these films were *Lawrence of Arabia* and *How the West Was Won*. Our local congressman paid a visit each year to talk to our classes.

The merit pay system at Rich East High School meant teachers were not compensated for extra duties. Instead, teachers were asked to "volunteer" for various activities, from club sponsorships to athletics. Theoreti-

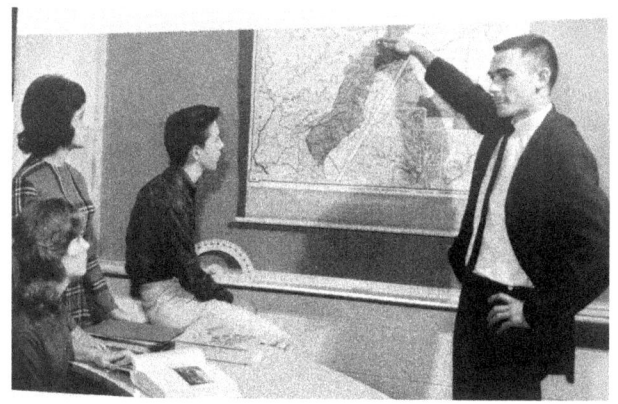

cally, compensation would be reflected in merit pay raises. It took only a few years for teachers to realize that this system was exploiting them, so they met to form a union. The extent and breadth of the extracurricular options for the students were amazing, especially when compared to my own high school experience, with clubs for everything from astronomy to playing bridge. These activities allowed me to get to know the students on a more personal level. As a single teacher, I frequently stayed after school. I helped with intramural basketball, track meets, and wrestling matches and ran the scoreboard at home football games. I also assisted the choir director, who orchestrated a major musical production each year. One of the lead student singers went on later to a Broadway career. I was the sponsor for the junior class, but my favorite assignment was serving as the sponsor for the student council. The student council was made up of some of the best and brightest students, many of whom I had in class. They needed very little guidance in organizing an array of school events, including the school prom.

During orientation on the first day of school, I met another teacher named Lou Schmitt. Lou had been a chemistry teacher for four years and had just returned from two years teaching at US military-dependent schools in France and England. Lou lived in a townhouse apartment in Park Forest with another teacher named Earl Hari. Lou and Earl had grown up together in a small town in northeastern Illinois called Cissna Park. Earl had just graduated from Illinois State and was starting his teaching career at a nearby high school in suburban Flossmoor. Lou and Earl became my close friends during our teaching years, and we remained friends throughout our lives. The following year, one of their other hometown friends named Bob Ruetter started his first-year teaching job and joined our little group. Little did we know then that, over the next five years, the four of us would take turns being in each other's weddings.

The average age of the faculty at Rich East High School was twenty-seven years old. A high percentage of the faculty were single teachers. This resulted in a very active social life with ski trips, weekend parties, and trips to downtown Chicago. We often celebrated surviving the teaching week by gathering at our favorite pub called Freeh's Inn after school on Fridays. One Saturday night, Lou and I drove to downtown Chicago to North Wells Street, which had become a new nightlife area, especially for jazz venues. We parked in front of a club called The Hungry Eye and walked in to listen to the music. After a long wait, Miles Davis sauntered out with his trumpet. On another evening, Lou, Earl, and I joined fellow teacher Bob Borich, who grew up in the Croatian community on Chicago's South Side. He took us to a club only he could find in his old but changing neighborhood. The experience was unusual for Lou, Earl, and me, as we were the only white guys in the packed house.

After our first year living together in the Chicago suburb of Monee, my roommate, Don Tolliver, decided to go back to EIU for a master's degree. Two fellow teachers at Rich East invited me to live with them in a house in Park Forest just a few blocks from the high school. Morrie Jones was the voice teacher and director of choral groups. Bert Gray was a biology teacher. Both guys were very talented, popular with their students, and

North Michigan Avenue (Miracle Mile), 1965

spent long hours at the school. Morrie also sang in the Chicago Chorale and arranged for us to attend his concerts. At later events at the symphony hall, we heard the popular French singing group the Swingle Singers doing their Bach routine and the Dave Brubeck Quartet.

Bert asked me if I would like to spend the summer traveling with him. I had no plans yet, so we spent time planning a ten-week trip for the summer of 1963. I thought the trip would be a big help for teaching American history. It turned out to be a great adventure. President Eisenhower's new Interstate Highway System initiated in the 1950s was now partially built, making our ambitious plan possible.

We started in Chicago, drove south to Mexico, then generally followed the coastline around the southern and eastern seaboard all the way to Canada. Our travels covered over ten thousand miles and took us to twenty-eight states. We focused on state capitals, Civil War battlefields, major university campuses, the nation's capital, and beaches. Bert fixed up his Volkswagen bus for camping, so we often would drive into the night to get to our destinations. We drove down the street by Dealey Pla-

House with Morrie and Bert

za in Dallas, not knowing that President John F. Kennedy would be assassinated there the following November.

Each state introduced us to something interesting and memorable. In Mississippi, we visited the Ole Miss campus in Oxford and then drove to see the state capital in Jackson. This stop resulted in one of the highlights of the trip. It was a hot Saturday in late June as we climbed up the steps of the Capitol. The cavernous first floor was cool but empty as we walked around looking at the murals. A woman's voice called out to us from an office with a friendly greeting on the second floor. We stopped to chat, and she said in her very pronounced Southern drawl, "Would you like to meet the guv'na?" We, of course, accepted, and she escorted us in to see Ross Barnett.

Governor Barnett was sitting behind a huge desk, but he stood and greeted us with a motion to sit down. He wanted to know where we were from and responded to Bert's mention of his home state of Minnesota as a place where he liked to go fishing. Barnett was a big man, a World War I veteran, and a strong segregationist. His reputation had been tarnished by blocking the entrance of Black student James Meredith to the University of Mississippi in the fall of 1962. Barnett went so far as to appoint himself as registrar of the university so he could personally reject Meredith's application. The courts ruled that his decision violated desegregation laws based on the 1954 Supreme Court decision in *Brown v. Board of Education*. Federal troops were brought in to enforce Meredith's entry, but a disastrous riot broke out when armed segregationists stormed the campus. Just a few weeks before our visit with the governor, the Black Civil Rights activist Medgar Evers had been murdered in Oxford. Against this backdrop, the governor's reaction was no surprise when I asked him for his thoughts about the Supreme Court decision. He immediately stood up with a totally changed demeanor and said, "Well, it was nice meetin' you boys," and promptly escorted us out the door.

We drove back down to the coast from Jackson to see Biloxi with its marina full of shrimp boats. Our subsequent travels took us around the Gulf Coast to southern Florida and the Everglades, then on to Key West, Florida. Of course, beaches were a big attraction, but historic sites and national parks remained on our agenda. In Brooksville, Florida, we stopped to see my uncle Lozier Stanley, Mom's brother, who ran a local diner. He treated us to a shrimp dinner. Going into Georgia after visiting Miami and Daytona Beach, we had a longer than anticipated time in Atlanta to repair the Volkswagen's engine. We were able to stay with Bert's cousin, who set us up with two lovely gals and loaned us his convertible. It was here, however, that we experienced signs of the growing Civil Rights movement when demonstrators marched in front of a theater we entered to see the new film, *Mutiny on the Bounty*.

After touring Georgia, Tennessee, and the Carolinas, we spent several days in Virginia hiking through a number of Civil War Battlefields. During the trip, we took turns driving. While one of us drove, the other would read aloud about the battles from the Civil War classic, *This Hal-*

lowed Ground by Bruce Catton. At the Petersburg National Battlefield in Virginia, I wanted to check out the Battle of the Crater that I had read so much about. The battle took place toward the end of the war as Union troops fought their way toward the Confederate capital in Richmond. The Union and Confederate soldiers were lined up in trenches across from each other for several weeks when a Pennsylvania colonel decided to have his coal miner soldiers dig a tunnel under the Confederate lines. They deposited a cache of dynamite in the tunnel below the Confederate line. A huge explosion resulted in a large crater that created an opening for an invasion. The Confederate soldiers recovered unexpectedly among the dust and chaos and turned the assault into a disaster for the North. Bert and I scrambled down into the crater that was grown up in large trees, but the scale of the hole was still impressive. The crater was better preserved in later years and the trees were removed.

In Washington, DC, we stayed in a classic Georgetown townhouse with Bert's cousin, John Strand, who shared the large apartment with two other federal employees, including an economist with the CIA. John was a Harvard graduate who worked as a systems analyst in Secretary Robert McNamara's Department of Defense. He was one of the "whiz kids" brought in by McNamara to revolutionize the department's planning and decision-making processes. John showed us around the town and gave us a tour of the Pentagon. We toured the major monuments, including the Washington National Cathedral, Arlington National Cemetery, the Smithsonian Institution, the FBI headquarters, the Bureau of Engraving and Printing, and Mount Vernon. We challenged ourselves by climbing the stairs to the top of the Washington Monument. We had the chance to see JFK's helicopter land in the Eclipse after his weekend at Hyannis Port. We were also able to watch the US Senate in session using the tickets given to us, as they did for other constituents who asked, by Illinois Senator Everett Dirksen's office. The government complex was

US Capitol, 1963

impressive, but the town was still a relatively sleepy southern city. There was no metro and no tall buildings, and the Capital Beltway that would become the city's outer limits was not yet completed. Nonetheless, I was quite taken by the experience in DC and left with an underlying sense that I might return.

After our immersion at the nation's capital, we completed our Civil War tours with visits to the battlefields at Antietam, Harpers Ferry, and Gettysburg. We then turned to the Atlantic Coast cities of Baltimore, New York, Philadelphia, and Boston. In New York, we visited my aunt, Ethel Johnson, who gave us a tour of Brooklyn. We then took in some of the Manhattan highlights from the Empire State Building down to the Statue of Liberty. We also drove along the Bowery to check out its skid row reputation. Leaving New York, we wound our way around the New England states and checked out everything from the Gold Coast in Rhode Island to Cape Cod, Martha's Vineyard, and Boston's historic venues. After Harvard Yard and Salem, we visited Maine, New Hampshire, and Vermont before entering Canada. We focused on Québec City, Montreal, Ottawa, and Toronto in Canada. We reentered the US at Niagara Falls and journeyed to Detroit to see the Ford Museum and tour a GM factory. Our long journey ended back in Park Forest in time for school to start.

My teaching load remained the same for my second year at Rich East in the fall of 1963. My new living arrangements with Bert and Morrie went very well, with the added benefit of a very short commute. The year was much the same as my first-year experience, though I felt more prepared.

Thanks to the influence of Lou Schmitt, I decided to apply for a position with the Defense Department military-dependent schools overseas. Two years of teaching experience were required, so I thought I was well prepared. The process started with an interview with a recruiter at one of the major bank buildings in downtown Chicago's financial district. It was a rainy Sunday as I drove down the empty LaSalle Street to the bank. There I received the bad news that I wasn't qualified. It seemed that, while I could teach seven subjects in the social sciences, I had to be qualified to teach in two separate disciplines, such as math or science.

To assuage the disappointment over the loss of teaching overseas, the superintendent for Rich Township, Dr. Robert Andre, nominated me for a Coe Foundation fellowship in American studies if I would return to teach for the 1964–1965 school year. I accepted his offer. The program was held on the DePauw University campus in Greencastle, Indiana. It consisted of four graduate-level classes in American history, political science, economics, and American literature that DePauw faculty members taught. One of the fun things was singing in a barbershop quartet for the closing banquet.

The more adventurous part of that summer's plan was one I cooked up with Lou Schmitt and Earl Hari. We decided it would be fun to attend the 1964 World's Fair in New York City. We had previously enjoyed spending our spring break together at Daytona Beach, Florida. At the start of the summer, I took my 1959 Chevy to Flora, and Uncle Harmon took it in trade for a new 1964 Corvair red convertible. It was not a Corvette, but it was the best I could do on a teacher's salary. After the summer session at DePauw, I drove the Corvair to Cissna Park to pick up Earl. We drove to New York City, where we met Lou, who was able to take a break during his summer program for chemistry teachers at Bowdoin College in Brunswick, Maine.

The World's Fair in New York was just as impressive as the one in Seattle that I had attended two years earlier. One lasting impression was watching a giant clock that counted the country's population growth. It spun around with the daily count that recorded the US population at 189 million. Since then, I've watched over the years as the US population reached 331 million people in 2020. While in New York with Lou and Earl, we toured some of the city highlights, and I was again able to visit Aunt Ethel Johnson, who was living across the Hudson in Brooklyn.

Earl, Lou, and I left New York City and drove to Providence, Rhode Island, Cape Cod, and Boston. We dropped Lou off in Brunswick, Maine, to complete his summer school session at Bowdoin. Earl and I drove on up the coast of Maine to Bar Harbor. Next was a visit to President Franklin D. Roosevelt's summer cottage on Campobello Island in New Brunswick, Canada. We toured Nova Scotia and Prince Edward Island, then drove along the St. Lawrence River to Québec City. We had a near-disaster along a stretch of highway in Québec when a large rockslide came crashing across the road right in front of us. A construction crew had set off an explosive to blast out a larger piece of roadbed but forgot

1964 Corvair

to close the highway! I had to contain my anger and find an alternative route to Québec City.

In Québec City, we visited the famous landmark hotel, the Château Frontenac. During World War II, England's Prime Minister Churchill and President Roosevelt met twice at the Château Frontenac to coordinate plans for conducting the war against the Nazis. Another memorable part of our experience at the Château was the ballroom's four o'clock tea and dance. Since many young men worked in Québec's forests for the summer, the young ladies at the dance were happy to see Earl and me. Leaving the fun at the Château behind us, Earl and I then made our way back to Park Forest for the fall start of the 1964 school year.

Before the school year started, Bert, Morrie, and I decided to give up our rental house in Park Forest. We invited another teacher, Timothy Sawyers, to join us in renting a house in a neighboring suburb called Crete. The house was larger and located on a golf course. It had a cozy atmosphere and was perfect for having parties with our teacher friends. I was now the lead teacher for team-teaching American history, and Tim was my partner. Living together made it easier for us to plan our lessons.

House with Morrie, Bert, and Tim

I was also in charge of a student teacher, Nancy Adelman, who was attending the University of Illinois. She was very bright and a quick learner.

Morrie, Bert, and I took a driving trip to New Orleans during spring break. Unfortunately, after we got back, I finally had to deal with my chronic tonsillitis. The surgery was performed by Dr. Aron Gerber, my former student's father, but I developed serious bleeding issues and had to stay in the hospital for seven days. A very nice nurse would sneak in ice cream to help me through the process.

By this time, I decided that I would leave teaching and move on to graduate school. I applied to the University of Illinois and Purdue University, where each had master of arts programs in social science. I received a full-ride fellowship offer from Purdue, but the University of Illinois only gave me a graduate resident assistantship for a residence hall counselor position. I ended up going to the University of Illinois anyway, thinking that the quality of the Illinois academic program made it the better choice.

The administration at Rich East supported my decision but urged that I take a year of absence instead of resigning. Superintendent Dr. Andre also supported my application for a summer program for teachers at the University of Illinois in Champaign. As a result, I received a scholarship to attend the first offering of a National Defense Education Act program for the humanities in the summer of 1965. The program was an American history institute for high school American history teachers. This was a perfect segue for me to continue at the university for a master's degree.

Leaving teaching at Rich East was bittersweet. I was excited to be moving on to a new part of my life, but it also meant leaving behind many friends and a comfortable groove. As a footnote, I later learned that Bert and Morrie left teaching at Rich East a few years later and revealed that they were gay. This was a bit of a shock to me since neither had given any indication of their sexual orientation, but it was a time when many repressed their identities. After Morrie and Bert eventually left teaching and went their separate ways, we lost touch with one another. Tragically, I learned that both had succumbed to AIDS in the 1980s epidemic. I mourned the loss of these old friends.

Chapter 11

GRADUATE SCHOOL

In June 1985, I started graduate work at the University of Illinois by attending the NDEA History Institute. The six-week program included forty high school history teachers. Dr. Robert Waller, a University of Illinois faculty member, was the director of the program, which included four courses focusing on foreign policy, economics, new interpretations of American history, and teaching methodologies. Dr. Waller taught the methods class in which we were required to write a paper. I wrote about team teaching and how it should be properly implemented. At the end of the course, Dr. Waller invited me to present the paper at a statewide conference for history teachers, which I did the following year.

Jerry Greer, 1965

The classes at the Institute were a good way for me to get back into an academic groove. My favorite class was the American history interpretations class taught by Dr. Gene Lewis. The course was based on an influential book by Richard Hofstadter called *The American Political Tradition*. Dr. Lewis had received his PhD a few years earlier from the University of Illinois and now was head of the history department at the University of Cincinnati. Dr. Lewis, now Gene to me, invited me to play tennis with him after class one day. This led to an invitation for martinis with him and his wife, Dottie. I was touched by their kindness, and over the summer, we developed a friendship that lasted throughout our lifetimes. Gene later invited me to come to the University of Cincinnati to work on a PhD.

Each of the professors for the University of Illinois summer program had an assistant that was chosen from leading high school programs from around the state. The American foreign policy course assistant was Gerald Greer (Jerry). Jerry was head of the history department at the prestigious Oak Park-River Forest High School on the West Side of Chicago. Jerry invited me to dinner one evening, where we discovered we had a lot in common. Jerry grew up on an Iowa farm and had an enormous dedication to his alma mater, the University of Iowa. He had a tremendous sense of humor befitting his Irish heritage. He was bright and quick, and he had a gift for storytelling that was unmatched in my experience. That dinner was the start of a lifelong kinship that only ended with Jerry's passing in 2021.

Jerry was a dedicated Catholic, and his only brother was a priest. A veteran of World War II, Jerry had remarkably recovered from a gunshot wound that left him in a coma for four months. He was part of Patton's Third Army and arrived in France as a second lieutenant in December 1944. Before the start of the Battle of the Bulge, his platoon was ordered to eliminate a German machine gun nest near Metz in Alsace-Lorraine. While he led his platoon up the hill, he was struck by a machine-gun bullet in the back of the head. A member of his platoon, Phil Pollack, later ran by what he thought was Jerry's body with a gunshot wound in the back of his head, but in the heat of the battle, he could do nothing more. Jerry was later placed on a pile of bodies awaiting triage at the field hospital. Fortunately, he was extracted when someone observed his body twitch. He was transported to a military hospital in England, where he made a complete recovery, although he was left with a permanent metal plate in the back of his head.

Jerry, a dedicated bachelor, asked if I had plans for August 1965 after the summer session. This led us to plan a trip to California, which I had not visited. After a brief visit with Mom and Dad in early August, I drove my Corvair out to San Francisco. Once there, I spent a couple of days with my great-aunt Margaret Frederick. She showed me around the University of California campus and other locations. She also treated me to my first Orange Julius in Berkeley.

Two days later, I picked up Jerry from the train station in San Francisco when he arrived on the California Zephyr. We checked into the Plaza Hotel near Union Square and proceeded to a sunset drink at the Top of the Mark on Nob Hill. We visited Alcatraz, Fisherman's Wharf, Sausalito, and other highlights of the delightful city, ending each day at a nice restaurant. As it turned out, Jerry had a knack for living the good life.

After touring the highlights of San Francisco, we drove the coast highway to Los Angles. Along the way, we drove the famous 17-Mile Drive and visited Carmel, San Simeon, and Santa Barbara. One of our favorite places to stay on the trip was the new motel chain, Motel 6, and yes, the cost was six dollars a night. Our last stop in LA was Disneyland before we started our trek back to Illinois, with stops at the Grand Canyon, Santa Fe, and Kansas.

I learned a lot from Jerry. Foremost was the value of friendship and how he made the time to maintain relationships through time and space. He maintained a prodigious amount of correspondence to keep in touch with his family and friends. Visits with Jerry's friends were filled with storytelling, laughter, and some pretty stiff drinks.

During the 1965 trip, we stayed with a couple of his World War II buddies who were in his Officer Candidate School class. Jim Coulter was a Lockheed engineer in San Jose who proudly showed us his backyard bomb shelter. The other was Ed Costello, a small-town banker and landowner in Kansas. Unlike Jerry, Ed had not been injured in the war. His platoon had been the first to reach Hitler's Eagle's Nest hideaway in southern Bavaria. He managed to bring back a couple of artifacts from the Eagle's Nest in his duffel bag, including an officer's Luger pistol and a book with original photos of Hitler with Eva Braun. I encouraged him to donate the photos to a museum, which he later did.

During the postwar occupation, Ed had several assignments, including serving as the mayor of a small Bavarian city. He also commanded a

Wedding: Lou and Chris Schmitt

convoy of four 2-1/2 trucks to pick up a group of German rocket scientists who had holed up in a small village near Garmisch-Partenkirchen in southern Bavaria. In the spring of 1945, it was clear to the Germans that the war was lost, so they relocated top scientists and their families to a location in southern Bavaria to avoid capture by the Russians. Among the scientists were Wernher von Braun and his associates, who later were instrumental in developing rockets for the US space program. The California trip was the first of many that Jerry and I were to take in the coming years.

In mid-August I arrived back in Illinois in time to participate in the wedding of Lou Schmitt and Chris Whan. The wedding took place in Peoria, Chris's hometown. Lou had met Chris when she was teaching elementary school in Chicago Heights near Park Forest. We had been friends before their wedding, and they remained my cherished friends for years to come.

Lou was the first of our quartet to marry, but Earl, Bob, and I each followed suit over the next four years. Both Earl and Bob were teaching at the Homewood-Flossmoor High School, also on Chicago's South Side. Before long, both of them met their life partners, Diane and Nancy,

Jim and Sally Long

who were also teachers at the Homewood-Flossmoor school. My friendships with Earl and Diane Hari, and Bob and Nancy Ruetter remain to this day, but my relationship at the time with a lovely elementary teacher, Tammy Thorne, did not last.

After Lou and Chris's wedding, I moved to Champaign, Illinois, to start the academic year at the University of Illinois. To fulfill my assistantship responsibilities, I moved into Snyder Hall, one of the men's dormitories. Each of the four floors had two graduate assistants who served as counselors. I had responsibility for the eighty undergraduates on my fourth-floor wing. While my graduate assistantship was great for paying school expenses, the job was not my cup of tea. At the end of the school year, I turned down an assistantship offer by the Director of Student services to lead a residence hall staff while continuing a PhD program.

The good news about the graduate assistant program was meeting Jim Long, my graduate assistant partner on the other wing of Snyder Hall's fourth floor. Jim and I escaped our duties on Saturday nights at a club in Urbana called the Rose Bowl. The Rose Bowl featured a legendary country singer and excellent guitarist, Sonny Norman, and the Drifting Playboys. Jim was an excellent athlete and turned down an offer to play minor league baseball. He would indulge me in playing basketball, and we attended the university football and basketball games together. After graduate school, Jim went into the Peace Corps in South America. He later married his fiancé, Sally, and became a math teacher in San Diego. My coursework focused on American history and economics in the university's master of arts program in Social Science. The graduate economics courses included basic micro and macro classes, US economic history, and the Soviet economy. My favorite courses, however, were American history and US diplomacy. The history class was taught by the department head, Robert W. Johannsen. Dr. Johannsen, a distinguished scholar and author, later wrote *Stephen A. Douglas*, a book still considered to be the definitive biography of Douglas.

Perhaps the most notable and popular professor in the department was Norman A. Graebner, who often lectured to standing-room classes in an auditorium that could seat 500 students-seat auditorium. His popularity was evidenced by the over 75,000 people who listened to his radio broadcasts. I took his courses on US diplomatic history, which had a lasting impact on my understanding of foreign policy.

His outstanding reputation as a teacher was based as much on how he presented his material as his considerable knowledge and worldview on how nations conduct foreign relations. He interpreted the role of US foreign policy through the prism of realism as opposed to idealism. He believed that nations pursued self-interest in a world of sovereign states in their relations with one another. Ideological goals as a part of a nation's foreign policy, such as making the world safe for democracy, were not achievable. End objectives, in his view, required the means to carry them out. His lectures on US diplomatic history reflected this view of geopolitical realities. The university administration at Illinois was highly upset

Professor Norman Graebner

when the University of Virginia hired him away the following year. He achieved even more recognition at UVA with his lectures, books, and role as an academic proponent of a realist foreign policy.

I decided to do my master's paper during a seminar on US economic history. The class was taught by Dr. Clark Spence, who had research interests in Western history, gold mining, and specifically, gold dredging in the West. By this time, Jerry Greer had invited me and Joe Cisco, one of his former students finishing graduate school at the University of Chicago, to spend the summer on a trip to Alaska. I decided to do my master's research on Alaska to learn more about the state before our trip. In consultation with Dr. Spence, he persuaded me to write about the history of gold dredging in Alaska. This choice led me to the ordeal of spending the entire spring break in the Mining Engineering Department's basement library, blowing the dust off of old mining journals to find primary sources. I learned more than anyone needs to know about the mechanics of dredges, permafrost, and the role of the price of gold. But it did have a payoff when we made the Alaskan trip during the summer of 1966. Moreover, Dr. Spence later wrote a book on gold dredging in Alaska called *The*

Northern Gold Fleet: Twentieth-Century Gold Dredging in Alaska, and he gained the reputation of being a premier historian for mining history in the US. Although he made no attribution to it, I like to think that he used some of my research in his project.

Oral exams were one of the requirements for my degree. Dr. Spence, who had given my master's thesis an A, also chaired the orals panel. The panel consisted of four of my professors. While they were generally kind, I was given one trick question on an arcane economics theory that I was able to finesse satisfactorily. I received all A's, except for one B in an economics class for my graduate coursework.

Graduate studies taught me a lot academically, but I also learned a lot about myself. At first, I was intrigued by academia and considered the prospect of obtaining a PhD. It so happened that the premier organization for American history, the Organization of American Historians (OAH), was being held at the University of Cincinnati in January 1966. Gene Lewis invited Jerry Greer and me to attend the conference that he was helping to organize. I drove to Chicago, and Jerry and I set off for Cincinnati, where we planned to stay with Gene and Dottie.

As we drove into Indiana with Jerry at the wheel of his 1960 Ford Falcon, the car engine blew up. Stranded, we took a bus back to Oak Park. Jerry was so upset with the "fulcan Falcon" that he decided to bail on the convention, so I drove to Cincinnati in my Corvair. Gene introduced me to some of his colleagues at the conference, including a department chair at Manchester College, a small Indiana liberal arts college. After a chat, I was offered a position teaching history at his college. At the same time, Gene offered me an assistantship to work on a PhD in his department at the University of Cincinnati. Still thinking about the prospects of an academic career, I joined both the OAH and the Montana Historical Society. My interest in history and my friendship with Gene continued. Many years later, Gene and I met in Helena, Montana, to attend an annual conference of the Montana Historical Society. Perhaps the most important thing I learned during my graduate studies was that the more I learned, the more I extended the boundaries of my ignorance.

The Index Card

Back in Champaign after the Cincinnati conference, I recognized deep down that I was not cut out to be an academic. Until this point, my goals for a career had primarily focused on education and the prospect of teaching at a junior college. Junior colleges were enjoying an expansion in many states, including Illinois, so changing to teaching at this level instead of high school seemed a reasonable choice. I decided, however, to pursue a different path for a couple of years to broaden my experience. I decided to get a job with the federal government in Washington, DC, and took the federal employee entrance exam. I then sent applications to the Bureau of the Budget and the Department of Agriculture, thinking I had some knowledge of each. One day, after a class in Gregory Hall, where most of the history classes were taught, I perused the employment flyers on the bulletin board. A handwritten index card caught my eye that said, "Central Intelligence Agency representative on campus, January 28, 1966, ph. xxx-xxx-xxxx." Intrigued, I called the number and made an appointment to meet the recruiter at a hotel. The interview seemed to go well, and I filled out an application form for the CIA that included a personal history statement that was extraordinarily long and detailed. A couple of months later, I was told my application was being processed, but after that—silence.

In the meantime, the Vietnam War raged on, and the mandatory draft for men up to age twenty-six stayed in place. During my three years of teaching, I received a deferment from the Selective Service board in Clay County. During graduate school, however, I was reclassified as 1-A. This gave me pause because, at twenty-five years old, I was still eligible to

| SELECTIVE SERVICE SYSTEM | SSS Form No. 2 |
| REGISTRATION CERTIFICATE | (Rev. 3-30-56) Approval not required |

THIS IS TO CERTIFY THAT IN ACCORDANCE WITH THE SELECTIVE SERVICE LAW

Darold Roy Herdes
(FIRST NAME) (MIDDLE NAME) (LAST NAME)

SELECTIVE SERVICE NO.: 11 | 95 | 40 | 49

RESIDENCE AT REGISTRATION: R.F.D. #3
(NUMBER AND STREET OR R. F. D. NUMBER)

Clay City **Clay** **Illinois**
(CITY, TOWN, OR VILLAGE) (ZONE) (COUNTY) (STATE)

June 5, 1940 **Clay Co. Ill.**
(DATE OF BIRTH) (PLACE OF BIRTH)

WAS DULY REGISTERED ON THE 5 DAY OF June, 19 58

Mae F. Reid
(SIGNATURE OF LOCAL BOARD CLERK)

---

be drafted. It turned out that Clay County had plenty of eighteen-year-olds, so older guys weren't being drafted, but I was unaware of this at the time. I wasn't opposed to military service, but I opposed the Vietnam War. Dr. Graebner had informed my view that national interests should be clearly defined and tools of diplomacy fully deployed. I wondered if my opposition to the Vietnam War might deter the CIA from hiring me. I decided, however, that I wanted to join the Agency and remained focused on this objective. The academic year ended, and I received my master's diploma. I still had not received word from the CIA, so I decided to continue with my plans for the Alaskan trip with Jerry and Joe Cisco.

Chapter 12

ALASKA

In mid-June 1966, Joe Cisco and I met Jerry Greer at his parents' home in Iowa City. Ever the inveterate planner, Jerry arranged to deliver a pickup-truck camper to Alaska. One of his army buddies, who worked for a Chevy dealer in Forest City, Iowa, had sold a ¾-ton pickup truck with a mounted camper to be delivered to a dealership in Anchorage. The camper had been manufactured at the Winnebago factory in Forest City. As part of the arrangement, the three of us could use the camper for the trip up the Alaska-Canadian Highway (Alcan) through Canada.

The Alcan was a World War II construction project that had been built to create a land route to Alaska. Until that time, Alaska could only be reached by sea or air. The highway was still a gravel road, notorious for broken windshields and flat tires. Instead of driving straight to Anchorage, we opted to keep the camper for about four weeks to explore the Yukon Territory and enter Alaska much farther to the north. However, we had a lot to see and do before we arrived at the start of the Alcan at Dawson Creek, British Columbia. It was, after all, a 3,300-mile trip from Forest City, Iowa, to Anchorage (barring detours which tacked on an additional 1,000 miles).

Fortunately, each of us in our trio was interested in history. Joe had just graduated from the University of Chicago with a graduate degree in

With Joe Cisco and Jerry Greer

history following his undergraduate study at Princeton. He came from a family with interests in history and government service. Joe's namesake was his uncle, Joseph Cisco, the Assistant Secretary of State for Near Eastern Affairs during the Johnson and Nixon administrations, who served in the State Department from 1951 to 1976. Joe had lined up a teaching position at a high school in a West Chicago suburb. This common interest made it possible to stop at almost all the historical sites along our planned route with complete unanimity.

Our first major stop was at the Theodore Roosevelt National Park in North Dakota. From there, we drove across Big Sky Country in Montana to Glacier National Park. Joe and I did most of the driving, and Jerry was the chief cook. Before leaving the US and crossing into Alberta, Canada, we had a pretty good grip on handling the logistics of camping with our rig. We checked out the Banff National Park and the Columbia Icefield en route to the start of the Alaska Highway in Dawson Creek. Driving the Alcan was a bit of a challenge, but the scenery and the sense of being in the wilderness kept our attention. One mishap we had was a flat tire.

Alcan Highway, a gravel road, 1966

I set about setting up the jack to change the tire. The jack, however, was suitable for the pickup, but not for the heavy camper. Instead of lifting the vehicle, the jack went the other way and sank into the ground. Service facilities were about fifty miles apart on the Alcan, but fortunately, we had just passed a service station. I walked back and persuaded the owner to let me borrow a proper jack that did the trick.

Camping along the way introduced us to another challenge: giant mosquitos. Stepping out of the camper at night meant preparing for a cloud of them to swoop around with bad intentions.

After leaving Dawson Creek, we drove almost nine hundred miles on the Alcan to reach Whitehorse, the capital of Canada's Yukon Territory. Whitehorse had a population of about 15,000 people and was located on the Yukon River. By then, we were ready for a break from the wilderness drive, so we spent a couple of days checking out the town. During the Klondike gold rush in 1898, Whitehorse had been the staging point for those going north to Dawson City. It was hard to imagine that 100,000 miners had descended on the area, hoping to strike it rich.

The miners could reach Whitehorse by taking a ship from Seattle to Skagway, Alaska, then hiking a hundred miles on a rugged mountain

A derelict gold dredge in the Klondike

trail. This trek got easier when an English company built a narrow-gauge railroad called the Chilkoot and White Pass in 1898. The miners took boats on the Yukon River from Whitehorse to Dawson City, another three hundred miles to the north. The traffic volume on the river was so great that large paddle-wheel boats were built to carry the miners and freight up to Dawson City. A road was later built so that vehicles could make the trip. While we were in Whitehorse, the town was relocating one of the abandoned paddle wheelers from its dry dock to a spot where it would be converted to a museum.

The Alcan turned westward from Whitehorse to enter Alaska. Anchorage was another seven hundred miles to the southwest. Not wanting to give up our camper just yet, we decided to travel north for the three hundred miles to Dawson City. When we got closer to the town, the road was built on the piles of gravel that had been left when gold dredges had dug up the river valley.

Dredging had been a popular way to find gold—a topic I had spent graduate time researching. I found it interesting to see the alluvial soils and gravel beds that the dredges had sifted to separate the gold. Some of the dredges were very large, and the gravel tailings left by the dredging operations extended for several miles before we got into Dawson City. Along the way, we came across a dredge that had been abandoned. I wasn't going to pass up the opportunity to explore the large machine, so we made our way out to it and climbed all over it, trying to figure out how it worked. Joe and Jerry were very accommodating with my peculiar interest in dredges.

Dawson City had about eight hundred people, including many native Indians. This compared to the forty thousand people who had lived there during the peak of the gold rush. There was a hill adjacent to the town named the Dome, where miners had built a road decades earlier. We drove to the top to look down on the town that still had an outline of the streets from the days when it had been a small city. The old wooden sidewalks were a bit of a hazard, and many of the old remaining commercial buildings were boarded up. Looking through the glass windows on some old, vacated buildings, we could see steel traps and other merchandise still on the shelves. The town did, however, restore the small but decorative opera house that had been built during the town's heyday. Since we were there in midsummer, the sun never dipped below the horizon. From our camping spot on the banks of the Yukon, we watched at midnight when the sun seemed to hover right over the water. It happened that we arrived in Dawson City on July 4, although it was not a holiday celebrated by the Canadians.

The most challenging part of the entire drive was the one-hundred-mile dirt road from Dawson City to the Alaskan border. Having observed the driving skills of my comrades, I insisted on taking the wheel. The road was about a lane and a half wide, which meant stopping or backing up when meeting the rare vehicle coming toward us. With no guardrails, parts of the drive could be quite thrilling as we went around the sides of some of the mountains and could see straight down over two thousand

With Joe Cisco, entering Alaska

feet to a valley floor. We were lucky that it wasn't raining, which would have made the path even more treacherous.

We entered Alaska with only a sign to welcome us. A few miles after entering Alaska, we spotted a moose standing in a marsh and munching on willow branches. I left the truck to take a photo, but the moose was not happy about it. He started to charge at me, but I was pretty fast getting back to our truck.

Our next stop was Fairbanks. We visited the University of Alaska's farm station, where we saw a herd of musk oxen. The muskox was native to Alaska, but they became extinct by 1900 because of overhunting. The university had received a grant to reintroduce the species with animals that had been imported from Greenland.

The more interesting stop for me was a visit to the headquarters of the Fairbanks Exploration Company, the largest gold mining company in Alaska until production was halted in 1964. The company compound was deserted, with dozens of abandoned vehicles lining the fences. When I knocked on the office building's door, I was invited in for a visit. I had a long discussion with the two remaining employees. They were the general manager and his assistant, both mining engineers. Their job was to oversee the maintenance of the company's mothballed gold dredging fleet, hoping for a profitable change in gold prices, which never happened. They were very friendly and extraordinarily knowledgeable, and they gave me an overview of the company's history. Their commentaries and papers they gave me would have been a *gold* mine primary source for me when I was writing my paper. Later I sent them a copy of my paper anyway. The company's dredges were considered behemoths and had been constructed at a cost of well over a million dollars each during the 1930s. The engineers gave us directions to the location of one of their dredges, but it was floating in a lake and out of reach.

We left Fairbanks and headed south, first exploring the Matanuska Valley and its Depression-era Matanuska Colony project. The colony was a New Deal program to lure American farmers to the valley to establish a farming economy. Most of the farmers were Scandinavians from Minnesota and Wisconsin who had farming experience in similar climates. We hiked on the Matanuska Glacier and chipped off some ice for our first glacier cocktail. A later group patterned after the Matanuska project called themselves the 59ers. They were blue-collar workers who were tired of the rat race in Detroit. In 1959, they banded together and formed a convoy for the three-week drive on the Alcan. They hoped to homestead on government land and receive 160 acres for free. Most of them failed, and my high school friend Hugh Lynn was among them. Hugh later discussed his adventure there with me and was very interested in the photos of my trip. After turning in our camper in Anchorage, we extended our stay and took the Alaskan railroad that connected Anchorage to Fairbanks. Our destination was the Mount McKinley National Park (now Denali). The sun came out, and luckily, we were able to see the highest mountain in the US on a clear day. We drove into the park to see the wildlife and watched a herd of Daw sheep crossing the road in front of us. From a high point on the road, we could see a herd of caribou grazing in one of the valleys.

Back in Anchorage, we plotted our trip back to the lower forty-eight, which took the form of several modes of transportation. We left Anchorage on a bus that took us back to the Yukon Territory and Whitehorse. The primary reason for this route was to take the Chilkoot and White Pass narrow-gauge railroad from White Horse to Skagway on the Inside Passage. It was an extraordinary ride with the roadbed clinging to the side of the mountains. The cars were still heated in winter by individual potbellied stoves. Looking down the toilet, we could see the railroad ties whizzing by, with the fortunate part being that the toilet was odorless. In Skagway, we watched a reenactment of Robert Service's famous poem, "The Shooting of Dan McGrew," that was performed in a saloon. Skagway was a relic of its gold rush past, but it was regaining life as the terminus of Alaska's ferry system.

The Alaskan ferries became our homes for the next week as we took them from Skagway to Prince Rupert, British Columbia. Established only two years earlier, in 1964, three ferries made the trip in eight-hour intervals. This meant that with our tickets, we could get off at ports along the Alaskan Panhandle then board the next ferry. There were no separate sleeping rooms on the ferry, so we slept in our seats.

At our stop at the state capital of Juneau, once again, Jerry had a contact for us. The family was originally from Chicago, and Jerry's friend had not lost his South Side accent. He took us up a stream outside Juneau

to watch the salmon struggle to get to their spawning grounds. At a small waterfall, a collection of fish took turns trying to hurl themselves over the falls. It was hard not to get in the water to give them a boost. After seeing the state capital, we boarded the ferry again to visit other coastal towns and see the totem pole park in Ketchikan. At Prince Rupert, we were treated to the most luxurious accommodations of the trip on the cruise ship that took us to Victoria Island.

 Finally, in Seattle, Joe departed to fly back to Chicago. Jerry and I boarded a Greyhound bus that took us down the Pacific Coast to San Francisco. There we took the San Francisco Zephyr Amtrak train going to Chicago. I left Jerry in Kansas City and took a train to St. Louis, where I caught a bus back to Clay County. The Alaskan adventure trip was a wilderness experience quite in contrast to the 1963 adventure covering the eastern United States with Bert Gray. The mountains, glaciers, wildlife, remoteness, and the sparse population were vivid reminders of how large and diverse our country is. It sparked a lifetime connection for me with the mountains and the wilderness. A few years later, when I moved back to Chicago, I rented an apartment around the corner from Jerry in suburban Oak Park, ensuring we'd have more time to swap stories.

Chapter 13

GAP YEAR

Following the Alaska trip, I returned home to visit Mom and Dad. There, in August 1966, I focused on what to do next. After all this time, I had not heard from the CIA, and I still had the 1-A Selective Service classification, which gave me some concern. While in graduate school, I had contacted the superintendent at Rich East High School and canceled my leave of absence. Without a job, I drove up to the University of Illinois placement office to see if any teaching positions were available. Coincidentally, the Maine West Township High School in Des Plaines, Illinois, had just sent a vacancy notice for an American history teacher. I drove to the school for an interview and was offered the job. The school in a northwestern suburb of Chicago was relatively new and reflected the growing number of families that were moving out of the city to the suburbs. The initial township school, Maine East, was where

Hillary Rodham Clinton had graduated two years earlier. My classes included teaching an advanced American history section, and generally, the experience went well. I knew, however, that I was simply biding my time for what I hoped would be a job in Washington, DC.

When I visited Maine West for the interview, one of the school secretaries said that her mother had a room for rent in her home near the school. I took the room, but soon the loneliness I had experienced while student teaching returned. Later in life, I learned that growing up as a twin makes it difficult to adapt to being alone. Fortunately, when visiting Lou Crane, my fraternity brother from Eastern, he invited me to live with him and two other guys in a townhouse development in Mount Prospect, Illinois. I seized the opportunity, not knowing at first that the complex called Boxwood Court had been the subject of an article in *Newsweek* Magazine. It seemed that Boxwood was one of the first developments designed for single adults. The primary feature was its proximity to Chicago's O'Hare Airport, which attracted many airline stewardesses. My three roommates, including Lou, were dating girls from this group, so there was a built-in social environment. This was never more apparent than when the great Chicago blizzard of 1967 dumped two feet of snow and closed down the whole city. Lou quickly organized a party at our townhouse and invited many of our neighbors. It turned into a three-day event. My legacy was learning to play bridge in a game that lasted all night. The legacy for Lou that resulted from his Boxwood experience was getting married to Carolyn Carlson.

Two weeks after school started in Des Plaines, Illinois, in September 1966, I finally received a letter from the CIA inviting me to Washington, DC, for interviews. I wrote back and said that I had signed a teaching contract obligating me to teach for the school year but that I remained interested. The response was that I could come for the interviews during

Christmas break. I arrived in DC between Christmas and New Year's on a cold, snowy day and checked in at a hotel on K Street.

There I received a call with instructions on where to report for the interview. A three-day succession of meetings, interviews, tests, medical and psychiatric exams, and a polygraph (lie detector test) followed. One of the officers who interviewed me was a case officer who had a penetrating line of questioning that gave me pause to consider my suitability for the job. However, I learned during our discussion that we had something in common: gold dredging. It seemed that he had spent a summer in Alaska working on one of the big gold dredges. While it may not have been relevant in the final decision, it was an interesting aside. After the interview, I was admonished not to disclose that I was a candidate for CIA employment.

The first positive sign that my application was going forward was hearing that a security clearance investigation was underway. Such a clearance investigation included interviews with people from my past. In April 1967, the Agency gave me a report date of June 27, 1967. When the school year ended in Des Plaines, I went home to see Mom and Dad and prepared to move to DC. The day before I was to leave, however, our neighborhood friend Jimmy Brown was killed in a motorcycle accident in Texas. His mom wanted me, Garold, and our mutual high school friend Hugh Lynn to serve as pallbearers. The departure delay was not an issue for my new employer. I was ready for the new adventure without really knowing what I had signed on to do.

Chapter 14

MARJORIE LYNN BURKE

While I was waiting for an elevator in November 1967, at a CIA training center in Arlington, Virginia, an attractive young woman was sitting nearby and reading a book. We started a conversation, causing me to miss the elevator, but it did give me time to get her name and phone number. A week or so later, we ran into one another again, and she chided me for not calling her. So I called. This started a romance with Marjorie Lynn Burke that led to our wedding in California a year later.

Mom and Aunt Mary in DC

Margie was twenty-three and had just joined the Agency after graduating from the University of Oregon. She came to the job because of her dad's urging, but her credentials were based on her time in the Middle East, where she had studied at the American University of Beirut, in Lebanon. We had an interesting year in DC, exploring many of the area's historic spots. A variety of outings, including canoeing on the Potomac, skiing in the Poconos, and hiking the trails in the Shenandoah National Park, helped solidify our connection.

Margie met my mom the spring after we met, when I sent Mom and her sister (my aunt Mary) tickets to fly to DC for a visit. This was the first time that either had been on an airplane. I also got them tickets to visit some highlights, including the White House and the Capitol. One evening, Margie and I took Mom and Aunt Mary to a seafood restaurant

1968 Oldsmobile Cutlass

near Capitol Hill for dinner. The most fun was seeing the expression on my mom's face when the waiter set down a whole lobster in front of her. It was the biggest crawdad she had ever seen, but she gamely took it on and enjoyed the experience. We also took them to my favorite restaurant, the Old Ebbitt Grill near the White House, which was still little changed from when Abraham Lincoln had eaten there.

Among other visitors to see me in Washington, DC, during this time was my old friend from EIU, Butch Swanstrom, and his new wife, Judy. He had finished veterinarian school at the University of Illinois and, after a tour in the Air Force, continued graduate work at Purdue. I also had a visit from Bob Reuter, who stayed with me while in town for an interview at the FBI. He was accepted and went on to have a sterling career. Earl Hari also visited while escorting high school students on a tour of the city.

Anticipating a trip from DC to Illinois, I traded my well-worn Corvair for a 1968 Oldsmobile Cutlass. The low-mileage car had belonged to an army general who sold it to me at a reasonable price. It seemed that he had a friend who worked for General Motors and bought a new Oldsmobile each year.

Our wedding in Pacific Palisades, California

Margie and I drove the Olds from Washington, DC, to Clay County to visit my parents. While there, we stayed at Mom and Dad's, and she met many of my relatives, especially my brother and his family. Taking what has become my standard roots tour, we visited the schools I had attended, the cemeteries where family members were buried, and other locations, including the Lathrop Church. The latter visit was fortuitous since it was the last time I saw the church before it burned down two years later. While in Illinois, we went to the Chicago area, where we visited several friends from my college and teaching days, including Lou and Chris Schmitt, Earl Hari, Bob Reutter, and the Swanstroms.

Subsequently, we flew to Los Angeles to meet her parents, who lived in Malibu. Although it was already clear that we came from widely divergent backgrounds, their house on Point Dume, just to the north of Malibu, was a vivid reminder. The introductions seemed to go well, and I met many of her friends. Margie and her mother were busy reviewing the impressive wedding plans that were already underway. I had previously

Wedding of Earl and Diane Hari

met her dad (Finley) when he was on a business trip to DC. He was an interesting man with more than a touch of arrogance, but we got along, and I learned a lot from him. He had a physics background and a PhD from MIT. During World War II, he had been part of a team at the naval laboratories in San Diego that developed sonar for anti-submarine warfare applications. Later, he was employed by the Air Force think tank, the RAND Corporation. At RAND, he used his underwater acoustics expertise to analyze the effects of underwater nuclear weapons testing, among other projects. He considered himself a gourmet and wine connoisseur, and over the years, we were treated to some of the finest restaurants in the cities where we lived.

Margie and I were married on November 28, 1968, at the St. Francis Episcopal Church in Pacific Palisades, California. Margie's maid of honor was her only sibling, Judy, who was four years younger. Three of

Bob and Nancy Ruetter

her school girlfriends were attendants. My brother, Garold, was my best man, and my three supporters were my high school teaching buddies, Lou, Earl, and Bob. They flew out from Chicago after frantically running through the Chicago O'Hare Airport on the eve of Thanksgiving to catch their flight. We all stayed in the Burkes' spacious house in Point Dume. After a reception at the St. Francis Church, our honeymoon started with a drive to Santa Barbara's Biltmore Hotel. From there, we drove the Pacific Coast Highway to San Francisco.

After returning to Washington, DC, we moved into her apartment. The apartment was the upper flat of a two-story building and only a few blocks from the apartment I shared with one of my Agency career training classmates. Things went smoothly for us until both of us became victims of the 1968 flu epidemic that laid us low for over a week.

We recovered from the flu in time for the inauguration of President Nixon on January 20, 1969. Attending such events was one of the advantages of living in Washington, DC. A little over two months later, we were again on the parade route for the funeral procession of President Eisenhower. It was a solemn occasion as we watched Raven, the riderless black horse with backward boots in the stirrups, follow the caisson bearing Ike's casket. These moments and the grandeur of the Washington Mall never ceased to be impressive to me. It wasn't long after that that I got my first field assignment with the Agency in Chicago.

Prior to our move to Chicago, we returned to Illinois for the weddings of the two remaining members of the gang of four: Earl Hari and Bob Reutter. Earl and his fiancé, Diane, were married in Cessna Park, his hometown. Lou, Bob, and I were happy to join Earl's brothers to make sure he didn't falter.

The last holdout, although the youngest, was Bob Ruetter. Although he had by now joined the FBI, Bob married his sweetheart from his teaching days in the Chicago suburbs. He and Nancy were married in her hometown of Wheaton, Illinois, with the old gang in the supporting cast.

Chapter 15

FAMILY EVENTS

The 1960s brought several changes in the Herdes family back home in Clay County. My granddad and grandma Herdes died two years apart. Granddad died in 1963 at age seventy-seven, followed by Grandma's death in 1965 at age seventy-five. After Grandma died, their farm was divided among their four children: Dad, Earl, Sadie, and Imogene. All agreed to sell their shares in the 120-acre farm to Dad. Once again, Mom and Dad moved back to the farm where Garold and I were born. They enlarged the house so that Mom finally had the kitchen she wanted, along with indoor plumbing.

In 1961, Garold and Elaine had their first child, Gregory Allen. Two years later, they had a daughter, Kimberly Lynn. Garold joined his father-in-law, Farrell Wolfe, and his brother-in-law Bill in a partnership that combined Farrell's farming and excavating businesses. Garold was principally involved with the growing farming operation that involved a feedlot and increasing acreage to produce corn and soybeans. He also started buying farmland, and his first purchase was land that adjoined his father-in-law's. There, he and Elaine built a new house where they raised their family. Although still in Clay County, their farm was located north of Clay City, near the village of Ingraham. They lived only a few miles from the farm where our mom had grown up.

Garold with Kim and Greg

Technology was rapidly changing most aspects of the economy, including farming in Clay County. Having transitioned from horses to tractors after the war, the changes in the 1960s brought about much larger and more complicated tractors and other machinery. At the same time, research advances developed by agriculture departments at all the land-grant universities in the Midwest were rolling out and being adopted in Clay County and throughout the farming region. New developments in soil science and fertility, plant genetics and hybrid seeds, herbicides and insecticides, and animal breeding brought dramatic increases in production. Individual farmers began to specialize their farming operations with larger machinery and increased acreages. As a result, the number of farmers across the Midwest dropped in half between 1950 and 1970. My dad was an example of this phenomenon. Instead of expanding, which required larger equipment, more capital, and increased acreage, Dad decided to retire from farming at age sixty-five. My brother, however, engaged in the ongoing changes and leased our dad's land. Dad then got a job in neighboring Olney, Illinois, working in the AMF factory that made bicycles. The revelation for Dad was that he enjoyed his work at the factory. There was camaraderie among his fellow workers, and his hard work ethic brought him compliments from his supervisors. Unfortunately, he had been born too soon for such an opportunity to have arisen earlier in his life.

Part Two

THE NEXT THIRTY YEARS: 1970–2000

PEOPLE AND PLACES

From 1969 to 1984, my career assignments were in three Midwestern cities including Chicago, Indianapolis, and Minneapolis, where I served a number of years in each location. These cities were enriching from a career standpoint and offered time for family, children, friends, homeownership, travel, church, and new hobbies. These factors led to a comfortable middle-class suburban lifestyle. Starting in 1984, my life took an unexpected turn. Divorce and new career opportunities disrupted life as I knew it, which had been mainly in the Midwest. Until my retirement in 1997, I had two foreign assignments in Germany, two interim tours in Washington, DC, then a return to a field position in the US as Chief of Station in Dallas. My last time tour with the Agency was teaching at the Air Force Academy in Colorado Springs, which concluded my thirty-year career. After the terrorist attack on September 11, 2001, I served an additional five years as a contractor for the Agency.

Chapter 16

CHICAGO

In the summer of 1969, after two years based in Washington, DC, Margie and I moved to Chicago, Illinois, to start my assignment. After visiting my new office in downtown Chicago, we drove west to Oak Park, hoping to find an apartment. Oak Park was an upscale suburb that bordered Chicago's West Side. It was noted for the several Frank Lloyd Wright-designed homes, including his personal residence.

We saw burned-out buildings and empty storefronts lining the street during the drive on Madison Street. The devastation had resulted from protests and riots during the summer and fall of 1968, and it still resembled a war zone. The assassinations of Martin Luther King and Robert Kennedy had rocked the nation. These events, combined with the anti-Vietnam war movement, led to widespread protests. The discontent came to a head at the Democratic Convention in Chicago during the summer of 1968. The Chicago police confronted a large group of protesters, and the consequence was widespread rioting, looting, and destruction. The protest leaders were later arrested and brought to trial. Referred to as the Chicago 8, the ringleaders—including Jerry Rubin, Abbie Hoffman, and Tom Hayden—became household names, as did the presiding federal trial judge Julius Hoffman. The highly publicized trial was conducted in the Federal District Court located in the Federal

Building. When going to work in this building, I tried to avoid TV cameras and the tightened security during the five-month trial.

Margie and I found an apartment in Oak Park. It was the top floor of a two-flat owned by an older couple, Mr. and Mrs. Peoletti. They were Italian immigrants and lived on the lower level. A front staircase reached our one-bedroom unit, but there was also an enclosed stairwell attached to the back. This stairwell was painted gray like thousands of other Chicago two-and four-flat apartment buildings. One thing I could count on when climbing the back stairs was encountering the distinct odor of stale tomato sauce. Mr. Peoletti was a retired cook who still plied his trade at home. The good part was that we were often the recipients of his Italian dishes. The apartment didn't have air conditioning, which meant that we joined many apartment dwellers who drove downtown at night to enjoy the breezes coming off of Lake Michigan in the hot days of summer.

The downside was that our apartment in Oak Park was on busy Lake Street in the days before the Clean Air Act. Between cars burning leaded fuel and the emissions from a soft coal-burning power plant on Chicago's South Side, the air was so polluted that an orange pall often encompassed the whole city. I could run my finger along our windowsill, and it would come away black from the soot. I used the elevated train (the L) each day for work. I had about a six-block walk to the train station, and during the heat of summer, the sunlight reflected the smokey air coming through Oak Park's magnificent trees that lined the streets. The impact of polluted air was probably the same as being a smoker.

Not coincidentally, our apartment location was just around the corner from where Jerry Greer lived. Jerry invited me and his colleague, John Ralph, to attend the season offerings at the Goodman Theatre located at the Chicago Art Institute. These outings were always preceded by dinner at the Berghoff, a classic German restaurant. Jerry was a big help in our orientation to the area. He also invited me to make presentations on Alaska to his classes at the Oak Park-River Forest High School.

The year we arrived in Oak Park, Jerry bought a lot on Lake Nelson in northern Wisconsin near Eagle River, where he planned to build a cabin. The area attracted thousands of vacationers from the Chicago metropolitan area. We joined them and drove up numerous times over the coming years, first to help with the building of his house and later to enjoy the peace of the Northwoods. The lake provided many opportunities to engage the outdoors—from fishing, canoeing, and swimming to cross-country skiing when frozen. Our visits always entailed sampling area supper clubs prevalent in the Northwoods of Wisconsin.

Jerry's next-door neighbor on the lake was Ken Eidness, who was of Norwegian extraction, not unlike many residents in the region. Ken, like Jerry, was a World War II veteran and worked as a mechanic on military aircraft. He helped build the bomb platform for the Enola Gay, the B-29 Superfortress that had carried the atomic bomb for the attack on Hiroshima, Japan, in August 1945. He and Jerry became close friends as they shared experiences and engaged in neighborhood activities, especially after Jerry made his home on Lake Nelson his retirement residence.

As we settled into Oak Park, Margie decided to return to school to become a Montessori teacher. She attended a Montessori training center in a nearby suburb, where she received her certification. She was later able to do some part-time teaching at the school operated by the training center. One of her classmates in the program was Lyn Dyck, who had been recently married and lived nearby. Lyn and her husband, Jim, became our friends with whom we shared many occasions over the coming years. They went on to have three daughters who matched well with our two girls.

Meanwhile, I joined the Oak Park YMCA to start a regular exercise program. At that time, fitness clubs were rare, though they would become ubiquitous later. At the Y, I quickly joined the judo club, where I met some interesting guys and unavoidably got in good shape. The judo master was a first-generation Japanese and a former competitor. I learned a lot about the etiquette and terminology of the sport and its practice. One of the club members became a candidate for the Olympic judo team and spent a year in Japan before competing in the 1972 games in Munich. While this five-year endeavor

gave me unwarranted confidence in my physical abilities, sparring with the 200-pound Olympian made me aware that I was still a relative wimp. I competed in a few tournaments and earned a brown belt, but a shoulder injury ended my engagement with the sport. The legacy, however, was that I developed a lifelong exercise routine.

I often needed my car for work appointments, so the time came for us to be a two-car family. We kept the 1968 Oldsmobile Cutlass while purchasing a 1972 Cutlass. I received reimbursement for work miles driven at the rate of fifteen cents per mile, which hardly covered the costs. Often, I had appointments that required overnight travel. In the late 1960s, government per diem was fifteen dollars per day, and Congress was reluctant to change it despite inflation. Staying at mom-and-pop motels and eating at Arby's restaurants made these trips forgettable. That Cutlass, however, was one of my favorite cars.

1972 Oldsmobile Cutlass

Working in Chicago's loop allowed me opportunities to explore the city, but I also traveled frequently throughout the region. Once a week, my office colleagues and I would depart from our usual cafeteria lunches to eat at one of the many downtown restaurants. The clientele at most of the restaurants were men in suits. Additionally, there were places, especially private clubs, where only men were permitted. One such posh club was called the Union League Club. An elderly and well-heeled friend took me there on a few occasions where the maître d' greeted him by name and seated us in the elegant setting. I quickly learned that the famous two-martini lunches favored by the executive class were not for me. Even the renowned department store—Carson Pirie Scott & Co.—had a Men's Grill. Most of my office mates preferred ethnic and local joints for our weekly outings. A perennial favorite was the ever popular Berghoff serving up authentic German dishes. However, our favorite place was a Czech restaurant under the L tracks on South Wabash.

When Margie's dad came to town, he always insisted on taking us to one of the best restaurants in town. One of these was operated by Louis

Szathmary, a Hungarian immigrant who had opened a restaurant called The Bakery. He had a bushy mustache and wore a very high-top baker's cap. His signature dish was beef Wellington, which earned him the sobriquet "the Duke of Beef Wellington." He always came around to our table, and not just ours, for a friendly chat.

Europe

One of our most significant undertakings in 1970 was my first trip to Europe. With considerable guidance from Margie's dad, we planned a journey that took us on a circular tour of the Germanic countries of Germany, Austria, and Switzerland, plus northern Italy and eastern France. Planning such an elaborate trip in the days before the Internet required a lot of library research, letter writing, and map study. We focused less on major cities and more on scenic and historic sites, plus mountain adventures.

Icelandic Airlines offered the cheapest flights to Europe with a couple of limitations. The flight stopped in Reykjavik en route, and its destination stop was in Luxembourg. We had a brief but cold stopover in Iceland, then flew to Luxembourg City. We rented a car at the airport, a German Opel, and proceeded to the German border. We entered the country near Aachen, and in the process of figuring our way out of town, I was stopped by a German *polizei* officer. It seemed that I had blown through a stoplight. I then found out that my college German was hopeless. The kindly officer had me pay him twenty marks (about five dollars) on the spot, and we ventured on.

Logistically, we decided not to make advance hotel reservations to have a more flexible schedule. For lodging, we usually found rustic guesthouses, sometimes above a pub. We paid around five dollars a night, which was a little more than the popular book *Europe on Five Dollars a Day* would have had us pay. Shopping in the local bakeries and grocery

Margie boarding Icelandic Airlines

stores for our picnic lunches was challenging but fun. Typically, we tried to arrive at our destinations by late afternoon and report to the train station tourism office for help in finding accommodations. We then would walk around the village or city, scoping out a dinner location. Often, we would be surprised by encountering local vocal and dance groups, especially in Germany, and street performers. Outside the cities, we visited very few people who spoke English.

In the city of Koblenz on the Rhine River, we took a riverboat tour to marvel at the hillside castles and wine villages. We stayed near the Deutsches Eck in Koblenz, where the Moselle River joins the Rhine. Walking around the pedestal where the statue of Kaiser Wilhelm II had been blown off during World War II reminded us that the war had ended just twenty-five years earlier. We followed along the Rhine River and then the Neckar River to Heidelberg to see the famous castle and have a beer at the historic Zum Roten Ochsen (The Red Ox).

Neuschwanstein

Next was a trip on the Romantische Strasse (Romantic Road) to visit "Mad" King Ludwig's Neuschwanstein Castle and view its beautiful setting in the Bavarian Alps. One of our favorite stops on the Romantische Strasse was the medieval town of Rothenburg ob der Tauber. We walked several miles around the old walled city, taking in the street scenes and unique architecture. We found a *zimmer frei,* room available, in a house near the city's center. After checking in, the lady proprietor asked us in German if we wanted an *ai* for breakfast, but my German failed me again. Frustrated, she went to her kitchen and brought back an egg.

Bavaria was totally fascinating to me. We toured Munich, the famous beer gardens, and the not-to-be-missed Hofbräuhaus. After visiting picture-perfect villages, including Oberammergau and Garmisch-Partenkirchen, we ended the German part of our trip in Berchtesgaden in the remote southeastern tip of the country to see Hitler's Eagle's Nest, his mountain hideaway. I had been eager to see this place after meeting Jerry Greer's friend Bob Coulter who had been among the first soldiers to reach the Eagle's Nest at the end of the war. We hiked up the steep trail to the top and enjoyed lunch seated at the outdoor café. Shortly, a pigeon

Eagle's Nest

flew over and dropped a present on Margie's head. It was more humorous to me than to her. At least it wasn't an eagle.

Hitler's house, which he named the Berghof, was located in the nearby area known as the Obersalzberg. When the war ended, his house—and those of his three henchmen (Goering, Gorman, and Speer) were bombed to smithereens by the British RAF. When we visited, the secret tunnels connecting the Nazi leaders' houses were still partially open, so we poked around in the damp passageways. They were spooky reminders of the area's dark past. The German government had taken great pains to clear the area to keep it from becoming a mecca for Nazi sympathizers. Sometime after our visit, the German government destroyed the tunnels.

We drove into Austria to the city of Salzburg, which became one of my favorite European places to visit. The Tyrolean Alps were almost as impressive as our Tetons, with picturesque mountain villages and manicured small farms. We drove from Salzburg to Innsbruck in western Austria, where the winter Olympics had taken place a few years earlier. We crossed over the Brenner Pass on the border between Austria and Italy into the Italian Tyrol toward Verona. We took a side trip to see the

Dolomite Mountains and the site of the 1956 winter Olympics at Cortina d'Ampezzo.

As we drove around the area, there were still signs of the South Tyrolean independence movement that was still trying to separate from Italy and form an autonomous German-speaking region. Bombings were going on despite the ruthless put-down of the movement by special units of the Italian carabinieri. Traveling in the area meant going through checkpoints operated by the carabinieri, through which we navigated without incident.

In Venice, we enjoyed the city of canals. The hot summer days, however, brought about unpleasant smells from the polluted waters. While we were there, the Feast of the Redeemer took place with fireworks and a boat parade on the Grand Canal of the Piazza San Marco. We next visited the city of Bergamo so Margie could visit the Maria Montessori International Training Center. Florence was unforgettable with its incomparable works of art, including Michelangelo's *David*, displaying his callipygian figure. After going to dinner at seven o'clock one night and

Kammerzell House

sitting in an empty restaurant, we learned to adopt the Italian style of eating late.

Leaving Italy, we entered Switzerland, the magical mountain country where it seemed most sizable towns, except for the capital in Berne, were on a lake. One of our destinations was Adelboden, a traditional Swiss mountain village with a cable car that traversed the valley with views of the town and surrounding small farms.

We left Switzerland from the city of Basel on the Rhine River, where the river exits the country and forms the border between France and Germany. After a visit to Freiburg in Germany's Black Forest region, we crossed the Rhine into the Alsace region of France and started the last leg of our trip. I found I could use my limited but improving German in Alsace's small villages since the older people still used the language dating from the area's German origins before World War I.

We stayed in the province's largest city of Strasbourg and visited one more magnificent cathedral in the town's center. We changed our remaining German marks, Austrian schillings, Italian lira, and Swiss francs into French francs. This allowed us to cap off our trip with dinner at the famous Kammerzell House, still standing since it had been built in 1427. We splurged on Chateaubriand and an excellent red wine for our most expensive meal at $20, or about $200 in today's dollars. Our departure town of Luxembourg City ended our four-week engagement with many memories and a new appetite for foreign travel.

Back in Chicago

In January 1971, Margie's mother died at age fifty-one. She had had several health issues and was quite frail, but her death was shocking. I never got to know her well, but she was a soft-spoken and very kind woman. Her death was difficult for Margie and occasioned more frequent visits by her dad to our home. He always spent the Christmas holidays with us, as did Margie's sister Judy. One of our Christmas traditions in Chicago was to take the girls downtown to see the window displays at the department stores, particularly at Marshall Field's landmark store on State Street. State Street was the dominant downtown shopping district before North Michigan Avenue's Magnificent Mile was developed a few decades later.

Visits with Margie's dad became somewhat fraught because of their complicated relationship. During Christmas break, I often chose to cover the workload at the office so my colleagues could take more time with their families. Another escape valve for all of us during these visits was playing bridge. Margie's sister Judy was an excellent player. We had some challenging and fun matches that lasted far into the night. Margie and I also joined a bridge group through the newcomers' organization and played monthly with several other young couples.

During our two years living in Oak Park, we learned a lot about the city of Chicago. Mayor Richard J. Daley was the dominant force in politics. Though controversial on many fronts, he was recognized as a politician who made the city work. One evening, after a meeting at the Palmer House Hotel, I rode down the elevator with him. At least for me, our conversation was inhibited by the two outsized bodyguards who stood on each side of him. One of Daley's endearing attributes that he played to good political effect was his attention to all the ethnic communities in the city. He made sure he rode in all the many parades that took place each year, honoring each group's heritage.

Mayor Daley's offices were in the Civic Center building that was completed in 1965 and later named after him. The structure was designed in the International Style, which added to Chicago's remarkable history of architecture. This building and the Prudential Insurance building near Lake Michigan were the two tallest buildings in the city. In the early 1970s, however, they were replaced by two more famous and much taller structures, the Sears Tower and the John Hancock Center. The Sears Tower was the tallest building in the world for the next twenty-five years. I was always captivated by looking at cities from the highest points I could find, and the observation decks of these two buildings were my favorite places to take guests. Like the Civic Center, the twin buildings of the Federal Center were also designed in the International Style by one of its leading advocates, Chicago luminary Ludwig Mies van der Rohe.

One of my office colleagues was Bill M. Like most of my older associates, he was a World War II veteran. His plane had been shot down over Germany during the war. He had been captured by the Germans and spent two years in a prisoner of war camp. His wife was a real estate agent, and the two of them befriended Margie and me. A couple of promotions that boosted my salary to $12,000 made homeownership financially feasible. Bill and his wife found us an affordable townhouse in a brand new development called Acacia. It was located in the Village of Indian Head Park near the West Chicago suburb of Western Springs, not far from Bill and his wife. It cost $28,000. We moved in during the summer of 1971. One of the benefits of moving into a new community was the ease of making friendships with our equally new neighbors. We also became involved with our homeowners' association, where I served as a committee chairman. I was also able to renew contact with some of my teaching and college friends who had remained in the Chicago area. Both Butch and Mick Swanstrom from our days at EIU had settled in nearby towns.

One of the features of our new community of Acacia Park was its recreation center, which included tennis courts and a swimming pool. Margie and I picked up our fledging tennis game, and after a time, we were able to play in the club's tennis tournaments. It felt good to be part of a community. Many young couples were starting families, so for us, the time was right for another chapter: parenthood.

On November 3, 1971, Christine Lynn was born. Her delivery was at a hospital in nearby Hinsdale, Illinois. In this era, fathers were not allowed in the delivery room, so the doctor told me when Margie was in labor to go to the lower-level cafeteria and have a cup of coffee. Little Christy came along so fast that she was already taking nourishment when I got a call from the doctor to come back. My mom came up from Clay County on the train to Chicago to help out. Christy's arrival changed our lifestyle in a good way. She was a bundle of energy and full of curiosity. Within a few months, one of her favorite activities was emptying all the kitchen drawers she could reach. Our townhouse had an unfinished basement, so I undertook a remodeling project to make her a playroom.

One of Christy's first trips was going around Lake Michigan the summer after she was born. We stayed a couple of days in Wisconsin's Door Peninsula, which forms Green Bay. There she had her first taste of the area's famous cherry pies. We also went to a fish boil. Fish boils are a

tradition thought to have originated with Scandinavian immigrants and involved boiling chunks of Lake Michigan whitefish in a large, black kettle. The fish cook in a wire basket and the oils and residue from the fish come to the surface. Before the fish are brought up in the basket, the head cook pours kerosene on the fire, causing the water to boil over, spilling the oils over the side, and leaving the tasty cooked fish. The meal usually ends with cherry pie and ice cream!

My commute changed after we bought our Acacia Park townhouse. I carpooled with a couple of our neighbors to the Burlington commuter train stop in Western Springs. Margie and Christy would often pick me up from the station in the evening. One of the joys was when little Christy would spot me and would come running for me to pick her up. When I went downtown, the train took us to Chicago's Union Station. To get to

destinations during Chicago's famous winters, I found passages through several office buildings in the winter months to minimize dealing with Chicago's weather.

The train ride on the Burlington was pleasant, and during the evening ride home, I could read the *Chicago Daily News*. The *Chicago Daily News* was an evening paper with a different political bent than the morning *Chicago Tribune*. Three Chicago columnists and authors that I enjoyed and admired were Sydney Harris, Studs Terkel, and Mike Royko. Studs Terkel was a man of many talents and wore many hats, but he was a pioneer of oral history. He wrote several books about the working man and life in Chicago. One of my favorites was *Division Street*, which was based on interviews with a cross section of Chicagoans dealing with class, race, and life in the city. A syndicated columnist for the *Chicago Daily*

News, Sydney Harris was a pithy and insightful writer with a philosophical bent in his observations about life and politics. I still have his book, *On the Contrary*. Like Harris, Mike Royko was a *Chicago Daily News* columnist. He gave a workingman's view of happenings around Chicago and was a beloved local figure. He was funny and pointed his humor and sarcasm at the absurdities of Chicago happenings, especially City Hall. His favorite hangout on Lower Wacker Street just below the *Chicago Daily News* building was the Billy Goat Inn. I still like to go there for a beer and hamburger when I am in Chicago.

As a footnote to the 1970s, the counterculture revolution of the late 1960s continued into the 1970s. The prolonged Vietnam War and the Watergate scandal that led to the resignation of President Richard Nixon caused an increasing distrust of government. Culturally and socially, however, there was a change in the views of the coming-of-age baby boomers. The generation born in the 1930s and 1940s grew up influenced by the Great Depression and World War II. This was my generation, and we learned from our parents the values of self-sacrifice, hard work, and saving money for the future. Those coming of age in the 1960s and 1970s were known as baby boomers. Many in this group were self-described as the "Me" generation. This generation was more self-absorbed and focused on self-fulfillment. During the 1970s, self-help books, sensitivity training, New Age religions, open marriage, and therapies around finding oneself were the rage, as were the women's consciousness movement, women's liberation, and the decline in traditional religious beliefs. Margie was very interested and engaged in many of these ideas. I participated in a few events with great discomfort, but pop psychology ideas didn't catch on with me. The combination of events and movements in the late 1960s and early 1970s created a new civil order, or a new disorder, that profoundly influenced American life and society for the next half-century.

Chapter 17

INDIANAPOLIS

We left Chicago in 1974 to move to Indiana after accepting a welcomed promotion to run my own Agency office. The state capital city at this time was a bit sleepy, but the layout was somewhat like Washington, DC, in that the roads angled in from all sides to a circle where a monument was erected to honor Indiana's Civil War veterans. Nearby was a historic landmark building, the Federal Court building later named the Birch Bayh Federal building. It was a magnificent structure and was on the National Register of Historic Places. The building had

Federal Courthouse, Indianapolis

House on Allisonville Road

been constructed in the Beaux-arts form in 1905, a popular architectural style at the turn of the century. At each entry, the high-domed ceilings were covered in mosaics and decorative murals painted by artists during the Depression years. I was fortunate to have my office in the building, although a new federal building had been built a few blocks away during the 1960s.

In December 1974, an investigative journalist found my unmarked office location and elicited my name from the building manager. She was following up on a national story about the Agency and was able to track me down. I refused an interview, but she wrote an article divulging my name and location. Fortunate the article appeared on Christmas eve, so it got little traction. However, it was not a very pleasant way to start my new job.

We had difficulty selling our townhouse in Chicago, so I commuted for several weeks until we decided to rent it. This made buying a house in Indianapolis financially tricky, but we finally bought one in an unincorporated area on the city's North Side. We paid $40,000 for the property. Our address was the town of Noblesville, which was located a few miles north of our house.

The house was a construction curiosity that posed constant challenges from the outset. The good part was that it was pretty large, with four bedrooms. We had three acres of land and a small stable that had accommodated the former owner's horse. The downside was that it had been built by a guy who had constructed it one room at a time in a rambling ranch-style form. An additional downside was its flat roof. Fortunately, the lady renting our Chicago townhouse decided to buy it, so we ended up with only one mortgage.

Over the next five years, I developed many handyman skills. Given my farm background, my approach has always been that if something was broken, just fix it. This became a questionable way to save money, apart from being a time sink. The many projects with the house included dealing with the pitched roof, the outdated septic system, the hard water well, an overgrown yard, tired kitchen appliances, the worked-when-it-wanted-to basement sump pump, and a crazy carried-home-in-a-lunch-bucket heating system.

Our house was definitely not mid-century modern, and the flat roof required re-tarring every two years. That meant I carried twenty five-gallon buckets of tar up to the roof and applied it with a broom every two years. I dug out and replaced the sewer line from the basement out to the septic tank that also had to be replaced. Our water came from a well in the yard that was heavy in iron content. Despite a water softener system, the water was barely potable and tended to leave rust deposits on dishes and clothes. The pump at the bottom of the eighty-foot drilled well had to be replaced.

I managed through most of these tasks, but the heating system was a mysterious monstrosity that I had to stare at for several hours to figure out. The good part was that it was a boiler system with copper pipes circulating hot water through the floor or ceiling of each room to create a uniform temperature. The boiler was heated with a fuel oil burner that required a pump and motor. The hot water boiler system had two pump motors and five zone valves. This meant ten copper pipes were coming in and out of the boiler, resembling a Rube Goldberg machine. All three motors malfunctioned in time, as did two of the zone valves. I found a repair guy who could fix the motors and pumps to lower the costs if I brought them into his shop. In the end, I figure the house qualified me for at least a community college degree in mechanical and electrical engineering.

The three acres of lawn tested my farm roots, but I was up to the challenge and bought a John Deere garden tractor with a sizable mower. The property had a row of pine trees along the frontage road and numerous flowering trees and shrubs. Pruning and caring for these plants resulted in a large pile of brush that I stacked in the back of the property. One spring day, I decided to burn the brush pile. I didn't account for the wind, and a gust blew burning embers and started a grass fire. I tried desperately to put it out, but I called the fire department when it spread to our neighbor's yard. They saved the day, but it took a long time to get over the embarrassment.

A surprising development occurred when I undertook replacing the dishwasher in our kitchen. I got the old unit out and had to do some plumbing work to get the new one in. This required "sweating in" a solid copper pipe connection for the water intake. To do this, I needed a copper soldering kit. Now six years old, Christy went with me on several trips to a hardware store for supplies. The store had just been opened by Central Hardware, a chain headquartered in St. Louis, Missouri. When going in for about the fourth time, Christy saw a fish aquarium near the front of the store. It was filled with nuts and bolts, and Christy asked me what it was about. The store's grand opening included a contest for a Caribbean cruise, a prize for whoever guessed the number of nuts and bolts in the aquarium. Christy urged me to fill out the contest entry, so I did a bird's-eye calculation of the volume and units per square inch. I then wrote down the number 949 and promptly forgot about it. A few weeks later, I got a call at my office from Margie screaming, "We Won!" She had just been informed by Central Hardware's office in St. Louis. It seemed that I had guessed the exact number of bolts and nuts in the aquarium.

The following winter, in 1978, my mom came to stay with the girls, and we went on the free seven-day cruise that included airfare to Miami. It was our first cruise and the last for me for another thirty years. But it was an enjoyable, if decadent, experience. We flew to Miami and boarded the Royal Caribbean ship for the adventure. The port stops were in Puerto Rico, the Dominican Republic, and St. Thomas. In St. Thomas, we took scuba diving lessons and went out for a dive. It was an experience to forget since I was never a water bug. The cruise involved a lot of eating and hanging out on the ship. The unfortunate part was that, back home, Christy came down with chicken pox. My poor mom did all she could to help her with the itching.

Not too long after moving to Indianapolis, I sold our aging 1968 Oldsmobile and bought my first sports car, a British MGB convertible. I got it from my boss in Chicago, an MG enthusiast. Christy and I loved to take rides with the top down, singing songs as we went. To this day, she and I can break into a chorus of "Christie and Me in our Little MG." The downside was that I needed to use it for commuting to work. This didn't work out so well because of constant maintenance issues common to the brand. I hated to give it up, but I had to sell, after which I got a Pontiac Firebird that made for a much better work car.

The year after we arrived in Indianapolis, Jacqueline Burke Herdes was born on April 27, 1975. Before she came along, Margie and I took Lamaze classes, a popular childbirth method at the time. The method emphasized using breathing techniques to assist with delivery, but we also learned a lot about child development. Jackie weighed 8.7 pounds, and

Christie and her snowman

much to my delight, she had red hair. She had redheaded grandparents on both sides, so it was in her genes.

Unlike during Christy's birth, I was allowed to be in the delivery room to welcome Jackie into the world. Mom came over from Illinois to help out since parental leave was not a concept at that time. Jackie's arrival was a challenge for her sister, Christy, but she adjusted and was a big help. From the start, Jackie demonstrated a different personality than her sister. She was calmer and didn't shake her crib so much to get out. The girls had bedrooms across from one another, but they often were together. We used the fourth bedroom as a TV room where we could all sit on the bed.

Margie's Montessori credentials led her to find a Montessori school that happened to be in the town of Noblesville. Christy started there and continued in the Montessori program during our time in Indiana. In addition, Margie made periodic trips back to Chicago. These trips gave me a lot of three-day weekends with the girls. Wintertime snow made for

Jackie, always smiling

much fun for them. I made a sled out of an old pair of skis to pull them around behind the tractor.

Now that we had children, we decided that it was time to find a church for ourselves and the girls. We landed at the All Souls Unitarian Universalist Church in Indianapolis. The main reason we joined and became active in the church was the minister, the Reverend Paul Beatie. Paul was an extraordinary intellect with broad-ranging scholarly interests in literature, psychology, the Greek philosophers, and ethics, in addition to religion. A prolific writer, he was most noted for his strong belief in religious humanism. He was active in several organizations and founded the Humanist Institute for training ministers. One of his closest friends was Rabbi Sherwin Wine, who was instrumental in the Humanistic Judaism movement. Paul would often invite Rabbi Wine to speak to our congregation. Paul's approach to his ministry was that the human situation—requiring intellectual, emotional, and spiritual reflection—could best be addressed by religious humanism. We got to know Paul personally, and we kept in touch after moving on from Indianapolis. He died unexpectedly at age fifty-four, and his obituary appeared in the *New York Times*. His wife, Lucinda, and I corresponded for a time after his death.

The All Souls Church offered another opportunity that we enjoyed: a range of discussion groups. An unusual offering was a yearlong program where the participants engaged in a different sport each month. There were seven couples in our group, and we had such a good time and chemistry together that we decided to continue. We did an array of activities that included bowling, volleyball, racquetball, golf, tennis, and cross-country skiing. Sometimes we would just meet at each other's homes for dinner and conversation.

Living in Indianapolis meant it was impossible to ignore the most famous annual event in town, the Indianapolis 500 auto race. Our friends from Chicago, Lou and Chris Schmitt, were racing fans, so they would come down to join us with their two girls to attend the event. Preceding the race was a grand parade through the city. My office on the second floor of the federal courthouse had floor-to-ceiling double windows that opened to the street below where the parade came by. We put harnesses on the girls to keep them from tumbling out onto the viewing stand below. We had a great time watching the parade and having a picnic before going to the race the next day. My friends at the FBI gave me a pass on the emergency route to the Speedway racetrack to avoid traffic, but that didn't keep us from getting soaked at the race one year that ended with a deluge.

Randy Schlack, a friend from our days pumping gas and fixing cars in Yellowstone Park (YP), proposed celebrating our fifteenth anniversary of working in the park with a winter trip. Randy and I flew out during the 1976 Christmas break to Jackson, Wyoming, to start our snow vacation. We took cross-country ski lessons in Jackson Hole before taking a bus up to the YP south entrance.

Three snowcats met our small group in a blizzard to take us to accommodations at Old Faithful. The lead driver was blindly trying to stay

Snowcat stuck in snow

on the road when his snowcat slipped off the road on its side. After much deliberation, the other two drivers hooked on to the stranded snowcat and finally got it back on the road.

Yellowstone Park in winter is truly a winter wonderland. We had several days of cross-country skiing around the geyser basins, on forested hiking trails, and along the Firehole River warmed by the thermal waters, which attracted birds and animals, including elk and bison. The trees around the geyser basins were shrouded by the freezing steam that made the trees look like ghosts. We took a long-anticipated trip in one of the snowcats to see the falls of the Yellowstone River. Seeing and listening to the Upper and Lower Falls in winter is way up on the list of amazing things to do.

During my first summer in Indianapolis, I was taking a walk during my lunch hour one day when I heard loud vocal music coming from Monument Circle, the downtown city center. I hurried over and saw this large crowd of men gathered around the circle singing while looking up at their director, who was standing at the top of a tall fire truck ladder. It seemed that Indianapolis was hosting the annual national convention and contest for the Society for the Preservation and Encouragement of Barber Shop Quartet Singing in America (SPEBSQSA). A local member was handing out literature for recruiting new members. I had always been intrigued by vocal quartet singing since I was about six years old. Our family had gone to a gospel quartet concert in the grade-school gym. I had been so taken by the bass singer that I hoped my voice would change so I could sing like him. Unfortunately, that never happened.

I did, however, attend the next meeting of the society's Indianapolis chapter which was called the Speedway Chorus. I learned that barbershop singers usually join a chorus, and that many form quartets. In short, barbershop singing is a four-part harmony genre sung a cappella. It features a lead voice singing the melody, with the tenor, baritone, and bass voices singing different parts but in harmony. The tenor sings above the melody line, which contributes to the unique barbershop sound. There were about six hundred chapters of barbershop choruses throughout the United States. The major event for the society was the annual convention that featured a chorus and quartet competition. The top twenty-five choruses and quartets had to go through preliminary rounds to reach the national competition. The Indianapolis chapter was a competitive chorus numbering about one hundred singers. There were also several quartets among the members.

After joining the Speedway Chorus, I was soon involved with the weekly rehearsals preparing for the next contest in the summer of 1976. I joined the lead section singing the melody line in the chorus, though after a year singing the lead part, I switched to singing baritone. The 1976 convention was held in San Francisco at the Cow Palace with several thousand attendees. Margie, Christy, and Jackie went with me for the weeklong event, and her dad came up from Los Angeles to join us. One of our show songs was "Song and Dance Man." It was a rousing number

Indianapolis barbershop chorus

with an ending that featured the tallest man in our chorus—at six feet six inches tall—popping up in the middle and dancing with a hat and cane as he came down to center stage. Our chorus placed fifth out of the twenty-five finalists that took part.

An interesting feature of the musical group was that the guys came from all walks of life and included doctors, plumbers, teachers, and businessmen. The commonality was that we all enjoyed singing and the associated camaraderie. Perhaps the most fun were performances for conventions and other venues during the year, including the state fair. We always performed the songs by memory without having sheet music in hand. The big event that eclipsed even the annual convention was the chorus' annual show. The event included three performances at Clowes Memorial Hall, a 2,000-seat concert hall on the campus of Butler University. We typically filled the auditorium, and the productions were very elaborate with decorative stage sets. Each year featured a different theme. One year, the subject was railroads, so the stage was converted to a railroad station with all the sound effects. I hadn't realized there were so many songs about railroads.

Another year, the chorus and participating quartets sang songs from the George Gershwin and Irving Berlin songbooks. Each year, a nationally known quartet was featured on the show, most often a group that had won first place in the annual competition. My favorite was a group called the Boston Common, but other first-place quartets at our shows included Grandma's Boys, the Bluegrass Student Union, and the Suntones, all of which had placed first in the national competitions. Although we were not a competitive group and no class act, my quartet performed at one of the shows, singing "Darkness on the Delta."

On Saturday night after the last show, the tradition was to gather at a venue for a celebration dubbed the "afterglow." In addition to eating and drinking, there was another round of performances. Reluctant to leave, many stayed until the wee hours singing tags.

A barbershop tag is a rendition of the last phrase of a song that ends in a ringing seventh chord that barbershop singers equate to seventh heaven. Properly executed with the right balance among the parts, the final note has a greatly expanded sound that makes it fun to create. I learned all four parts to several tags so I could teach others. It was fun to try at parties, but finding four willing guys who could carry a tune was not always easy.

I was helped in my barbershop singing efforts by attending Harmony College. Each year, the society took over the campus of Missouri Southern State University in Joplin for a weeklong event. The curriculum included about forty courses, from ear training to the physics of sound. It was all a lot of fun, and I would go on to enjoy barbershop singing throughout my life.

As part of my focus on fitness that had started in Chicago, I joined the Indianapolis Athletic Club to work out at lunchtime when I wasn't traveling around the state on business. The athletic director conducted a workout class for a regular group of guys, followed by a volleyball game. We had a lot of fun with a mixed group that included a couple of race car drivers. One of the participants was Rick Mears, who went on to win the Indianapolis 500 four times. One older gentleman in the group was always disheveled and wore an old pair of tennis shoes that were on the verge of falling apart. The class pitched in and bought him a new pair. The irony was that he was extremely wealthy, having sold his textile company for millions of dollars.

Fritz, one of my business contacts, who became a good friend, had been a helicopter pilot in Vietnam and worked as an international salesman for a company that manufactured helicopter engines. I accepted his invitation to take the family for a helicopter ride, and we met him at a local airport where he was waiting with his Bell Ranger equipped with a bubble canopy. There were only two passenger seats, so he took Christy and me first to fly around the area. He asked for directions to fly over our house, which turned out to be a reconnaissance mission. When we returned to the airport, he picked up Margie and Jackie and, in a surprise move (especially for our neighbors), landed in our backyard.

Another work-related friendship came about with a guy my age from an old-line Indianapolis family. Fred worked for a small private investment firm and was well-connected. We usually had lunch every week or so and attended lectures sponsored by the Council on Foreign Relations chapter in Indianapolis. He invited me to join him and his dad, both pilots, on a trip in their twin-engine plane to St. Louis. It seemed his dad needed to take his skeet and trap shotguns to the Browning factory for repairs. Each year, I accompanied him to his University Club's annual Christmas goose dinner, another men's-only affair. Overall, he was a tremendous source of information about the city's and state's political and business affairs. Not least, Fred got me started on a more informed strategy for investing in the stock market.

A phenomenon during the 1970s was the popularity of CB radios, or citizens band radios. These radios were a two-way communication system that used a push-button to talk on an open channel over short distances. After the oil crisis of 1973, CB radios became very popular among truckers who could communicate with one another about where gas supplies could be located. Since personal mobile car phones were rare, costly, and bulky, the public adopted CB radios as a communication tool. In addition to helping in communicating with fellow travelers about traffic conditions, they became the source of fun and mindless chatter. One afternoon, Fred and I installed the radios in our vehicles. CB users each had a nickname or "handle," and mine was Polecat. Most amusing was the lingo that CBers used in their chatter that tried to mimic that used by truck drivers. So, "Roger that, Polecat, but you have a bear on your back door, so pull to the granny lane, turn off your chicken lights, and hammer down on the double nickel. That's a big 10-4, Texas Drifter, catch you on the flip-flop. I'm gone."

One advantage of living in Indianapolis was our proximity to Clay City, about a three- to four-hour drive away. We were able to take the girls on several trips to see Mom and Dad on the farm and to visit my brother and his family. Although Dad had retired, he kept a herd of cattle, and Mom continued to raise chickens. The girls enjoyed visiting their grandma and helping her gather eggs. Dad, however, remained troubled and in a constant state of worry. He and Mom had difficulty communicating with one another, and Mom stifled most of her feelings to the point where the internal stresses likely led to her getting diabetes. Regulating her glucose levels became very problematic despite her disciplined efforts to maintain an appropriate diet. On more than one occasion, she lost consciousness and had to be hospitalized. The disease plagued her for the rest of her life with its devastating side effects. Still, she remained engaged with her clubs and was active with her church's quilting group. She loved being a grandma and took tremendous delight in spending time with Christy and Jackie.

During this period, I understood and recognized that my troubled relationship with Dad had a lot to do with my lack of understanding. I

Christmas, 1978

saw that his absence during my growing-up years had resulted from his mental illness, and that he had struggled to do the best he could. We never spoke about it directly, but I think we both sensed a closer connection. Nonetheless, his condition worsened as he aged, and our infrequent visits did not make me sufficiently aware of his increasing mental deterioration.

Chapter 18

MINNEAPOLIS

As five years in Indianapolis approached in the summer of 1979, my division headquarters directed me to return to Washington, DC, as chief of staff for the division. We scrambled to put our house on the market to make the transfer. The housing market was slow and difficult because of rising interest rates for home mortgages. I was able to delay taking the position right away, but in midsummer, I received a call from the head of our division. It seemed that the chief of the Minneapolis office had to be replaced unexpectedly, and he wanted me to change course and take the position. Not only did most field officers try to avoid returning to a headquarters assignment in Washington, DC, but field chief positions were coveted and much sought-after. I immediately accepted the assignment that typically required a tour in Washington. Coincidentally, a week later, we sold our house!

Ironically, the 1979 Barbershop Convention was to take place two weeks later in Minneapolis. We decided to plan our house-hunting trip to Minneapolis to coincide with the barbershop contest. We left the girls with Mom, and Margie joined me on the trip. My former chief in Chicago, Vern Sando, had since retired and was working as a real estate agent in Minneapolis. After he showed us several homes, we entered one and knew immediately it was the house for us.

House on Meadowbrook Lake

The new house in Minneapolis was on a quiet side street and overlooked the Meadowbrook Lake and Golf Course. It was located in the suburb of St. Louis Park that adjoined Minneapolis on the city's west side. The home cost $90,000, and the interest rate on the loan was 10 percent. It was also about midway between my office and the Montessori school that Margie had scoped out for the girls to attend. We were all set to start a new life in the far north.

At this time, Christy was seven (soon to be eight) years old, and Jackie was four. We enrolled both girls in the Lake Country Montessori School, which was housed in a school building on the grounds of the Basilica of St. Mary in downtown Minneapolis. Founders of the school were Larry and Pat Schaeffer, who followed their vision of creating a model school. Lake Country was only three years old and small, but it had an excellent staff and reputation. Both girls thrived in the coming years with first-rate teachers. As enrollment grew, the school moved to a new location closer to where we lived. Jackie's first teacher in the pre-school program was Kathy Coskran. She was a remarkable woman and would later become principal of the school, among many other achievements.

Minnesota

I found the history of Minnesota to be much more interesting than that of Illinois or Indiana. Settled a half-century later than the lower Midwest, a large influx of immigrants from Germany, Norway, and Sweden had arrived in the state after 1880. Minnesota is known for its Scandinavian heritage, but the number of German immigrants was larger than those from either Norway or Sweden. The German settlers were mainly attracted to the better farmland in the southern part of the state. At the same time, the collectively much larger Scandinavian group populated the northern two-thirds of the state.

The economic development of the state had several distinct, if overlapping, phases. Agriculture remained the backbone of the economy. Wheat was a dominant crop, and General Mills and Pillsbury started the flour milling industry in Minneapolis. These companies utilized waterpower from the falls on the Mississippi River at the townsite of Minneapolis. Once, as a guest, I was treated to a view from the Pillsbury board room overlooking the company's Pillsbury A-Mill constructed in 1880 on the banks of the Mississippi River. The company's A-Mill had replaced the General Mills Washburn A-Mill as the largest flour mill in the world.

Following the Civil War, lumbering became a significant activity in Minnesota. Vast swaths of the virgin white pine forests covering the northern part of the state and neighboring Wisconsin were clear-cut during this time. Many Midwestern cities were built from the lumber coming from this region with the help of Paul Bunyan and Babe the Blue Ox.

In the late 1800s, Minnesota's Iron Range near Lake Superior became a significant source of iron ore and produced over half of the iron ore in the US over the next half-century. Many immigrants from Eastern Europe and countries with declining mining operations provided the primary source of labor for the new industry. Bob Dylan grew up in Hibbing, a relatively large town on Minnesota's Iron Range. Duluth was the shipping point for ore boats taking their cargo through the Great Lakes to the steel mills in Chicago and in northern Indiana and Ohio. Later, with the St. Lawrence Seaway opening, Duluth's port had access to international trade, especially for grain exports.

After World War II, manufacturing grew in importance, and a group of companies played a major role in developing the state's high-tech and computer industries. Honeywell, Control Data Corporation, Sperry Rand's Univac Division, the Cray Corporation, and IBM's installation in Rochester made Minnesota a high-tech hub. Technology paved the way for companies like Medtronic and 3M to prosper. They helped create a diverse manufacturing base in the Twin Cities of Minneapolis and St. Paul.

The Minneapolis-St. Paul International Airport was southeast of downtown, near the Fort Snelling military base. Fort Snelling was deactivated after World War II, and much of the land was taken up by the airport. The adjacent site of the original frontier army outpost was preserved as a National Historic Landmark and is referred to as Historic Fort Snelling. The location is at the confluence of the Mississippi and Minnesota Rivers and across the Mississippi from St. Paul. My commute to the federal building was reasonable with favorable traffic, and it was approximately the same distance to the Montessori school where Margie drove the girls. I was still driving the Pontiac Firebird, and she had a new Chevy Nova.

Running the Minneapolis office allowed me to develop my management style and establish a wide range of relationships in the business and academic communities. Thomas, one of my work contacts, and I developed a personal friendship. Like Fred in Indianapolis, Thomas was a man who would rather be doing what I was instead of pursuing his own career. A Harvard graduate, he had come back to his hometown of Minneapolis to practice law. He was quite knowledgeable and interested in foreign affairs, and he brought good insights into the goings-on in the political and economic communities in the region. He was a bit of a gourmet, so he was in charge of locating restaurants for us to sample. The Scandinavian food traditions were still a feature in some restaurants, especially during the holidays. I had my first exposure to the supposed delicacy lutefisk as well as lefse, gravlax, Swedish meatballs, and *krumkake*. Lutefisk defied my efforts to like. My office colleagues and I enjoyed an annual Christmas lunch with our FBI colleagues. Our destination was a St. Paul restaurant on the Mississippi River, famous for the best liver and onions in the Twin Cities.

Based on the positive experiences Margie and I had had with the Unitarian Church in Indianapolis, we started attending the First Unitarian Society of Minneapolis. After attending several services, we decided the place was not for us. As its name implies, it was not a church but more an ethical society. The congregation had an intellectual bent and was primarily composed of atheists and agnostics focused on social justice issues and leftist political causes with no spiritual attention. Instead, we found a family-friendly church home in the First Universalist Church and enjoyed a comfortable and welcoming atmosphere. Not coincidentally, Kathy Coskran and her husband, Chuck, attended this church. Chuck and I hit it off immediately. He soon invited me to go with him to his family's cabin for the opening of fishing season in May 1980. We started what would become a meaningful and long-lasting friendship.

The fishing opener in Minnesota is akin to a state holiday. An estimated one-quarter of the population takes to the highways going north to the state's many lakes on the second weekend of May. Chuck's family cabin was on Lake Mille Lacs, the state's third largest, located about a two-hour drive north of Minneapolis. The cabin, which his mom and dad had purchased in the 1950s, was a small, two-bedroom home located on a large wooded lot with over 150 feet of lake frontage. After his dad died, Chuck assumed responsibility for its maintenance, and his mom continued to live there during the summers.

Not having fished on a lake before, I learned a lot. Chuck was a good, if not always patient, teacher. I soon learned the difference between drifting and trolling, and how to rig up our fishing rods for each method. Chuck's favorite spot was a rock ledge located about a quarter of a mile offshore from the cabin. We would push his aluminum boat into the water from the backyard, and he nurtured the old boat motor that had belonged to his dad to propel us out to the rocks, where we spent many hours fishing and solving the world's problems.

Mille Lacs is known as a walleye lake. Fishing for walleye is rewarding, mostly for catching the fish to eat. Pulling them to the surface is more placid than landing a spirited northern pike and, as I later learned, the thrill of landing a rainbow trout with a fly rod. Chuck's mom would often join us and always seemed to bring us good luck.

I became fascinated with the subculture of Minnesotans' attachments to the lake country, summer cabins, and the small fishing resorts. Years later, after visiting Sweden, it was clear that the immigrants had carried on old country traditions. A quarter of a mile up the lakefront from Chuck's cabin was Fisher's Resort. Chuck's dad and the resort owner, "Copple" Fisher, had been close friends and World War II veterans. Copple, who was of Norwegian descent, was a colorful figure on the lake and spoke with the recognizable accent of northern Minnesota's Scandinavian population. Chuck had a long friendship with Copple's son Greg, who ran the resort when his dad died.

Fisher's Resort was a typical lakeside family enterprise that featured cabins, campsites, boat launches, rental boats, bait shops, and guided fishing trips. The restaurant and bar were gathering spots for tall tales repeated by old-timers who came to Malmo Bay each year. Over the years, I accompanied Chuck to the cabin for the opener and fall fishing, winter

Chuck trying to keep up

ice fishing, and cross country skiing. It became one of my favorite places to spend time with Chuck.

Chuck and I also undertook a number of cross-country ski outings each winter. Minnesota's state parks converted their hiking trails to well-groomed ski trails during the winter. We were using long skis that required waxing, and there was an element of competitiveness when we took on more challenging trails. Although he was bigger, we were pretty evenly matched. I took advantage of the fact that he was still a smoker.

On one January weekend, we took a trip to the north shore of Lake Superior and stayed at the Cascade Lodge near the Cascade River State Park. The lodge was located on the lake where the Cascade River débouchés into the lake after tumbling down several small waterfalls. We started our ski trip into the interior early in the morning after a light snowfall. The trail was challenging with forested hills. Our destination was an inland lake, where we stopped for lunch. The highlight was following wolf tracks out on the lake to where the wolf had left the remains of a prior deer kill. Farther up the lakeshore from Cascade was the town of Grand Marais, the terminus of the Gunflint Trail used by French fur trappers. Margie and I took the girls on an outing with a group of other parents from the Lake Country school to a resort on the Gunflint for winter fun.

One midwinter, we took our girls and joined Chuck's family at the cabin that turned out to be our coldest time in Minnesota. At –34°F, and following a major snowstorm, Chuck and Kathy's three children built a snow cave in a large drift outside the cabin with Christy and Jackie in tow. Lighted candles on shelves carved on their cave walls, along with hot chocolate, kept them warm. Meanwhile, Chuck and I spent the night in a fish house on the ice we had rented from Fisher's Resort.

Ice fishing has its subculture, and at its peak, there were over four thousand fish houses on Mille Lacs. Fisher's rented cabins, but they also pulled privately owned houses out on the lake, which they arranged in orderly rows so that they could keep the ice roads plowed after snowstorms. Some of the private cabins were quite elaborate with TVs and carpeting. Fisher's cabins were bare-bones and were rented from 6 p.m. to 6 a.m., or the reverse for daytime fishing.

The fish house that Chuck and I rented was equipped with a propane heater, a double bunk bed, a card table, and two chairs. In each corner was a six-inch hole drilled through the thirty-inch-thick ice. We dropped weighted lines with baited hooks down each of the holes that were attached over the holes to a coffee can filled with rocks. When a fish took the bait, the can rattled and took us away from our card game. Hot soup, a six-pack of beer, and a deck of cards were vital to the experience. After crawling into our sleeping bags for a few hours of sleep, we were abruptly awakened around 2 a.m. by the clanging of the coffee can. Chuck bounded out of his bunk and, with great effort, pulled up a three-foot-long eelpout that slithered around on the cabin floor. Minnesotans consider eelpouts to be the ugliest of fishes and a general nuisance. We threw it outside on the ice, where it froze and resembled a stick of firewood the following day.

Chuck's dad had been an Irish cop in Minneapolis, and his mom was a Norwegian immigrant. Before coming to the United States, her family had lived first in Saskatchewan, where her father homesteaded and built a sod house where the family lived. Chuck had worked his way through college and received a master's degree from the University of Minnesota. He taught high school history for a couple of years before joining the Peace Corps.

Chuck served for two tours in the Peace Corps, first in Ethiopia and later in Kenya. He met his wife, Kathy, in Ethiopia, and after they married, they lived in Washington, DC, where he was Deputy Director for the African Division of the Peace Corps. In the mid-1970s, they relocated to Minneapolis, where he made his career with the Minnesota Department of Education.

His experiences gave us a lot in common, as he retained a keen interest in international affairs. It must have been the mixture of the Irish and Norwegian that gave him a temperament that was at once stubborn and impatient but equally accommodating and generous. He was well-read, honest to the core, loyal to family and friends, and never a day went by that didn't end with a heavy dose of whiskey, Irish or not. We would spend hours out on the water and in the cabin, solving the domestic and international issues of the day. He'd be the first to say that his biggest treasure was his wife, Kathy, followed quickly by his children and grandchildren. Kathy had a superior intellect, keen curiosity, and a calm and engaging manner that put everyone she met at ease. The two of them lived their values. After their first two children were born, they adopted a baby boy from Colombia. Over the years, they had several foster children from Africa and several foreign exchange students. Chuck was as frugal as they come, but his and Kathy's generosity to others was boundless.

Warren

Not long after we settled in Minneapolis, I joined the SPEBSQSA barbershop chapter known as the Minneapolis Commodores. It was also a large and competitive barbershop chorus and home of the 1975 quartet champions, the Happiness Emporium. The chorus had excellent leadership and disciplined singing. I sang with the baritone section and arrived as the chorus was preparing for its annual show.

The chorus' annual shows, held at the city's Orchestra Hall in downtown Minneapolis, were well attended but not as elaborate or as much fun as those in Indianapolis. The chorus practiced intently for the district and national competitions scheduled for the summer of 1980. After winning the district competition, we flew to Salt Lake City for the national event. Our chorus placed third among the twenty-five choruses that reached the finals.

There were two highlights at the convention that were especially memorable. The winner of the quartet competition was my favorite, the Boston Common. They had been the featured quartet on our Indianapolis show a year earlier. Their voices blended in an incomparable sound. The second highlight was a performance at the Mormon Tabernacle by Dallas's perennial barbershop chorus winner called the Vocal Majority. They were on the program with the Mormon Tabernacle Choir, and the acoustics of the tabernacle made their performance unforgettable to all of us who filled the auditorium.

When I joined the chorus, the guy standing next to me, also singing baritone, became one of my best friends. Warren Wildes and I developed a tradition of having a beer together after the weekly rehearsals. Warren had wide-ranging interests, and he always seemed to arrange his work life

With Warren, the adventurer

around his hobbies. I was never able to get over my tradition that work comes first.

Unlike Chuck and I, Warren had been born with a silver spoon. He grew up in Midland, Michigan, where his father was an executive with Dow Chemical. His high school summer job had been working as a caddie on a golf course. He had attended the Ivy League school of Cornell on a navy ROTC scholarship and majored in mechanical engineering. After his navy service, he worked for a large corporation and spent two years living in Scotland. His first wife, Cisela, was from Sweden, and they had two children.

Warren had an independent streak that made him ill-suited for the corporate world, so he set up his own engineering firm in Minneapolis. He kept the company small but efficient enough to provide a comfortable living and a flexible schedule. He played competitive golf at a country club and squash and tennis during the long winters. His house was on Lake Johanna in Arden Hills, where he kept a sailboat and a motorboat for water skiing. To add to his duties, I appointed him director of anti-submarine warfare on his lake. He had a strong passion for duck hunting and always had an English black Labrador highly trained as a retriever who served as a companion. He pulled his duck boat with an RV to Canada and elsewhere for duck or goose hunting during the fall. He was also a dedicated powder snow skier and maintained a condo at the ski resort in Steamboat Springs, Colorado.

While Warren could be irritating and abrupt, he was also engaging and fun to be around. He was interested in international affairs, politics, and foreign travel. In addition to our mutual interest in barbershop music, Warren and I got together occasionally for family visits and engagements with some of his activities. Christy and Jackie loved to water-ski behind his boat. Warren and I went on fishing trips to Lake Superior, where I learned about using downriggers for deep-water fishing.

During the summer of 1981, Warren and I traveled together to Seattle, where the barbershop chorus competed in the annual competition once again. We took a side adventure with a rental car and toured the nearby Cascades before the contest. Going to the auditorium for our contest performance, three of us were loading gear in the car trunk. Our partner slammed the trunk lid down, hitting Warren on top of the head. Blood was streaming down his face and onto his tux. He somehow shook off his headache, and we cleaned him up and went on with the show. It was just one more example of his exuberant, full-speed-ahead approach to life.

Dad

In November 1981, I was scheduled to fly back to Washington, DC, for the annual meeting of field chiefs. It was an anticipated occasion for keeping up with the latest substantive and organizational issues and camaraderie. A couple of days before I was to leave Minneapolis, Mom called and said Dad was in the hospital. I rearranged my flight to go through St. Louis and drove from the airport to Clay City just in time to bring him home. The diagnosis was ulcers, which were successfully treated. It was clear when we got home, however, that Dad's mental state had degenerated. He was having hallucinations and lacked focus. I hurriedly arranged for psychological assistance with the county health department and stayed for the first consultation before resuming my trip to DC. Unfortunately, Dad told the nurses on their second visit not to come back. By this time, Mom was still struggling with her worsening diabetes. It was a troubled household, so I made regular calls to check in and tried to assist.

In early June 1982, I received a frantic early-morning call from Mom informing me that Dad had killed himself. She was waiting for my brother and official help to arrive. It seemed Dad had gotten up early and went to the garage where he started his car with the garage door closed and waited for asphyxiation. I quickly made arrangements with my office and drove Margie and the girls to Clay City. It was a sad occasion, but my brother was on hand to make the arrangements. Dad was buried in the Smith Cemetery next to the graves of his dad and mom.

I stayed on to help Mom with legal and financial matters, but the more significant issue was about living arrangements for her. Diabetes had left her so fragile that allowing her to live alone out on the farm was not an option. For an interim few months, she lived with her widowed sister Mary. Without the stress of living with Dad, her health improved, and she was subsequently able to live on her own in an apartment in Clay City. The rental income from the farm allowed her to live comfortably. Rather than trying to rent the farmhouse, we decided to sell the house and the adjacent five acres to give her a financial cushion. In addition, we had a farm sale to sell the farm equipment and remaining household stuff. It was a painful transition on many fronts, but Mom and Garold remained mainstays for me on the home front over the next couple of decades.

Divorce

There was an increasing deterioration of my relationship with Margie by this time, as my tour in Minneapolis was coming to an end. Statistics showed that 50 percent of marriages ended in divorce during this period, and it was unfortunate that ours was one of them. I suppose there were several commonalities for this phenomenon, including the upheaval in roles and different expectations resulting from the social disruptions of the 1970s. Still, understanding these social issues provided no comfort for the emotional trauma and devastating impact on our family.

The unraveling reached the breaking point during the summer of 1983. We started with counseling, but we reached an impasse when Margie was unwilling to discontinue her outside relationships and insisted on pursuing her notion of having an open marriage. After the failures of counseling and mediation, she filed for a divorce. The discussion about "dividing the spoons" became what I viewed as an unnecessary struggle. Ultimately, the division of the lives we had built together was resolved by court guidelines.

The initial step we took was a separation agreement that rightly focused on the girls. During the proceedings, I attempted under the circumstances to gain custody of the girls. But the times and a female judge were in no mood to take little girls from their mother. The resulting joint custody agreement granted limited visitation, hefty alimony, and continued child support obligations. I felt I had no option except to move out of the house, where I was soon replaced.

On a cold and snowy December night, we arranged an overnight visit with friends for the girls. With the help of Chuck and Warren, I rented a truck and loaded the family-room furniture for relocating to an apartment. The saving grace as Christmas approached was returning to the house for our traditional holiday celebration. It was indeed a strange phenomenon to live by myself again in a one-bedroom apartment. The pullout couch in the combined living room and kitchen was comfortable enough for the girls when they came for weekend visits. They tolerated my cooking as we sat at a card table and ate "Daddy sandwiches," a Dagwood compilation of a fried egg with bacon and cheese, or frozen pizza.

The apartment building was an older, somewhat seedy building but retained some of its early elegance. It was called the Calhoun Beach Club and had served as a private residential club in an earlier epoch. After several iterations, including serving as a retirement home, it had been converted to rental apartments. Some remnants of its more upscale days were a gym, an indoor swimming pool, and a second-floor restaurant and bar. Happy hour in the bar, complete with hors d'oeuvres, became my regular dinner outing. The swimming pool had been covered over in some early phase but was more recently discovered, so it made an excellent place for the girls, who were both water bugs, to swim. While I usually picked them up from school, the emotional downer was delivering them back home, then driving away.

I chose to break the news of the divorce to my mom in person, so I drove to Clay City to see her. She, as usual, was sympathetic and understanding, but she was extremely sad and concerned about the girls. Ironically, my twin brother had also just separated from his wife, Elaine. They later divorced as well, so we had much to commiserate about. Coincidentally our high school class was having its twenty-fifth reunion during my visit. Garold and I went together and had a good time reminiscing with old friends.

During the ensuing months, the emotional impact was much more difficult to deal with than I would have imagined. I looked into a career change to stay in Minneapolis to be closer to the girls, but I had no interest in returning to teaching. The limited prospects were not financially feasible, so I continued my career path with the agency that, fortunately, was going exceptionally well. I attended several divorce workshops, including one at our church. The sad yet, in some ways, comforting part was that so many people were in the same boat. I was also surprised at the number of unsolicited calls from women I barely knew, with some offering meals and even flowers. Among them was a former Miss Nebraska, a concert pianist, who was interesting but complicated. During this time, my Yellowstone Park friend Randy Schlack came on one of his annual visits. He had learned that another YP friend, Sandy Schauder, lived in Minneapolis. She was the college girl I had escorted at the Miss Yellowstone contest during our college days. It turned out she was also going through a divorce. Although we saw each other a few times, there was no thought of anything serious.

The mainstays of my support, however, were my friends Chuck and Warren. Chuck was the real rock and a compassionate listener to my trials, usually over a beer. Ironically, Warren was also going through a divorce. His new girlfriend was Mary, a tall and beautiful woman who shared his passion for music. They got together due to her participation in a jazz band he was forming. Warren renewed playing his trumpet and created a Dixieland band, with Mary performing as the band vocalist. As the spring and summer of 1984 came along, I spent many Sunday afternoons at their house enjoying cookouts on their deck overlooking the lake. Warren and Mary were also very tolerant of the occasional lady friends I brought along. A couple of years later, when I was in Minneapolis during a tour overseas, I was privileged to participate in their wedding.

The summer of 1984 marked the end of five years leading the Minneapolis office. The Agency signaled that it was time to move on to a new assignment. One of the dreams I had long harbored was serving in Germany. The professional stars were aligned for this to become a reality when I learned of a position opening during the summer of 1985. By leaving Minneapolis in the summer of 1984, I could participate in the required year of language training in Washington, DC, before transferring overseas. I was saddened to move farther away from the girls, but it seemed like the best option given the circumstances. So I made the overture with the head of our division, who approved the assignment.

In August 1984, as I prepared to move to Washington, DC, I drove the two hundred miles to Camp Kamaji, a girls' camp near Bemidji in northern Minnesota, for the last visit with Christy and Jackie, who were spending several weeks at the camp. The sight of them trudging back to their cabin after the visit remains a painful memory.

Chapter 19

WASHINGTON TO BONN

Washington

Washington, DC, was as hot in August as I remembered when I arrived there in 1967 to start my Agency career. I found a one-bedroom apartment near my old neighborhood in Arlington, Virginia, conveniently located across the street from the library. Now a divorced dad, staying connected to Christy and Jackie was challenging from a long distance. Still, I managed to get back to Minneapolis during language training when vacation time allowed. They were also able to visit me in DC where, according to them, I proceeded to walk their legs off as we explored the city.

During my year in Washington, I reconnected with many work colleagues. In particular, my friendship with Lloyd Salvetti was cemented during this time, and we went on to share many experiences over the coming years. Lloyd had completed a tour in headquarters and was now the chief of our division's office in Washington, DC. He joined the Agency shortly after serving in the Air Force, including a Vietnam tour. He and his wife, Gail, had three children, and they often invited their bachelor friend to dinner. One of our traditions was having Thanksgiving dinner together, an event always preceded by a game of touch football.

Musing with Einstein

My immersion in the study of German was intense, but fortunately, my apartment building was within walking distance of the language school. The lack of a long commute enabled me to play tennis and take frequent bike rides across the Potomac to explore the nation's capital. On Sunday mornings, I would ride with a cup of coffee and the *Washington Post* to a park bench in front of the Federal Reserve building on Constitution Avenue. There, beside the gnarled statue of Albert Einstein, I could enjoy the quiet and try, unsuccessfully, to think big thoughts about time, space, and my place in the cosmos.

Before leaving for Germany in the summer of 1985, I bought a condo in a building that was to be built not far from my apartment location. The structure was across the street from the metro stop in the Ballston neighborhood of Arlington. The building would be one of the first of what would become a burgeoning complex, not unlike what was occurring on most of the planned subway stops linking the area's suburbs to the city. The realty lady selling the condo agreed to handle the apartment rental while I was overseas.

Condo building in Arlington, Virginia

Bonn

I arrived in Bonn to start my first overseas assignment on a beautiful day in early July 1985. My friend and colleague Jon Aaronsohn, whom I had also replaced in Indianapolis, got me oriented to the area. Some referred to Bonn as a bucolic place, and it was indeed an unlikely city for Germany's capital. But its touristic charms and historical traditions were quite appealing. Its location on the Rhine River was an added attraction with biking and walking paths alongside passenger and barge traffic. The embassies and capital city buildings belied the feel of the small historic downtown.

My apartment was in the US embassy's housing complex in Plittersdorf, a small district to the south of downtown Bonn. Because of my rank, I was assigned representational quarters equipped with a 600-square-foot living room. My meager furnishings hardly made a dent in the space, but fortunately, it was filled from the embassy's warehouse. The location was terrific. I was in easy walking distance to the American Club, tennis courts, and the walkway along the Rhine. I didn't ship a car over to Germany, so right away, I bought a new BMW 318 with German specifica-

Plittersdorf apartment

tions for only $9,000, thanks to the strong dollar with an exchange rate of over three deutsche marks to the dollar. The BMW didn't match the Mercedes autos that flew past on the outside lane of the autobahns at 240 kilometers per hour, but it performed well.

Gastronomically, the food along the Rhine was not exactly Parisian, but there were several very nice places. Early on, I happened upon a restaurant in a historic location in Bad Godesberg, an upscale district in Bonn, where several embassies were located. The restaurant was called Im Aennchen, and the building had been built in 1792. It was located at the foot of Bad Godesberg's high-point landmark, the sixteenth-century ruins of a medieval castle.

The restaurant had just been taken over by a new owner, Hans Hoefer, who had moved to the area from Hamburg in northern Germany. Hans and I struck up a relationship, and when he spotted me coming in the door, he would throw up his arms in greeting, calling me Herr Herdes. When I would bring frequent guests, especially lady friends, he would seat us with a complimentary drink and a rose for the lady. A few years later, when I took my future wife, Elizabeth, on a drive from Munich to show her my old haunts, he immediately gave me the old familiar

Hans Hoefer's restaurant, Bad Godesberg

hallo. His restaurant had become extremely popular and quite upscale by this time, and no tables were available. Hans graciously took us to the large center table, where he seated us next to the British opera singer Rosalind Plowright and her husband, Tony Kaye. Kaye had just flown in on his plane to see her performance at the Bonn Opera House. After a pleasant evening, Hans's parting gift was a bottle of wine with his autographed label.

One of Germany's favorite sports is fitness walking, or *wanderungs*, called *Volksmarches*. Many villages have walking clubs that organize an annual *wanderung* that attracts hikers from other clubs and is open to all. One of my colleagues, Steve Montgomery, and I spent many weekends participating in these events that followed marked trails of ten or twenty-three kilometers. We usually walked the ten-kilometer route but missed a turn on one occasion and went the longer distance. One attraction for us was celebrating with the German hikers at the end, where the organizing club sponsored a fest with bratwurst, beer, and oompah mu-

Mary and Warren at Berg Eltz Castle

sic. In addition, participants, who were properly marked with ink stamps along the way, received medals, a very German tradition. The hikes themselves were the real reward, as they typically traversed forests, river trails, small farms, and quaint villages.

On one midwinter weekend, the station's chief of operations and I drove to the famed Nürburgring, Germany's Grand Prix racetrack, to cross-country ski. He and I negotiated the fifteen-mile track with its sharp turns when we came to one with a steep drop covered with ice. Near the bottom of the drop, my feet flew out from under me, and I landed squarely on my back. I soldiered on, but later the displaced vertebrate had to be unceremoniously popped into place by a German doctor. The injury came back to haunt me in my later years when I needed surgery to deal with an arthritic lumbar spine.

While in Bonn, I had several friends and work colleagues visit. Among them were Warren and Mary from Minneapolis. I took them to some of my favorite spots, including the Berg Eltz Castle in the Moselle Valley. The Moselle Valley itself, with its picturesque wine villages, never ceased to amaze. The Moselle River flows out of France and winds its way through the vine-covered hillsides to its confluence with the Rhine at Koblenz. We also had an interesting visit to the nearby Benedictine Abbey of Maria Laach on the shores of the Laacher See. We arrived in time for evening vespers and heard the monks perform Gregorian chants. The monastery is noted for having harbored Konrad Adenauer from the Nazis, although it didn't prevent his later arrest. However, he later became the first head of state for postwar West Germany.

Two classmates from my career training class came to visit during a business trip together. Earl Tomlinson and Bill Wenger were good friends, and we continued our friendship after retirement. I took them to a very well-appointed multilevel spa in downtown Bonn that featured coed thermal baths, pools, and all manner of hydrotherapies. The spa was great, but the real fun was watching them acclimate to the Germans' unabashed nakedness when luxuriating in the thermal waters.

My most important visitors, though, were my daughters. Thanks to an allowance for a once a year visit, I would get to see them in Germany as well as on annual trips back home. I planned our time together to introduce them to Europe. Christy and Jackie's first visit was for Christmas in December 1985. Fortuitously, my nephew, Greg, was stationed with the US Army in Frankfurt as a captain in the military police. In October, Greg and his wife, Meredith, who had given birth to their daughter Rachel, joined us in Bonn for the Christmas celebration. It was wonderful to have a family gathering, and the girls were able to meet the newest family member.

Christy and Jackie, now ten and fourteen, were accustomed to having Dad take them on extended walks, but they retain not fond memories of their first hike along the Rhine. Across the river from Bad Godesberg

Christy and Jackie, Christmas, 1985

is the resort town of Koenigswinter. A hiking trail starts in the town that ascends a small mountain called the Drachenfels, or Dragon Rock. The trail was a three-mile hike with an elevation gain of a thousand feet. At the top are the ruins of an old castle and spectacular views of the Rhine Valley. Hiking to the top in the winter weather was not their idea of a fun time. I don't think they will arm wrestle to see who gets my Drachenfels lithographs.

The following summer, Christy and Jackie were able to come for two weeks. The first of two trips we took was a drive to Bavaria to see Neuschwanstein Castle and other sights along the way. During our stay in the quaint woodcarving town of Oberammergau, we selected a wood sculpture that may well result in an arm wrestle. It is a sculpture of a woodsman with his gun and dog that now stands guard in our dining room.

Jackie and Christy in Paris

But their favorite trip was a week in Paris. Both girls had studied French at their Montessori school, so we took the train to explore the city. The Parisian highlights, including the Eiffel Tower and the Louvre, were obligatory, but I think they most enjoyed the ambiance of the street scenes on the Left Bank and hanging out around the Centre Pompidou. Christy was able to keep us from getting lost on the metro as we navigated the town. They also enjoyed the Impressionist paintings at the Jeu de Paume. Shortly after our visit, the artworks were relocated to the revamped d'Orsay train station on the Seine.

On our way back to Bonn, the train's ultimate destination was Warsaw, Poland. Our car had standing room only, with many Polish visitors returning home. The aisles were packed with suitcases filled with consumer goods to take back to their relatives behind the Iron Curtain. It was a teachable moment.

During their visit toward the end of my tour, we traveled to Holland to visit the capital at the Hague and, more importantly, the Scheveningen Beach. During this visit, the most fun part was meeting with a German family I had come to know. On one of my business trips, I met a German who was well-placed in the defense industry. We were both attending the Hanover Trade Fair, one of the world's largest trade shows, and Dieter and I sat together for an address by the German Chancellor, Helmut Kohl.

As our relationship developed, he invited me to bring the girls to his home for an outing. We went to a small private airport where he kept his plane. He gave the girls a ride circling over the beautiful countryside below. Afterward, he and I went up in a sailplane with two single-file seats. The plane lifted slowly upward with its tiny engine laboring away as he manned the foot pedals that maneuvered the ailerons. Up a few thousand feet, he cut the engine, and we glided around in perfect silence. One thing the girls and I remember about the visit left us a bit askance. Before going out to dinner with Dieter and his wife, they gave their two small children sleeping pills and left them home.

One affliction, or maybe benefit, of being a bachelor was the desire of my married friends to play matchmaker. Mary and Ben Fischer were friends with a woman they referred to as the "Persian princess." Zareen had come to Germany from Iran with her parents when her father received an appointment at the Free University of Berlin. She had studied in London but returned to Germany and made her home in Bonn. We enjoyed each other's company, and she had a number of connections at the British embassy that enabled us to attend diplomatic functions together. Of additional help to me was her friendship with a woman whose husband was the president of Ford Germany. Participating in dinner parties at their home in Bad Godesberg made for interesting conversations and relationships.

A more interesting contact was with a woman I met without a matchmaker's benefit. Katia was a somewhat enigmatic person with a

Traveling with Katia

complicated past. She had been born and educated in Bucharest, where her family had moved a couple of generations earlier to escape the pogroms in Russia. When the Communists confiscated her father's factory after World War II and forced him to retire, she left her job as a tour guide for foreigners and moved with her parents to Israel. There she married a fellow Romanian who was a nuclear physicist. After successive moves that ended in divorce following his appointment to the University of Bonn, she established a private practice as a psychologist in Bad Godesberg. English was the fourth-best of her eight languages, so she made a great traveling companion.

She was a true Francophile, and our trips to France were the most fun. Moreover, Katia got along famously with Christy and Jackie during their visits to Bonn. She, too, had joint custody of a daughter similar in age to my girls. Assuming that she had a connection with the Israeli intelligence service, I remained a bit cautious. My suspicion seemed to have been misplaced, however. When it came time for me to return to Washington, she plotted a potential job at the International Monetary Fund

1988 Saab 9000

(IMF) in DC as a way to join me there. Before that could come to pass, we stopped seeing each other. She was far too complicated.

Harking back to my barbershop singing days, I attended a concert one evening to hear a German men's chorus. At a reception following the concert, I had an extended discussion with one of the singers who was a veteran of the German army during World War II. Horst said that he had been part of Operation Typhoon, the German military plan to capture Moscow in late 1941. He drove a fuel truck as part of an armored column that headed the advance. The weather was extremely cold, and the windshield on his truck broke out in a blinding snowstorm. He lost track of his unit but kept driving east, not knowing that he had driven right through the Russian defensive line. When the snow cleared, the Russians captured him and sent him to a POW camp. Fortunately, the camp commander thought that since Horst was a truck driver, he must be a mechanic, so he put him to work in the motor pool. Despite four years as a prisoner, he survived, unlike most of his comrades.

After two years in Bonn, I received an assignment back in Washington, DC. I said goodbye to friends and colleagues and made arrangements for my return. I sold my BMW, albeit at a less favorable price with the intervening decline in the dollar's value. Instead of ordering a new BMW, I took advantage of a discount and bought a Saab 9000. It would later be shipped to the US from the Scania factory in Sweden. I introduced my replacement in the Bonn office to my network of contacts and, with some apprehension, contemplated my upcoming appointment in Washington, DC, that would come with considerable responsibility.

Chapter 20

WASHINGTON TO MUNICH

Washington

The coming year was eventful on many fronts. Most significant was meeting my future wife. My friend Lloyd Salvetti and his wife, Gail, often invited me to their house for dinner. When I returned from Germany, Lloyd picked me up one evening at my condo since my Saab had not yet arrived from Sweden. It turned out that another guest was a woman connected to a friend of his in California. Elizabeth Buechler had been a young lawyer working at a law firm in Santa Barbara when she met Lloyd. She had just arrived in Washington to pursue her interest in working on Capitol Hill.

After a very pleasant evening, Lloyd cleverly asked Elizabeth if she would drop me off at my apartment on her way home. This led me to ask her to dinner, and a few days later, we met at the Berlin Café in the District. Our first outing came a few days later when my Saab arrived, and we drove to one of my favorite historic sites at Harpers Ferry in West Virginia. I approached the relationship with considerable hesitation because she was only thirty years old and seventeen years my junior. However, she didn't seem to be dissuaded, and we continued. She was up for all manner of outings and visits to historical places, and we had great chemistry. We

had shared interests in playing tennis, biking, movies, and travel. I was impressed with her intelligence and work ethic.

Elizabeth went about her job search with considerable networking at the Capitol. I introduced her to my old roommate Ron Tammen who, by this time, was chief of staff for Senator William Proxmire of Wisconsin. In the end, with considerable diligence, Elizabeth landed a position on her own through California Senator Alan Cranston's office. She was hired as a staff attorney on the Committee on Veterans' Affairs. She worked on many issues, including legislation to assist Vietnam veterans dealing with PTSD. Most importantly, she helped create a new court system within the Department of Veterans Affairs. For the first time, veterans could appeal adverse decisions; heretofore, they had no recourse.

At this time, Lloyd served on the White House staff as Director of Counterterrorism on the National Security Council. He invited Elizabeth and me to join him one evening for a tour of the West Wing. With mostly just Secret Service agents still in the building, we visited the Oval Office and my favorite, the Lincoln Room. My most memorable moment was sitting in Reagan's seat at the table in the Situation Room, where I made some consequential decisions not yet surfaced. Our White House visit took place during the 1988 election campaign. Soon, George H. W. Bush would be occupying the chair in the Oval Office. President Bush assembled a first-class team of national security officials, including General Brent Scowcroft, James Baker, Colin Powell, and Bob Gates. Lloyd was able to interact with this esteemed group that presided over the end of the Cold War. Some years later, in 1999, Lloyd invited me to a conference he organized called "US Intelligence and the End of the Cold War" that included these major players and President Bush as the keynote speaker.

I took advantage of accumulated leave to spend as much time as possible with Christy and Jackie in Minneapolis, and my mom and brother in Illinois. Garold had remarried, and he and his new wife, Glenda, had moved to Clay City. He was no longer in the farming business and worked for an oil company. Our mom's health had further deteriorated, so it was a great relief to have him and Glenda nearby.

Christy was a junior at her high school in Minnesota and was thinking about colleges. She was interested in going out of state, so during her spring break in 1988, she came to Washington so we could look at campuses. Since I was a Virginia resident, she was eligible for in-state tuition. We visited the College of William & Mary, the University of Virginia (UVA), and James Madison University. She was accepted at all three but wisely chose to select Thomas Jefferson's UVA in Charlottesville. She started in the fall of 1989 and pursued a major in philosophy. She and

Jackie, now an eighth-grader, came in the summer to take more walks with me to see the historic wonders of the nation's capital.

In the summer of 1988, I was able to negotiate a change in work positions. This allowed me to terminate my time in DC and accept a position back in Germany. After additional training, I was set to move overseas in January 1989. Elizabeth was aware by this time that I was not ready for any commitment. Still, we spent Christmas together at the Greenbrier resort in West Virginia before heading west to see my mom in Illinois. While we were there, Mom had a heart attack. We took her to the hospital, where she recovered, though she was much weakened. It was a sad goodbye, but she could recuperate at my brother's home that was only two blocks from her house. Back in DC, with my belongings packed and the Saab shipped, I flew to Munich during the first week of 1989.

Germany

After some searching, I found an apartment on the west side of the city in quite a grand building. It was a stop for tour buses as the exterior displayed the coats of arms of regional cities, and decorative friezes surrounded each floor of the five-story building. Our landlord, Herr Hans Gustav Zink, was an architect and had redesigned and restored the building. Hans later invited us for drinks at his penthouse on the top floor to show us his apartment. We learned he had been born to a prominent family in Romania, and his mother had been a member of the Romanian parliament before World War II. An uncle who had escaped to the West paid a bribe to get Herr Zink, then twenty years old, out of the Communist-controlled country. He was smuggled out in a large luggage chest.

Herr Zink studied architecture at the University of Stuttgart's Institute for Design and Construction and established his own design firm. After a lucrative business building mansions for Saudi royalty, he reduced his operations and began the three-year renovation of his build-

Our apartment building

ing in Munich. His apartment was furnished with family antiques that had been hidden in barn lofts when the Communists came to power in Romania and confiscated private property. He was subsequently able to smuggle out the family treasures. I was impressed by an elaborate set of architectural drawings mounted in his turret office. They appeared to be an original copy of an eighteenth-century renovation of the Louvre in Paris. Hans didn't deny my observation about its originality.

On occasion, Herr Zink would rent his apartment, or the building itself, for a movie set. One evening, I returned from work to find the entrance roped off and the sidewalk blocked by a red Ferrari convertible surrounded by a camera crew. The director stopped the filming so I could enter the building and, incidentally, exchange greetings with a beautiful actress who was making her way to the Ferrari.

Elizabeth, on left, in her dirndl

The building was in a mixed commercial and residential neighborhood with a convenient subway stop just steps from the entrance. Although I had shipped my Saab for vacation and weekend trips, the public transportation system was amazing. We were two stops on the subway from the central train station, which was convenient starting point for both work trips and for exploring local attractions.

The apartment was also within walking distance to the Löwenbräu and Augustiner beer gardens, as well as those of the Spaten, Hofbräu, Hacker-Pschorr, and Paulaner breweries. After considerable sampling, I decided my favorite beer, albeit by a slim margin, was Augustiner. The Spaten brewery had the best restaurant. The Augustiner beer garden in our neck of the woods was very large, with picnic tables under a canopy of trees. The convivial atmosphere would grow more so as the evening progressed, as people enjoyed the liter steins of beer, the popular rotisserie chicken, and beer hall music.

Perhaps more fortuitously was our proximity to the Oktoberfest grounds, a thirty minute walk. The annual festival, which takes place mainly in September, features enormous tents erected as beer halls. Each of the Munich breweries had two tents seating between five and ten thousand revelers. We generally avoided the rowdiest tent taken over by planeloads of Australians, but the popular annual event was not to be missed.

Elizabeth and I continued to exchange letters, and she came for a visit during Easter 1989. Our travels included a trip to the top of the Zugspitze, the tallest peak in the German Alps. The Zugspitze is in the Wetterstein Mountain range that forms the border between Germany and Austria to the south of Munich. After her visit, we decided that she would join me, even though her job on Capitol Hill was progressing well.

In midsummer, I picked her up at the airport, along with twenty-two boxes of her belongings, and we began cohabitation and a new adventure together. Lacking a work permit from the local government, Elizabeth got a job as a secretary at McGraw Kaserne with AAFES, the Army Air Force Exchange System that didn't require the documentation. Six months for her was enough in that job.

By chance and networking through a German lawyer friend, she applied for a secretarial job at IBM Germany. At the start of the interview, she was asked if she would be interested in a job as an attorney rather than as a secretary, a no-brainer. A few minutes into the interview with the head of the project, he hired her as his lawyer at a surprisingly lucrative salary. The IBM project was a contract with a consortium of four European airlines to develop a new reservation system. The project language was in English, and she became the principal in contract resolution issues. This introduction to corporate law would influence the rest of her career.

We set about exploring our fantastic city with its plethora of museums, parks, and historic landmarks. Some of our favorite walking and biking destinations in the city were the extensive gardens, river trails, and the university and bohemian quarters. We frequently hiked the two-mile distance to our favorite park, the Olympia Park, and often took guests to tour the nearby BMW plant. We even went to a Rolling Stones concert at the olympic stadium. The next day after that concert, there were noise complaints from villages up to thirty kilometers outside the city.

Biking on a Sunday afternoon often took us to our favorite beer garden. It was a great place to people-watch and listen to German traditional band music. A side distraction was the nude sunbathers taking in the rays on the grass meadows of the Englischer Garten. A large year-round market in the city center was always a fun destination for fresh and unusual edibles. We passed on the horse meat butcher-shop offerings but enjoyed bratwurst or a *weisswurst*, a white veal sausage, and a Spaten in the beer garden. About a half-day's drive outside the city was a real treasure, the Andechs Benedictine monastery. The monastery had a beautiful Baroque chapel and an outstanding brewery. Sitting on the deck overlooking the expansive grounds with a sample of the monks' exceptional brew was a great way to put life in perspective.

We also enjoyed the city's array of history, art, music, and museum venues. Hitler and the Nazi influence was a significant part of its past, so we checked out the places where well-known incidents had occurred that bore his signature. The most notable was the Luitpold Arena where the Nazi Party had its headquarters and where the massive rallies and parades saluting the führer took place. Although heavily bombed during the war, many buildings and the entry gate have been restored.

Fittingly, we learned during a 2019 visit to Munich that the City has erected a new building on the rubble site of the Brown House (former Nazi Headquarters). The building exhibits provide a frank portrayal of Nazi crimes against humanity. Called the Munich Documentation Center for the History of National Socialism, the exhibits and documents give visitors and researchers a deeper understanding of Nazi oppression, its societal impact, and the atrocities carried out under Hitler's leader-

Hiking in the Leutasch Valley

ship. Time in the museum is a requisite for understanding this dark chapter in German history.

The starkest remembrance, however, is the site of the concentration camp in the town of Dachau. We visited other camps, and one that is particularly haunting is called Mauthausen—or "Stairs of Death"—located on the Danube River near Linz, Austria. Prisoners had been forced to carry stone blocks up a steep rock staircase from a quarry below and often fell to their death. The camp was one of the most notorious, and 120,000 of the 200,000 prisoners brought here didn't survive.

On a lighter note, and as I had learned during my time in Bonn, Germans are inveterate hikers. The countryside, and especially the Alps, offered many opportunities for hikes. Our favorite hiking area, however, was the Leutasch Valley in Austria. Located over the border from the old violin-making town of Mittenwald, Germany, the Leutasch Valley was just to the north of Innsbruck. In addition to hiking and cross-country skiing in the picturesque valley, the north side had mountainous hiking trails in the Wetterstein range that divides Austria and Germany.

One of our favorite hotels in the area was called the Interalpen-Hotel Tyrol, a magnificent wooden structure in a remote but gorgeous setting. The hotel was the dream project of Dr. Hans Liebherr, entrepreneur, industrialist, and head of Austria's equivalent of Caterpillar. The hotel was at its most spectacular in winter. The principal town in the Leutasch Valley is Seefeld, the center of many of Austria's winter Olympic events in 1956 and again in 1976. Seefeld had many great restaurants, mostly in hotels, including the Klosterbräu Spa, another of our favorites. Even in small towns, many restaurants benefited from chefs trained at Vienna's many culinary schools. The fine cuisine was a way to attract tourists—as if the country's beauty was not sufficient.

One of our favorite recreational activities was playing tennis. We joined the German-American tennis club—made up mostly of Germans who spoke English—and enjoyed the play as well as the camaraderie. The club met monthly at a local pub for beer and schnitzel and, incidentally, activity planning. The fundraising endeavor for the club was operating a stand at the annual festival sponsored by the US military. The American-style festival featured a midway with rides and a host of eateries offering American food and drinks. Our tennis club sold baked potatoes with all kinds of toppings and soft drinks. Germans flocked to the fest by the thousands, and our club made an unbelievable amount of money each year selling spuds. It was fun to serve the public, shout out *"heise Kartoffel"* ("hot potatoes"), and serve the very popular Dr. Pepper. With ample funding, we could play tennis year-round on indoor courts and enjoy tournament play.

Now that Christy and Jackie were a bit older, they could gain more from their trips abroad. They became very familiar with the subway system in Munich during their visits, and most enjoyed (I'm sure) the independence to explore the city on their own. One of their favorite destinations was the university and bohemian quarter with its crowded sidewalk cafés and art displays. After an initial visit by train to Salzburg, Austria, with me on an earlier visit, Christy, at seventeen, made the trip on her own with great confidence. But they were also in tow to the many places that I thought important for them to see, including Dachau and Hitler's hideaway near Berchtesgaden in Bavaria's southeast corner. Also on the list was a visit to St. Johann Kirche. This elaborate Baroque chapel was tiny compared to many of the cathedrals in the city. Still, the stunning interior made an unforgettable impression even for those churched-out on European cathedrals. It was also our place to be for Easter services.

Both girls were athletic and now better hikers, so the Alpine adventures were fun. Christy's first couple of visits were cut short because of summer activities back home, but Jackie stayed longer and was accompanied by girlfriends. Jackie was able to navigate with friends to her favorite spots. She was there when the German soccer team won the World Cup in the summer of 1990. When the game ended, German fans poured into the streets all over the city. Jackie and her friend Heidi viewed the action from our balcony window.

Christy became interested in studying in France for her junior year in college. When she visited that summer, we traveled to one of the schools she was interested in, the University of Strasbourg in the Alsace region of France. Just across the Rhine River from Germany, Strasbourg became the seat of the European Parliament a couple of years after our visit. Christy, however, was not impressed by the campus, which had an industrial feel, and later made a wiser choice. While in Alsace, we visited the Vosges Mountains and stayed in the picturesque village of Obernai. Many of the older folks in the area still spoke German, which persisted from when Germany ruled Alsace before World War I. Neither Jackie nor Christy was enamored with the local charcuterie cuisine.

Christy in Wernigerode

Christy later decided to spend her junior year in the university town of Aix-en-Provence in southern France. Before starting in the fall semester of 1991, she came for a visit. Since the wall had come down two years prior, we thought it would be great to take a trip to the town of Wernigerode in what had formerly been East Germany. Wernigerode was the town where the Herdes family coat of arms had been registered centuries earlier. We stayed in the neighboring town of Goslar in the Harz Mountains of central Germany. The old city center buildings in Goslar are unique, with siding made from slate that is abundant in the area. It was a short drive to Wernigerode that was still very much at the start of recovering from forty-five years of Communist rule. We were both impressed by the contrast between East and West when comparing Goslar to unreconstructed Wernigerode.

After returning from our trip, Elizabeth and I drove Christy to her new adventure in southern France. Our trip took us over the Brenner Pass on the border between Austria and Italy, a journey that was familiar

With Lloyd Salvetti

to us. We drove south through Italy to the Mediterranean and then into southern France to reach Aix-en-Provence. Christy dealt with some precarity about what she would encounter, but she soon acclimated. In addition to her studies, she learned a great deal by living with a French family. It was telling that she wasn't ready to go home at the end of the academic year and opted to spend the summer in Switzerland.

Elizabeth and I were privileged to host many of our friends. Among them were Jerry Greer, Gene Lewis, Chuck Coskran, Lloyd Salvetti, and Paul Ropp. Lloyd was also stationed in Europe, so we had reciprocal visits with him and Gail. Luckily, Paul Ropp and his wife, Gayle, were in Madrid at this time, so they hosted us for our introduction to Spain, where we especially enjoyed our visit to Barcelona. Elizabeth and I also traveled to London to explore the city with Warren and Mary Wildes.

I also arranged for my brother and his wife, Glenda, to join us for an overseas experience. We traveled with them to our favorite spots in Salzburg, including the Goldener Hirsch (Golden Elk) hotel and restau-

Glenda and Garold in Berchtesgaden

rant. The restaurant is not to be missed for the best chocolate mousse in Europe. For my fiftieth birthday, Elizabeth started a tradition by taking me to the Hotel Schloss Mönchstein restaurant located on the fortress overlooking Salzburg's enchanting old city center. We returned to celebrate both her fiftieth and sixtieth birthdays at the former castle.

Elizabeth also took advantage of being overseas to entertain her closest friends. Beverly Tiffany, Carol Stroup, and Audrey Smith had lived together with Elizabeth while going to law school at Pepperdine University. They continued their friendship over the years and got together frequently. Before bringing them to visit, Elizabeth met them in Paris for a week. I think Elizabeth was looking to them for approval of our relationship when they made their visit. In any case, I approved of them, and we had a good time showing them our favorite spots. Carol was the only

With Mom and Garold before her death

one married, but that changed when Bev, Audrey, and Elizabeth were later married within a two-year period, starting in 1995.

For Christmas 1990, Elizabeth and I flew back to the US. We traveled first to California, where I met Elizabeth's mother and other family members. I then returned to the Midwest to visit the girls and family in Illinois while Elizabeth went to Hawaii to attend a college friend's wedding. Elizabeth joined me in Clay City before our return to Germany. Unfortunately, Mom had another heart attack as we were about to leave. We were glad to be there for her, and with Garold and Glenda, but we were sad at the turn of events. Fortunately, Mom returned home after a few days in the hospital, and we flew back. However, two weeks later, my brother called with news that she had died. Fortunately, she passed away peacefully in her sleep.

I made arrangements for my daughters and me to fly back for the funeral. It was a sad occasion as my brother and I reckoned that we were now the older generation in the family. Mom was buried in the Smith Cemetery next to Dad in the winter of 1991. The site would become a place for many pilgrimages, as the quiet hilltop offered a place of solace and reflection.

Chapter 21

DALLAS TO COLORADO SPRINGS

After three years overseas, my next assignment was back in the US. I was honored to be appointed Chief of Station for the domestic division station in Dallas. Both Elizabeth and I recognized that our time overseas had given us tremendous opportunities to expand our horizons and our relationship in ways we could not have imagined. Together, we looked forward to our next adventure. Our relocation back to the US occurred in December 1991.

When Elizabeth and I arrived in our new location, we moved into an apartment until we could buy a house. During this process, we visited a new subdivision located in the upscale area of Los Colinas. The gated community of Hackberry Creek was located not far from the airport. We liked what we saw and contracted with the builder for a new house. The community had a golf course and tennis courts, and we quickly joined the club to play tennis and engage in other social activities, including playing bridge. Elizabeth was just learning bridge, but she became a better tennis player than I was. I played doubles on one of the men's club teams that won the city division in USTA tournament play. One of our Hackberry Creek neighbors was Troy Aikman, the quarterback for the

Our new house

Dallas Cowboys. After a winning season and a new contract, he soon moved to a large ranch outside the city.

We enjoyed participating in a gourmet group sponsored by the country club. One of our neighbors in the gourmet club was Bjorn Heyerdahl, who said he was the son of Thor Heyerdahl, the famed Norwegian explorer. He spun quite interesting stories about his father and his own experiences managing his father's ranch in South Africa and, more recently, a large ranch in west Texas. He lived with a wealthy woman who had inherited a chain of gentlemen's clubs. She later made him chairman of her Million Dollar Saloon corporation. Somehow, his story about being the son of Thor Heyerdahl didn't ring true, and indeed I learned that even though he had the same name as one of the explorer's sons, he was an imposter. I never confronted him about his deception, and apparently, his benighted lady friend was never the wiser.

Elizabeth and I were able to entertain friends, but our special visitors were my girls and my brother. The girls could come for Christmas, and Garold and Glenda also came. We took the girls to see local attractions and one of my favorite Dallas landmarks, an elaborate sculpture known as the Mustangs of Los Colinas. It became the equivalent of the Drachenfels for provoking an "Aw, Dad" gibe. They were not destined to become Dallas cowgirls.

One of our favorite tourist destinations was the Fort Worth Stockyards, which now featured a historic district with shops, restaurants, and the giant Gilley's saloon. The saloon covered three acres that included a bullfighting ring and a concert venue where we saw the likes of Jerry Lee Lewis. It was quite a memorable concert. In contrast, we also saw Luciano Pavarotti in concert at the performance hall located nearby downtown Fort Worth. While we never learned to speak Texan, the friendliness and social atmosphere made our time in the area most enjoyable. Elizabeth had become an accomplished hostess and chef by this time while furthering her legal skills as a corporate lawyer.

We took a trip to Italy in the spring of 1994. We flew to Rome for a marvelous few days in the city with Lloyd and Gail Salvetti. Elizabeth and I then drove down to the Amalfi Coast to take the challenging but truly stunning Amalfi Drive. The downside was not having a sports car for the adventure. We stayed in the delightful cliff-hugging village of Positano. Not to be missed in this part of Italy is Pompeii, and our visit there satisfied the curiosity I had harbored since elementary school.

By this time, my daughters were no longer girls but young women. Christy graduated from the University of Virginia in the spring of 1992. It was a proud moment to see her in procession on the campus lawn. She returned to Minneapolis and spent a few years with a consulting firm before joining her friends in New York City for a different life and work experience. We visited her at her tiny Park Slope, Brooklyn, apartment in the year 2000, and she showed us the highlights of her city. She took us to the World Trade Center's observation deck in Lower Manhattan, not knowing that the infamous and world-changing 9-11 terrorism disaster

Our wedding, April 29, 1995

would soon destroy the Twin Towers and kill three thousand people. Later, Christy would return to Minneapolis, where she enhanced her career prospects by earning an MBA at the University of Minnesota and entering the corporate world.

Meanwhile, like her sister, Jackie wanted to go to an out-of-state college and enrolled at the University of Iowa in the fall of 1992. She pursued her interest and talent in art and started a passion for long-distance running. She was encouraged in the sport by her boyfriend, Shawn O'Shea. They would later become triathlete competitors, and Jackie would often lead her age group in these events. Shawn competed in Ironman competitions both in the US and overseas, including the renowned world championship event in Kona, Hawaii. I enjoyed seeing her in Iowa City and going to Hawkeye football games at the famed Kinnick Stadium. After graduating in 1996, she and Shawn moved to Denver, Colorado, to start their careers. She had a stint in the corporate world, but it decidedly was not her cup of tea. She pursued her passion for children by studying to become a Montessori teacher. She received her master's degree in education at Loyola University in Baltimore.

The most epochal event during this time was when Elizabeth and I got married. We were married at the First Unitarian Church on April 29, 1995. We decided to have a small intimate wedding that included Christy, Jackie, Chuck Coskran, and his wife, Kathy. Elizabeth chose her best friends, the law school sisterhood of Beverly Tiffany, Audrey Smith, and Carol Stroup. The setting was an outside venue in the garden of the church and involved a traditional ceremony officiated by the church pastor. It was a moving moment as our important people surrounded us.

After the ceremony, we all piled into a limo to ride to the acclaimed Adolphus Hotel, which had hosted Queen Elizabeth and Prince Phillip from England a couple of years earlier. We had a magnificent dinner, all seated around a circular table. There were tears of joy and much laughter as we renewed our commitment to one another. Elizabeth and I departed the hotel the next day and flew to Puerto Vallarta, Mexico, for a wonderful week at a resort hotel.

Elizabeth and I gave considerable thought to where to live following my retirement. In the fall of 1994, we flew to Albuquerque, New Mexico, and rented a car to drive north along the Front Range of the Rocky Mountains through Colorado. Our destination was Boulder, Colorado, because of fond memories of visiting there during my college days. We liked Boulder, but the housing costs and political environment left us skeptical that it would be the right place to settle. As we drove south through Denver to Colorado Springs, we stopped to visit the Air Force Academy. While looking at the campus from an overlook at an elevation of seven thousand feet that took in the totality of the place with the spectacular mountainous backdrop, a light bulb went off in my head—I could

Left: House in Colorado Springs
Right: 1995 Ford Explorer

teach here! Shortly after that, we decided to pursue my dream of living in Colorado, which had developed when I'd represented my fraternity at a convention at the Stanley Hotel in Estes Park thirty-five years earlier.

Colorado Springs

In July 1995, Elizabeth and I moved to Colorado Springs. I successfully received an appointment to teach at the Air Force Academy as a CIA officer, so we left many friends and pleasant memories for new adventures in the mountains. We found a house on the north side of Colorado Springs that would shorten my commute to the academy. The house had been built fifteen years earlier by a builder for the Parade of Homes. Surrounded by towering pines, the house was near a large, open space with hiking trails. But it had a downside that was not readily evident to us in July. It had a steep north-facing driveway. Living in Minnesota should have warned me that we were in for trouble, but we were impressed with its mountain-lodge atmosphere. We purchased a new Ford Explorer SUV with four-wheel drive to more properly deal with winter driving.

We soon joined a nearby tennis and fitness club called Lynmar. Elizabeth became very active in USTA tennis, and after a couple of years, her

David Barber (left) on site

team advanced to the final round of the USTA regional tournament in Salt Lake City. With great regret, I gave up playing tennis. I ruptured my Achilles tendon while playing a doubles match and decided after a long recovery to try other sports.

Elizabeth worked remotely for her software company employer, but this soon proved unsatisfactory. She took the Colorado bar exam and became licensed to practice in the state. Her job search was highly successful, and in the summer of 1997, she became in-house counsel for a pipeline company called Colorado Interstate Gas (CIG). Her new position continued her career path as a corporate lawyer. CIG, which had a network of pipelines in the Intermountain region, was acquired by a Texas company called El Paso Corporation shortly after Elizabeth joined the firm. She advanced rapidly after the acquisition and ultimately became a recognized expert on pipeline safety and risk assessment.

Our dream home in Colorado

Elizabeth and I had developed a habit of looking at model homes, but we finally decided to build our own. The open space near where we lived was called the Houck Estate, so named because it had been a ranch in the Houck family since the late 1800s. The land had been gifted to Johns Hopkins University, which fortuitously sold the property to a local developer in 1997. We immediately bought a lot and started plans to construct our dream home. Elizabeth's good friend and tennis partner, Kathy Van Inwegan, introduced us to her husband, David Barber, an architect. We hired him to lay out our vision on the lot, which was on a bluff that faced America's Mountain: Pikes Peak. All of this occurred as I was retiring after thirty years with the Agency. My full-time obsession in 1998 was the construction of the house. Thanks to guidance from David Barber and Charlie Patterson, the builder we contracted to construct the house, we had a pleasant and gratifying experience. It became the place for many gatherings and happy times.

To landscape the lawn at our new house, I attended conferences on xeriscape gardening to learn a new type of agriculture. We placed first in a local xeriscape contest that led to a TV interview.

With my brother on one of our last visits

My Brother

The most devastating event for me was the death of my brother, Garold, on August 17, 1998. Elizabeth called me with the news. I had gone to Montana to fly-fish with my old friend John A., who had a cabin on the Madison River near the small town of Ennis. It was a difficult moment as I absorbed what had happened. Garold had died immediately after a massive heart attack. Elizabeth quickly made travel arrangements for us, Christy, and Jackie to fly back to Illinois. We stayed with my brother's wife, Glenda, and were soon joined by his children, Greg and Kim, their spouses, and his stepdaughters, Leslie and Kelly. It helped us all to be surrounded by family and close friends. Garold was well-known and respected in the small community, so it was not surprising that over five hundred people came to his visitation. Standing with his family at his coffin as people came by was quite emotional, but it was comforting to see that so many cared so much for him. He was buried at the Smith Cemetery next to our mom and dad the next day. Garold's death was life-changing for me. It made me realize that time on earth is finite. I decided to make up for his shortened time and maximize what I could do with mine.

Part Three

1967–1997

MY WINDOW ON
WORLD EVENTS

During my career in foreign intelligence, I served under fourteen CIA directors and nine presidents, including Johnson, Nixon, Ford, Carter, Reagan, Bush, Clinton, Bush, and Obama. When I joined the CIA in 1967, the dominant issue was the ongoing Cold War between the United States and the Union of Soviet Socialist Republics (USSR). The Cold War lasted from the end of World War II in 1945 until the USSR collapsed in 1991. Although no direct armed conflict occurred between the powers, the Cold War created a bipolar world in which countries aligned with two very different worldviews. The USSR advocated the worldwide spread of communism with its authoritarian style of government and a planned economy. Countering that view was the US's promotion of democratic governments and capitalism with market-based economies. The ideological divide led to confrontations on several fronts, including a nuclear arms race, a divided Europe with competing alliances, and third-world military confrontations that included wars in Korea and Vietnam.

The CIA is a global intelligence service responsible for monitoring and assessing security and economic issues worldwide that impact US interests. These concerns changed dramatically when the Cold War ended, but none more so than the rise of terrorism. The direct attack on the US on September 11, 2001, challenged US intelligence agencies in new and different ways. Although I had retired in 1997, I joined many of my retired colleagues who were asked to come back on contract to assist with this crisis. This extended my career as an intelligence officer for an additional five years.

Chapter 22

PERSPECTIVE ON THE 1960S AND 1970S

In the election of 1960, John F. Kennedy was elected President of the United States, replacing Dwight D. Eisenhower. The primary foreign policy issue confronting President Kennedy and his successors over the next three decades was managing the Cold War between the United States and the Soviet Union. The Cold War played out on three fronts. The most complex and vulnerable of these was the division of Eastern and Western Europe by the Iron Curtain imposed by the USSR. The focal point was Berlin, a situation worsened by the installation of the Berlin Wall in 1962 by the Soviets. An exciting moment for me was being in Germany when the Berlin Wall came down in 1989.

The second confrontation between the superpowers related to a troubling arms race that led to the buildup of vast arsenals of nuclear weapons. Through espionage penetrations of US research and development laboratories, the Soviets were able to steal US technology to advance their development of nuclear bombs. The US nuclear strategy for deploying this weaponry was matched by the Soviets and centered on a triad of delivery systems: land-based, submarine-launched, and strategic aerial bombers. The most effective of these was underwater missiles based on submarines. Next was nuclear-tipped air-to-ground missiles mounted on aircraft, and lastly, land-based intercontinental ballistic missiles (ICBMs) hidden in underground silos. The devastating potential of this weaponry was so grim that only the prospect of mutually assured destruction prevented its use. President Kennedy faced one of the Cold War's most dangerous standoffs when the Soviets planned to install nuclear weapons in Cuba n 1962. During the later stages of the Cold War, some progress was made in negotiating arms reduction treaties.

The third front involved the persistent hot "proxy" wars, which started with the Korean War then extended to Vietnam and beyond. The Korean and Vietnam Wars were the most devastating of these conflicts for the US. However, the confrontation between the East and West included other areas such as propaganda, economics, and espionage.

Inside the United States, the 1960s was a period of continued economic growth. Democratic presidents Kennedy and Johnson dominated the political era. Many still see the passage of the Civil Rights Act of 1964,—which officially ended segregation and discrimination based on race, color, religion, sex, and national origin—as the crowning achievement of both men's administrations. Ultimately, though, it was a series of unfortunate incidents that shaped the legacy of the decade. The nation was stunned by the unthinkable assassination of John F. Kennedy in November 1963, followed by the assassinations of Martin Luther King in April 1968 and Robert Kennedy in June 1968. The escalation of the Vietnam War and the legitimacy of fighting, which many Americans had come to question, resulted in civil unrest and demonstrations in the late 1960s. This unrest and the questioning of government responses—combined with changes in social and cultural norms, such as free speech, gay rights, and women's equality—caused a great sense of uncertainty and apprehension.

Similarly, the late 1960s into the early 1970s was a time of challenge on the international front. The continued casualties from the prolonged Vietnam War increased under President Richard Nixon's administration, as did public anti-war and anti-government sentiments. The seminal political event of the 1970s was the so-called Watergate scandal that occurred during the presidential election of 1972. Although reelected, Richard Nixon ultimately resigned in ignominy from the presidency in 1974 after being caught in the cover-up of election improprieties. His vice president, Gerald Ford, succeeded him as president and served the remaining two years of Nixon's term. Combined with the Vietnam War, the Nixon scandal initiated an erosion of confidence in the US government and a lingering public distrust. President Ford took various steps to diminish the US's role in Vietnam. Still, eventually, the war ended with humiliating scenes of helicopters flying off the roof of the US embassy in Saigon in April 1975.

The Vietnam War was the most unpopular up to this point in our history. It cost the US almost sixty thousand lives of its men and women in uniform and untold civilian casualties. It seemed that we all knew someone who had been lost. The war also heightened mistrust in the US government, which we continue to suffer from today.

Academics from the realist school of international politics saw the outcome of the war in Vietnam as inevitable. Policymakers assumed that a Communist takeover in Vietnam would lead other countries to the same fate. This so-called domino theory was widely held at the time but would later prove to be faulty. The tragedy of this point of view was reinforced for me when I discussed the matter with a former Office of Strategic Services (OSS) officer. He had met with Vietnamese leader Ho Chi Minh in Vietnam shortly after World War II. During a meeting around a campfire, the officer said that "Uncle Ho" pleaded for support from the United States in his efforts to free his country from colonial control by the French. The US rejected Ho's overtures because of his Communist leanings and sided with the French-supported opposition against Ho's efforts for independence.

After a negotiated pullout by the French in 1954, Vietnam was divided into two countries, not unlike the resolution in Korea in the preceding year. In the ensuing civil war between the north and the south, the US sided with the forces in the south fighting Ho's efforts to unite Vietnam under a Communist regime. Shortly after our training, many of my colleagues were assigned to the region to engage in intelligence supporting the war effort.

Colonial empires were coming to an end worldwide during the decades after World War II. Unfortunately, many independence movements were caught up in the Cold War standoff between the US and the Union of Soviet Socialist Republics (USSR). The Soviets were often successful in exploiting nationalist movements and extracting commitments from emerging nations to become part of the Soviet sphere of influence. Such was the case in Vietnam.

Meanwhile, the Cold War continued between the US and the USSR. The overall US policy of containment, or the effort to prevent the spread of communism, was replaced by a détente in the early 1970s. This approach, which brought about a thaw in our relationship with the Soviets, was implemented by President Nixon's secretary of state, Henry Kissinger. The thinking was to find areas of mutual interest on which the countries might agree. Consequently, arms control, increased trade, and scientific and academic exchanges opened up more contact with the USSR. These developments had a great deal to do with my work activities during this time. By the end of the decade, however, the Cold War hardened during the presidency of Jimmy Carter from 1997 to 1981.

In December 1974, the *New York Times* reported that the CIA was engaged in activities within the US inconsistent with its charter. The reporting indicated that a CIA covert action project had opened the mail to US citizens from the Soviet Union. Additionally, the *New York Times* reported that the Cold War had led to other questionable programs over the decades since World War II. These reports adversely impacted the CIA's reputation, making it more difficult for its domestic divisions to carry out their responsibilities. It also led to the well-publicized senate hearings on the disclosures undertaken by the Church Committee starting in 1975 and the subsequent creation of congressional oversight committees to review CIA activities. This permitted more legislative branch authority over the Agency's activities.

As a follow-up to the *New York Times* article, an investigative reporter discovered my identity as an Agency officer during my assignment in Indiana and published my name in an article. Fortunately, the article appeared on Christmas Day, so it was largely ignored.

The US domestic economy was shaken by an oil crisis in 1973 and again in 1979. The underlying issue was that the US economy depended on foreign oil imports for half of its requirements. US oil reserves at that time were believed to be insufficient for current as well as future needs. US actions in the Middle East were exploited by oil producers placing embargoes on exports to the US. In the first instance in 1973, US support for Israel during their Yom Kippur War with Egypt and Syria led to an embargo on oil shipments to the US by Saudi Arabia. In 1979, Jimmy Carter had defeated Gerald Ford and was elected to the presidency in 1976. When the Iranian Revolution occurred in 1979, the US supported the Shah in Iran when revolutionaries overthrew him. Major oil-exporting countries in the Middle East backed the new Iranian government and placed an embargo on oil exports to the US. Iran, meanwhile, blatantly took employees of the US embassy in Tehran hostage.

The embargoes on oil coming into the US led to a dramatic increase in prices. Our family (and almost everyone across the US) was impacted by having to wait in long lines to fill up our cars with gas. Not only did gas prices nearly double, putting a strain on household budgets, but many stations limited the amount one could buy. To deal with the scarcity, states implemented a scheme in which consumers with license plates ending in an odd number could purchase fuel on odd-numbered days and even-numbered license plate numbers on even-numbered days.

More broadly, however, the oil crises contributed to economic difficulties in the US in the late 1970s and into the early 1980s. By the end of the decade, interest rates on loans eventually reached as high as 20 percent. This made getting a mortgage to buy a house a costly undertaking, and it impacted many of my colleagues in the domestic division (and me) when transferred to new locations.

As a footnote to the 1970s, the counterculture revolution of the late 1960s continued into the 1970s. Culturally and socially, there was a change in the views of baby boomers as they came of age. The generation that grew up with the influence of the Great Depression and World War II during the 1940s and 1950s (including me) learned the values of self-sacrifice, hard work, and saving money. Many baby boomers, who grew up in the 1960s and 1970s, embraced individual freedoms and social change and gradually abandoned traditional cultural norms and religious practices. Some referred to this group as the "me" generation. They were more self-absorbed and focused on self-fulfillment. Self-help books and pop psychology movements like EST, New Age religions, open marriage, and therapies around finding oneself and getting in touch with one's feelings were the rage. The birth control pill paved the way for women to embrace more sexual freedom, and the women's consciousness and liberation movements were transformational. The combination of events and movements in the late 1960s and early 1970s created a new civil order, or disorder, that profoundly influenced American life and society for the next half-century. Living through this period was unsettling without the benefit of hindsight analysis. My life was unavoidably caught up in these issues as I focused on my career, marriage, and children, and the logistics required to deal with them.

Chapter 23

TRAINING

In June 1967, I reported for orientation at the CIA headquarters. The Agency was housed in a new building in Langley, Virginia. The building, which had opened only five years earlier, was located in a wooded setting east of the Potomac River and north of downtown DC. Outside the entrance was a statue of Nathan Hale, the American spy who was executed by the British during the Revolutionary at the age of twenty-one. He is remembered for his last words, which were, "I only regret that I have but one life to lose for my country."

CIA headquarters building

Agency seal at front entrance

Walking into the building's entry, I had my first look at the impressive inlay of the Agency's logo on the floor. More solemn was the wall of stars, each of which represented an Agency employee who had been killed in the line of duty. Also on the main lobby wall was the inscription of a biblical verse and the Agency's unofficial motto that all agency employees take to heart: "And ye shall know the truth and the truth shall make you free." The motto was augmented by the often-used phrase, "Speak truth to power."

The induction process included getting photographed at the badge office for the ID necessary to enter and wear while in the building. The next step was taking the oath of office. With a group of new hires, I stood tall as we affirmed our pledge to "support and defend the Constitution of the United States against all enemies foreign and domestic." We then had a week of briefings on administrative issues and an overview of the agency's history. I was then ready to start the career training program and, as with my classmates, I was referred to as a "CT." The class before mine included Bob Gates, who would later become director and subsequently secretary of defense.

By 1967, the Agency was hiring and adding officers to its ranks. Part of this buildup was to support the Vietnam War. In addition, there was a looming departure of officers who were approaching retirement age after beginning their careers when the agency had been founded in 1947. At the outset, many employees were recruited from Ivy League universities. In a policy change by the Agency to recruit a force that better reflected US society, hiring was extended to universities across the country. My roommates, for example, came from state schools in Florida, Indiana, and Washington. One of my classmates had the distinction of having degrees from Harvard, Yale, and Princeton, but we retired at identical ranks. Eastern Illinois University was not exactly the Harvard of the Midwest, but my education at Eastern and the University of Illinois served me well.

Our CT training class was composed of ninety students, seven of whom were women. In the classrooms we were seated in alphabetical order. This meant that initial friendships formed with colleagues tended to be with those seated around us. Seat mates with last names starting with D, E, H, and K became part of my lasting career network. Several of my classmates were former military officers and were eventually deployed to Southeast Asia.

Seated in front of me was Alan Fiers, a former marine who played football for Woody Hayes at the Ohio State University. He was assigned to the Near East Division and had a meritorious though somewhat controversial career. His ascendency ended with his involvement in the Iran-Contra affair in the late 1980s during the latter stages of the Cold War. Although he was convicted following a congressional investigation, he was later pardoned by President George H. W. Bush.

The first several weeks of the CT training program took place in a commercial building away from the main headquarters building. We referred to the building as "Blue U" because of the blue panels on the building's facade. There we attended numerous presentations on the organizational structure of the Agency as well as the US government's foreign policy and national security apparatus. Our heads were soon buzzing with the dozens of alphabetical abbreviations for the various components.

The main elements of the Agency were its four directorates, each headed by a deputy director reporting to the Director of Central intelligence, who at that time was the legendary Richard Helms. Helms had been with the Office of Strategic Services (OSS) during World War II. My only personal proximity to him as a trainee was when working out at the Agency gym, where he would ride a stationary bike with a look that said, "Don't bother me." And I didn't.

The four directorates were the Deputy Directorate Operations (DDO), deputy directorate intelligence (DDI), deputy Directorate Science and Technology (DDS&T), and the Deputy Directorate Administration (DDA). The DDO, or the clandestine service, was the intelligence collection and covert operations component and was the ultimate destination for most CTs. The emphasis of the clandestine service was on collecting what is referred to as HUMINT, or human intelligence collected by recruiting spies. The intelligence directorate performed the analytical function and prepared finished intelligence reports for the president and other national security officials. The DDS&T provided scientific and technical support for the DDO and other missions. The first spy satellite for photo-reconnaissance was developed by the DDS&T and was referred to as the Corona Project. Support functions, such as finance, personnel, logistics, and security, were the mission of the DDA. Each directorate had numerous divisions and subcomponents that led to the proliferation of the alphabet soup we tried to digest. However, the introductory briefings gave an excellent overview that served us well and provided clues as to where we might want to be assigned.

The training also engaged us in more substantive topics with the USSR, China, and Communist theory courses. Our China lecturer was born in China, where his parents were missionaries during the 1920s and 1930s. Because of his language skills, he was again in the region with the OSS during World War II. Our briefers from the DDS&T gave us an overview of technical operations involving the collection of ELINT, SIGINT, and COMINT (or electronic, signal, and communications) intelligence.

John McMahon, the ELINT presenter to our class, was very impressive. He could recall everyone's names in the room after the briefing based only on the short introductions everyone gave at the beginning of the class. He later rose to become the Agency's deputy director, the second-highest position. John's boss at the time of our training was Carl Duckett, Director of the DDS&T and an expert in missile and satellite technologies. Unwittingly, I met him when I went to his house to pick up a date, a young lady who worked at the headquarters building. She introduced me to her uncle Carl, who stood by his fireplace with an amused look on his face as he grilled me on what I did. Not realizing who he was, I struggled mightily, if unconvincingly, to maintain my cover. I worked closely with Carl's daughter later in my career. She also had an outstanding career with the company, our term for the Agency.

The bulk of our training took place at the Farm. The Farm is the informal name for the Agency's training center located in southern Virginia. The training was intensive and focused on tradecraft, the techniques of espionage. We learned the vocabulary of spycraft, but the primary objective was to spot, develop, and recruit agents to provide secret information for understanding the threats and intentions of foreign adversaries of the United States.

One night, my roommate and I were rudely awakened in our barracks room by a group of commando-dressed guys with weapons who blindfolded us and transported us to a remote site where we were interrogated separately. The purpose was to see how we responded under duress and how well we maintained our covers against accusations of espionage. We both passed the test. In other instances, we sometimes received surprises at postmortem sessions when we were captured on film performing a clandestine activity.

More fun was learning how to conduct secret communications with agents using dead drops, brush passes, and car pickups. Street operations in other cities involved training in surveillance and countersurveillance. One team exercise was conducting surveillance on an assumed spy known as the "rabbit." The goal was to catch him in the act of planting a dead drop or placing material or communications in a hidden location prearranged by the officer and his agent. We failed miserably, as our rabbit was a classy and admired case officer of Russian descent.

Interestingly, this officer had been exiled to the Farm because he was under suspicion of being a mole or working as a double agent inside the agency. He was under suspicion by the Agency's paranoid chief of counterintelligence, James Jesus Angleton. The officer was later exonerated, but his career was ruined.

A significant part of the training was writing reports on our activities. Often, this meant late nights at our classroom desks working with a concomitant bit of grousing. However, preparing clear and accurate information was a crucial aspect of the work.

During our training, we were often regaled by war stories. Perhaps most notable was the recounting of how two Soviet spies were handled by one of the Agency's more celebrated case officers, George Kisevalter. George was born in St. Petersburg, Russia, before World War I and came to the US during that war when his father was on a military assignment in DC. His family stayed in the US when the Bolshevik Revolution occurred in Russia and the Communists took over the government during the war. George was in the US Army during World War II, where he used his fluency in German and Russian and subsequently joined the Agency.

For five years during the 1950s, George lived in Vienna, Austria, where he would meet with a Soviet military intelligence officer, Major Pyotr Semyonovich Popov, a member of the Soviet military's primary intelligence service, the GRU. Popov volunteered to spy for the US and provided prodigious amounts of valuable intelligence on Soviet and Warsaw Pact military forces. George's meetings with Popov were held in a safe house when Popov traveled outside the USSR, especially in Vienna, where Popov was allowed to travel. George was a very colorful figure, and what I most remember from his briefings was how his night meetings with Popov required downing at least two bottles of vodka. George later handled an equally important GRU agent who volunteered his services, Colonel Oleg Penkovsky. Penkovsky was most notable for providing information on Soviet missiles, and his report was critical when President John Kennedy confronted the Soviets during the Cuban Missile Crisis in 1962. Penkovsky's story has been recounted in several books, including *The Spy Who Saved the World*. The sad endings for both Popov and Penkovsky were that they were both caught and executed by the Soviet KGB.

Free time at the Farm could also be enjoyable. We had time for exercise, sports, and socializing. I was able to play a lot of basketball and tennis, but a key evening activity—when not working or listening to fireside briefings—was gathering at the social club or recreation center. We had time to relax and unwind, often playing pool and other table games or hanging out at the bar. It was also a time when instructors might appear to get their assessments of us in a nonclassroom setting.

Weekends were often free, with many married trainees driving back to DC. I liked to stay and explore the area. I rode a bike for miles on the many trails and backroads and a path along the river. On one occasion, I rode around a roadblock with an off-limits sign. It turned out I had found the location where Yuri Nosenko, a Soviet defector, was being held under suspicion that he was a KGB plant.

Noskenko's three-year incarceration at a location on the Farm was abetted by the chief of counterintelligence, James Angleton. Angleton's hyper aversion to potential Soviet assets resulted from his engagement with Kim Philby. Philby rose to a high position in the British service, MI6, and secretly spied for the Russians for years. As a double agent spying for the Soviets, he rose to head counterintelligence for MI6 and was stationed in Washington, where he frequently interacted with Angleton. When Philby later suspected he was under suspicion, he defected to Moscow. After being duped by Philby, Angleton became increasingly paranoid and leery of potential Soviet volunteers, to the dismay of many case officers. Controversy over the Nosenko case continued despite his later exoneration. I never got any credit for risk-taking by discovering his sequestration purdah. After completing the training program at the Farm, it was decision time for what would come next on our career paths. Two-thirds of the class went to the operations directorate and stayed at the farm for more in-depth training in tradecraft and paramilitary operations. About thirty of us elected to go to the Directorate for Intelligence/Analysis. I thought my academic background was more suitable for this part of the agency's mission. We then started additional training, including short-term interims in some DDI components. I was most intrigued by the Office of Current Intelligence (OCI) which focused on global events in real-time.

During my interim assignment in OCI, I was tasked to assess a looming Soviet-Sino crisis over a border issue on the Amur River. Technical intelligence revealed a buildup of tank forces by the Chinese along the Amur where there was a dispute over ownership of river islands. After this initial alert, Agency analysts confirmed in the following spring of 1969 that hostilities had occurred, signaling a decade-long split between the two countries.

The US was able to exploit this perceived split between the Soviets and the Chinese. It resulted in the opening of a relationship between the US and China when Secretary of State Henry Kissinger in the Nixon administration made a secret trip to China in 1971. The 1972 visit of President Nixon followed his trip. This early breakthrough in relations was referred to as "Ping Pong" diplomacy since one of the first visits to China was by an American ping-pong team. Subsequent developments led to the opening of trade and an increasing commercial relationship between the US and China.

During this part of the training, I became aware that one component of the DDI was involved in intelligence collection. When I heard the initial briefing at the Farm by this component, the Domestic Contact Service (DCS), I thought it was interesting. Still, I had the impression that positions in this component were reserved for more senior officers. It turns out that DCS was seeking recruits from our CT class. I jumped at the opportunity—along with three of my classmates, Jon W., Carl Tolonen, and Earl Tomlinson. In later years seven more of my CT classmates would join this division.

We reported to duty in December 1967. Training in this component occupied us for the next year and a half. A few years later, DCS was moved out of the Directorate of Intelligence and into the Directorate of Operations. DCS was renamed the Domestic Collection Division (DCD) in the reorganization. The change reflected that the division was engaged in intelligence collection and not analysis. This repositioning occurred when Richard Helms was replaced as the DCI by James Schlesinger in 1973. Schlesinger held the office for only five months, but he made other significant organizational changes during his tenure. The transition to the operations directorate was to have important consequences for my career.

Chapter 24

DOMESTIC DEPLOYMENTS

The mission of the Agency is to gather foreign intelligence, so it may, at first, seem an anomaly to have a domestic division. Indeed, the Agency is prohibited from spying on Americans. To the extent that any federal agency is conducting surveillance on Americans, it is performed by the Federal Bureau of Investigation as part of its counterintelligence mission. Authority for domestic activity by the Agency was granted early after its formation in 1947. During my initial tour in headquarters following CT training, my colleagues and I received the necessary training on field operations to represent the Agency. Our intelligence collection priorities were issues involving the USSR and other countries posing threats to national security. Information on scientific, technological, and economic matters was necessary, but of particular importance was assessing Soviet research capabilities for developing advanced weapons systems.

Another significant advantage of my time in headquarters was developing relationships with my colleagues, especially those in the domestic division. Jon W, one of my CT colleagues, was a regular lunch partner, and our friendship extended to getting together with our girlfriends. I was in his wedding when he married Alice S., and later in our careers, Jon played a major role in one of my more interesting assignments. I was fortunate to have long-term friendships with many of my CT mates, especially Earl Tomlinson, Karl Ruyle, and a later CT class member, Lloyd Salvetti, among many others. Although we often were in far-flung assignments geographically, our paths frequently crossed as our careers advanced. Although networking was not part of the vernacular at that time, by any other name, we were networked.

One of my first supervisors in headquarters was Vadim S., a World War II veteran like most of the older officers in the CIA. Vadim was a first-generation White Russian whose family immigrated to the US after the Communist revolution in 1917. Vadim alleged that he was from Russian nobility, and he played the role well. He smoked cigarettes using a long holder with an affected upward position, and his favorite time of the week was Friday lunch at Chez Francois in downtown DC. He gave me an assignment as liaison to the State Department on security issues related to the exchange program with the USSR. This gave me an insight into the importance of cooperation among governmental departments. My initial headquarters tour as a desk officer also allowed me to work closely with DDI analysts and learn more about the substantive issues I would be dealing with as an intelligence officer in the field.

The Agency was very good at providing additional training on a variety of subjects. My training in the field included a two-week stint in the Boston field office. The chief of office there was quite colorful. Many chiefs in the domestic division field offices in the early days of the Agency had been senior businessmen in their communities before agreeing to work for the Agency. The Boston office chief was one of them. He was a right proper Boston Brahmin whose wife was serving as interim president of a well-known university. He invited me to his house for dinner, loaned me a car, and one evening invited me to his office after the workday, where he pulled out a bottle of a very fine whiskey. We then had dinner before going to the symphony, where he promptly fell asleep. The field training in Boston, though, was terrific, as I accompanied officers to a variety of interviews and learned the value of knowing where to park and find a restroom.

It soon became clear to me that the preferred assignments for most officers were in the field and not in headquarters. Becoming chief of a field station was the exalted position to which to aspire. A fortuitous situation for me and the other young officers coming into DCS was the looming departure of almost half of the division's officers through retirement. Like many components, the original officers in the division had joined the Agency when it had been formed some twenty years earlier. The aging of the leadership was evident when a group of us junior officers was invited to sit in on a session of the annual conference of the field chiefs. Most were getting a bit long in the tooth. However, two of the younger chiefs stood out as exceptionally talented and were key participants in the discussions. They were Jack Horton and Joe Shugrue. Jack, who headed the New York office, would soon be appointed chief of DCS. He was bright and articulate and made a great impression. When Jack retired from the division chief position almost a decade later, he was succeeded in the post by Joe.

My good fortune was to embark on a series of assignments that would encompass fifteen years and a field chief position before returning to our headquarters in Washington. I spent five years each in Chicago, Indianapolis, and Minneapolis, the latter as chief of station.

When I arrived in Chicago in late summer 1969, the town had not yet recovered from the riots and destruction that plagued the city in the aftermath of Martin Luther King's assassination in April 1968 and the riots occurring during the Democratic Convention that summer. A continuing reminder of the convention riots was the trial of the Chicago Seven, (who were considered the ringleaders of the uprising) that was going on in the federal building where our offices were located.

When I arrived, the chief of the Chicago office was a former businessman who had made his fortune. After selling his company, he was hired by the Agency to start an office in Indianapolis; later, he came to Chicago. He was an officer in the navy during World War II, but he was not well versed in intelligence matters. I learned very little from him except to note what not to do when my turn came to enter management.

Sam was old-school and a natty dresser in his Hickey Freeman suits. He was a master bridge player who took an extended leave of absence to play on the tournament circuit with the notable Easley Blackwood, Sr. Sam liked to gather a group of officers for lunch at his favorite restaurant, Binyon's, which was an upscale place in Chicago's South Loop. Sam always started lunch with a martini and Binyon's famous green turtle soup. The restaurant was excellent but far above my pay grade, so I soon retreated to the building cafeteria. Fortunately for me, Sam retired shortly after I arrived and was replaced by a more professional officer. The new chief, Vernon Sando, was a great mentor and was instrumental in my advancement.

As a first tour officer in Chicago, I learned how to deal with a range of people. The job required me to interview people in positions to provide useful intelligence on issues of the day. I honed my interviewing and report-writing skills. While most comfortable dealing with executives, I became more adept at dealing with the more challenging collection of scientific information. A major objective of meeting with experts was to gain insights into the strengths and weaknesses of Soviet scientific programs that supported advanced weapons development. My education was enhanced by many visits to factory floors and laboratories, plus patient briefings on arcane subjects by my interlocutors, including two Noble laureates. My goal was to be the most productive officer in Chicago. I received five promotions in five years that set me up for a new position. This led to a move from Chicago during the summer of 1974.

Vern Sando arranged for me to head the Chicago suboffice in Indianapolis. The head of an office acts as a representative of the DCI, and these responsibilities allowed me to develop a range of liaison relationships with key individuals in the business and academic communities. One of my responsibilities was developing relationships with the heads of other federal agencies, including the Secret Service, Immigration, DEA, and most importantly, the FBI. There was off-and-on tension between the headquarters of the FBI and CIA, especially during the J. Edgar Hoover years. He opposed the Agency from its formation and terminated relations between our respective field offices while I was still in Chicago. The precipitating incident occurred in 1971 when the chief of our Denver office, Mike T., disclosed classified information he received from the FBI about the disappearance of a Czech professor at the University of Colorado. Mike told the president of the university that the professor had been sighted in his home country of Prague. This disclosure caused Hoover to blow a gasket and call Richard Helms to terminate all contact between bureau agents and agency officers. The story of the Czech professor is a tangled web and a mystery never resolved, but the incident involving Mike created quite a rift. Despite Hoover's admonition, field officers continued their relationships. Over the years, my dealings with the FBI were nothing but cordial and cooperative.

My time in Indianapolis was overly long, and I was more than ready to move back to a staff position in headquarters during the summer of 1979. Serendipity intervened, however, and I was tapped to take an unexpected opening for chief of the division's office in Minneapolis. This extended my time in the field and set me up for another promotion. I was in the enviable position of receiving eight promotions in the years since coming on board in 1967. As chief of the office, I had my first crack at a more senior management position. The office was relatively small, so the good part was that I could continue doing fieldwork as well. I quickly learned that my success was dependent on the performances of my officers. Dealing with subpar performance was unacceptable, but it took a couple of years for me to assemble a first-class team. The ultimate reward for me was being recognized by the division chief for having the best-managed field office in the division.

Another lesson I learned was the importance of the support staff for having a smoothly run operation. I was fortunate when I was in Indianapolis to have a first-rate secretary. Elouise Leaders was an older woman who had been valedictorian of her high school class. She was capable and patient in making sure the office ran smoothly. In addition, she took dictation in shorthand and typed my reports and other correspondence in proper governmentese. The same good fortune continued in Minneapolis. My administrative assistant, June Randall, had served in an overseas embassy where she met her husband, a marine guard. They settled in Minneapolis, where he was a corporate executive. June was older but a classy woman who, like Elouise, would in a later time have gone to a university and on to a professional career rather than to a secretarial school. June did a great job supervising the support staff, and her infectious good cheer helped make for an office environment that was collegial and efficient.

Cubans

In April 1980, Cuban leader Fidel Castro decided to let Cubans leave the country. Those eager to escape Communist repression gathered at Cuba's Mariel Harbor. They traveled by boat to Florida after President Jimmy Carter agreed to accept the immigrants. The operation was referred to as the Mariel boatlift, and some 125,000 Cubans arrived at the port in Miami over the next six months. Before long, processing facilities in the Miami area could no longer handle the influx, so four additional military bases, including Fort McCoy in Wisconsin, opened in succession around the country to receive the Cubans.

One evening during the summer of 1980, I received a call at home in Minneapolis from Joe Shugrue, now the division chief in DC. I was tasked to be at Fort McCoy the following day at 10 a.m. for an initial meeting with the organizations responsible for dealing with the expected arrival of up to fifteen thousand Cuban refugees. I started early for the three-hour drive along the Mississippi River to La Crosse, Wisconsin, and turned east to Fort McCoy. The military post was in a rural area between the two small towns of Sparta and Tomah.

The army contingent at Fort McCoy scrambled to prepare for the influx of Cubans and would remain in charge of logistics and security after their arrival. The federal government placed the Federal Emergency Management Agency (FEMA) in charge of the operation, and several government agencies were involved. Part of my job was to attend morning meetings conducted by the retired general who represented FEMA. Several planeloads of the refugees arrived at the airport in nearby La Crosse and were then transported by bus to the fort. The Immigration and Naturalization Service (INS) handled the initial processing, and each Cuban was required to fill out an extensive form. After receiving a package of toilet articles and clothing, they were sent to living quarters in the fort barracks. A major objective of the program was the resettlement of the refugees in the US. This undertaking fell to several nongovernmental organizations (NGOs), primarily the Red Cross, Lutheran Church Charities, and Catholic Charities. While many of the Cuban refugees made arrangements to travel to Miami to join relatives, many were placed by the NGOs with volunteer families around the US who facilitated their resettlement.

Why was the Agency participating in such an operation? The FBI was in charge of screening individuals for counterintelligence and criminal risk. We participated in these debriefings to determine whether any refugees could provide useful intelligence based on their prior occupations or military service. My job was to set up and manage the equivalent of a new field office complete with secure communications, reports officers, military debriefers, and a cadre of Spanish linguists from across Agency components. We had a separate building to house our activities and managed to be operational in two days. A significant undertaking was scouring the area for hotel rooms and rental cars in competition with other agencies to house our rotating roster of over twenty-five officers. We worked long hours, starting at 6 a.m., but secured our building at around 7 p.m. for the high point of the day, finding a Wisconsin supper club within a fifty-mile radius for dinner.

The initial arrivals in Miami were mostly dissidents and professionals escaping the oppression of the Castro regime. Castro's revenge, however, was to send criminals and people with mental health conditions among the later arrivals. Many of them ended up at Fort McCoy. The cantonment was divided into separate areas for families and single men separated by barbed wire-topped fencing. The FBI identified several criminals, and they were sent to a federal prison in Georgia.

One day, a military police patrol responding to a disturbance in the single men's compound left their jeep unoccupied. They returned to find that some of the younger men had drained the radiator of their jeep and were drinking antifreeze cocktails. The result was that several were hospitalized with liver failure, and a few died.

One of the impressive characteristics of the Agency was its ability for quick reactions to deal with crises. The Cuban activity was but one example where operational elements could be organized and functional on short notice. It was also an example of the importance of cooperation among government agencies and, in our case, working closely with the FBI.

Soviet Émigrés

With a bit of a thaw in the Cold War relationship between the United States and the Soviet Union with the initiation of the détente in the early 1970s, the Soviets were interested in expanding trade. A new trade agreement was signed in 1975. It included an amendment, known as the Jackson-Vanik amendment, that required the Soviets to relax their restrictions on people, especially Jews, wanting to immigrate. Senator Henry "Scoop" Jackson, a Democrat and strong opponent of the USSR, pushed through the amendment. The consequence was that many Soviet Jews, who confronted repression and lack of opportunity, were allowed immigration visas for Israel. After leaving the USSR for Israel, many were able to change their destination. Over the years, some 300,000 were resettled in the US. Despite limitations on their professional careers in the USSR, many had access to information of intelligence interest. This led to a national debriefing program led by the Agency and conducted by our domestic division.

During my time in Minnesota, one of the émigrés I interviewed had been an engineer at the famed Paton Welding Institute in Kyiv, known as the Ukrainian SSR Academy of Sciences Electric Welding Institute. The metallurgical advancements at the institute were first-class and critical to the Soviet military's weapons development programs and space projects. After several meetings, the engineer confided that he had brought out a welding sample disguised as a boot jack or a boot puller from his research lab. In fact, the boot jack was made of layered alloy materials for developing explosive reactive armor. The product was designed to protect tanks against penetration by projectiles such as artillery rounds. I persuaded him to turn over his treasure to me, which ended up at the US Army Aberdeen Proving Ground.

Many Soviet émigrés did not have sufficient English, so Russian speakers, primarily retired Agency officers, were hired on contract to assist the debriefing program. Many of the debriefers were polished case officers with Russian heritage. During this time I developed a friendship with John A. that continued during our retirement years. John had a background in electrical engineering and had earlier developed secret communications equipment. His family had come from Finland, and he was a fluent Russian speaker. John's retirement home was in Montana, where he could indulge his passion for the outdoors. He was an expert marksman and adroit at hunting big game. More important to him, and for me as well, was his interest and expertise in fly-fishing. When we both were retired, I spent twenty summers visiting him in Montana for fishing trips and to pursue our mutual interest in visiting Montana's historical sites.

The Great Grain Robbery of 1972

In the summer of 1972, a Soviet trade delegation met in Washington, DC, with US officials to negotiate the purchase of US grain, primarily wheat and corn. Thinking the purchase would help farmers, the US agreed to subsidize the purchase and signed a secret deal in which the Soviets would buy $750 million of US grain over three years. Unbeknownst to US officials, the Soviet delegation stayed on in the US and met with the five major grain trading companies. They ended up buying approximately 1 billion dollars' worth of grain. This sudden enormous purchase caused grain prices to skyrocket and cost the US over $300 million for subsidizing the purchase. The trading companies profited when the government had to pay the difference between the price guarantee for the Soviets and subsequent market prices. The Soviets pulled the wool over the US government's eyes by not disclosing that the USSR had suffered a major drought and that the population was on the brink of famine. Information collected by DCD field offices revealed what the Soviets were up to. Their sudden entry into the international grain market disrupted commodity markets worldwide. Consumers bore the brunt of high grain prices. American homemakers were outraged when the cost of bread doubled from thirty to sixty cents a loaf.

So, what did this have to do with the CIA? It was clear that the Russians could not be trusted in such negotiations. Hence, the intelligence objective was to independently assess Soviet grain production to determine its impact on future entries by the USSR into the international grain market. The US government had just released the first Landsat satellite in 1972 for observing the Earth's surface. This resource was directed to collect photographic and sensory data on Soviet agriculture regions. The Agency assembled a task force to utilize all source data and created a model for forecasting Soviet grain production. I suppose my background gave me a greater interest in this project than most of my colleagues. In the Midwest, debriefing agricultural research scientists at the major land grant universities who visited agriculture regions in the USSR provided ground truth information. Many visited under the auspices of the US-USSR scientific exchanges program. One of my reports was generated sitting on the back of a pickup truck in an experimental cornfield in Indiana. The plant geneticist was hard at work at his research plots after just returning from Odessa in the Ukraine, so our conversation took place over lunch under a shade tree. The result of the program was that the Agency soon had a better understanding of expected Soviet grain harvests than the Soviets themselves. The consequence was a return to normalcy in the commodity markets.

US-USSR Exchange Programs

When I was a desk officer during my initial assignment in Washington, one of my duties was relaying the CIA's position to the State Department on Soviet exchange visitors to the US. The two superpowers had initiated an agreement during the Eisenhower administration to increase people-to-people contacts to reduce tensions. Starting with cultural exchanges during the 1950s, the program was expanded to include scientific and technical exchanges during the Nixon administration. The State Department administered the program, which sought input from other agencies, including the CIA, on whether the visits would be detrimental to US interests. One of the jokes about the program was that the US sent graduate students in art history to the USSR while the Soviets sent forty-year-old postdocs in nuclear physics to study in the US. An underpinning of the exchanges from the US point of view was that visiting Soviets were exposed to an open society, and a much higher standard of living would help weaken the repressive nature of the Soviet system. The downside was the potential for the Soviets to gain valuable scientific information that would benefit their military capabilities.

Over fifty thousand Soviet citizens visited the US under the auspices of the exchanges. Most US participants were receptive to sharing their observations with the Agency. Some academics believed that science knew no borders and that collaboration should be free of government involvement, notwithstanding their participation resulted from taxpayer largesse. Following debriefings, the challenge for me was to sort out the intelligence significance of the scientific observations. What I learned contributed to my community college degree in the sciences.

Transition

Headquarters officials enjoy visiting field locations in part, I suppose, to get a break from the routine of office confinement and endless meetings. The interactions were beneficial for both sides, especially when more senior officers visited the field. One of my favorite visitors was Vernon Walters, Deputy Director for the CIA from 1972 to 1976. He visited the Chicago office while I was there and displayed his ability to put everyone at ease with his charm and his vast storehouse of stories. He had a commanding presence as an army general, and his liquid speech and fluency in six languages led to his serving as an interpreter for five presidents. I enjoyed following his career as he became ambassador to the UN, a troubleshooting roving ambassador during the Reagan administration, and finally the US ambassador to Germany as the Cold War ended.

Later, I met with several CIA directors. My first was hosting Stansfield Turner when I headed the Minneapolis office. Turner was one of the more unpopular DCIs, and his navy admiral demeanor didn't enhance his image. He was appointed by President Carter seemingly due to their association as classmates at the Naval Academy. That said, Turner had an impressive intellect and was a serious thinker about national security. His objective at the CIA was to promote technical means of collecting intelligence over HUMINT (human intelligence). He drastically cut the clandestine service, which led to his dislike within the Directorate of Operations. My contact with him, however, could not have been more pleasant. I met him on the airport tarmac when he arrived on the Agency plane and drove him to our office. After a private session with me, he briefed my officers and was very complimentary in his remarks. I then accompanied him to the Minneapolis Club, where he delivered a speech to the city's business elite. He was then hosted by the CEO of a leading Fortune 500 company, Ed Spencer. Ed was a friend of Turner's dating back to their days at Oxford University, where they were both Rhodes scholars. I still have Turner's note of thanks he sent following his trip.

During my initial fifteen years in the CIA, I was introduced to an extraordinary range of ideas, people, organizations, and current issues impacting our national security interests. After college, I had sensed that I had limited knowledge of the actual workings of politics, the economy, and international affairs. My career pushed back the extent of my ignorance about these things to a considerable degree. More importantly, I developed a skill set around dealing with people from various backgrounds and belief systems to gain their cooperation. While my strength was dealing with economic issues, much of the information we sought dealt with scientific and technical information. Fortunately, most of the executives and scientists I interviewed were patient in explaining the significance of their insights. I conducted hundreds of interviews and wrote as many intelligence reports.

In the spring of 1984, I laid the groundwork for a dramatic change in the direction of my career in the Directorate of Operations. This required a move to Washington, DC, in August.

In reflection, one of the most rewarding aspects of intelligence operations was the relationship that developed with our sources of information. Although some contacts required only a single meeting, many were in positions to assist on a continual basis. The downside was saying goodbye when the time came to move on. But whether domestically or overseas, transitioning meant turning over these valuable assets to our successors. The knowledge I had acquired and the friendships made during fifteen years in field assignments underscored how privileged I was to have a role in our country's intelligence service.

Chapter 25

THE 1980S

The 1980s brought about the culmination of the Cold War between the East-West superpowers, the United States and the Union of Soviet Socialist Republics (USSR). Historians and pundits disagree on the cause of the Soviet collapse, whether it came about because of inherent flaws in the system or from pressures by the US. Perhaps the more accurate view is that the ultimate failure of the Soviet system was inevitable but hastened by a series of measures undertaken by the US during the 1980s. The end of the Soviet Union as we knew it came in 1991. The collapse was preceded by the fall of the Berlin Wall in 1989 and the resultant transition of the entirety of Soviet-dominated Eastern Europe from the yoke of communism.

    Based in Germany during both of these seminal events, I had a closer look at this enormous change that impacted Germany, in particular, but also the entire world. With the passage of time, I sometimes think that we forget the importance of the Cold War victory as one of the most significant events of the twentieth century. The Cold War was the dominant issue during my first twenty-four years of service as an intelligence officer. Given that the Agency was a comprehensive global intelligence service, there remained still many issues requiring the attention and engagement of the intelligence community, not the least of which was the growing terrorist threat. Most of my contemporaries and I, however, considered ourselves Cold War warriors.

When Ronald Reagan became president in early 1981, US foreign policy took a distinct turn toward the Soviet Union, which Reagan denounced as an "evil empire." In addition to stepped-up anti-Soviet rhetoric, he supported major increases in the defense budget. He was supported by two key appointments, Casper Weinberger as his Secretary of Defense and William Casey as Director of the CIA. Casey was a member of the OSS during World War II and a strong anti-Communist. He was also a great believer in HUMINT instead of emphasizing technical operations advocated by his predecessor. Casey's approach was met with enthusiasm by the clandestine service. More importantly, he was a director with excellent access to the president. My only personal meeting with him occurred when I was in Bonn, where I briefed him on my program during one of his visits.

Dealing with the Soviets in the early 1980s was made very difficult by changes in their leadership. Between 1982 and 1985 there were four different heads of government going from the longtime leader Leonid Brezhnev, former KGB Chief Yuri Andropov, and the aging Konstantin Chernenko, all of whom died while in office. Mikhail Gorbachev became the last Soviet leader when he replaced Chernenko in 1985. Gorbachev represented a dramatic change from the three old men he succeeded. While he tried to introduce reforms, such as perestroika and glasnost, to salvage the deteriorating Soviet system, he presided over its demise.

Most historians agree that the closest the US and the USSR came to an exchange of nuclear weapons was during the missile crisis in 1962 when the Soviets attempted to place nuclear missiles in Cuba. Others argue that the "War Scare" of 1983 brought us even closer to the brink. For a combination of reasons early in the Reagan administration, the Soviets thought the US was preparing for a nuclear strike. With Andropov, former head of the KGB, now heading the government, the Soviets gave serious consideration for a preemptive attack on the US. They were guilty of cognitive bias, as the KGB conducted Operation RyaN to prove that the US planned an attack. The US, perhaps unwittingly, contributed to the Soviets' paranoia by a series of plans that included placing intermediate-range nuclear missiles in West Germany, testing Soviet air defenses by flying US Air Force jets to their borders, and supporting the opposition to Soviet intervention in Afghanistan. The Soviets also became aware of their technological deficiencies when President Reagan announced the Strategic Defense Initiative (SDI), called Star Wars, to put a defensive shield around the US to protect against incoming missiles. The most alarming concern from the Soviet's standpoint was a large-scale military exercise in Europe undertaken by the US and NATO called Able Archer 83. The Soviets thought it was a cover for an attack. Fortunately, the situation de-escalated when a US military commander changed the scope of the exercise, which caused the Soviets to hold their powder. Some years later, my Bonn colleague Ben Fischer wrote an unclassified analysis of the war scare of 1983 that revealed how it was indeed a year of living dangerously.

On the domestic front, President Reagan held the office for most of the decade until his vice president, George H. W. Bush, succeeded him in 1989. Reagan introduced a different approach to the government's economic role by adopting supply-side economics. Economic growth did take off after the early depression of the decade, but the agricultural sector continued to suffer. There was somewhat of a backlash to the social movements of the prior decade. Young urban professionals (or yuppies, referred to as the Y generation), were characterized as affluent professionals who liked to dress in preppy clothes and show off their possessions. The movie *Wall Street* was based on the greed and corruption that many believed was occurring in the financial sector.

Chapter 26

BONN, GERMANY

My opportunity to change career directions resulted from a relatively new program by my division, now called the National Collection Division (NC), to expand overseas. I was selected for a posting in Bonn to be preceded by language training in DC. I started the intensive study of German in the fall of 1984. Striking to me was how much the Washington, DC, area had changed from the somewhat sleepy southern city of the 1960s when I had lived there for initial training. Now the town was a rapidly growing metropolis. The infamous Beltway was no longer the city's boundary, with conurbation extending in both Maryland and Virginia. Tysons Corner in Virginia was no longer a cornfield, and construction of the Metro, the city's subway system, was well underway.

Although I tested above average in language aptitude, I quickly learned that my college German got me through about two days before I was in new territory. I was in a class of four students, and our two women instructors were native speakers. Erica was originally from Bielefeld, and Helga was from Berlin. Both Erica and Helga were excellent teachers, and we all formed a tight-knit group after nine months of intensive study together. Erica and Helga gave us essential information about the culture, customs, and quirks in Germany, in addition to our language training. Erica later became a staff officer, and we subsequently served together when we were stationed in Germany. One of my classmates was also slated to go to Bonn as the Deputy Chief of Station. David Duberman was a senior officer, and we later connected in Bonn, playing tennis and having frequent dinner outings accompanied by his Swedish wife, Inger.

Germany

After World War II, Germany was divided into four sectors controlled by Britain, France, the US, and the USSR. The Soviets refused to consider the reunification of Germany despite years of occupation by the Allied Powers. The formation of the Federal Republic of Germany, known as West Germany, came about in 1949 and was composed of the American, British, and French sectors. The eastern sector controlled by the Soviets was named the German Democratic Republic and was referred to as East Germany. Germany was essentially divided into two countries. Bonn was selected for the capital of West Germany at the behest of Konrad Adenauer, the newly elected chancellor—so named by German tradition as opposed to the title of prime minister. He successfully oversaw the establishment of a democracy in West Germany compared to the Soviet transformation of East Germany into an authoritarian Communist state.

Since Western occupation officially extended in West Germany until 1952, the US military's occupation government, known as the US High Commission for Germany (HICOG), moved a significant contingent from Frankfurt to the new capital city. In some ways, Bonn was an odd choice for a capital. It was a relatively small university town without much infrastructure, as opposed to Cologne, just twenty-five miles farther north of Bonn, Germany's fourth largest city. A large building on the Rhine River south of downtown Bonn, built as a German military hospital during the war, became the new seat of the US occupation government. The military then built a large housing complex on the Rhine River in the Plittersdorf district of Bonn. When military occupation

US embassy, Bonn, Germany

came to an end, the HICOG headquarters building became the US embassy. The building and grounds were well protected by perimeter fencing and controlled entry.

I arrived at the Cologne Bonn Airport in early August 1985, where I was met by my predecessor in the position, Jon Aaronsohn, a colleague and longtime friend. We drove to his (and soon to be my) apartment in Bonn, where we dropped my luggage then immediately departed for lunch in Belgium. I wondered how that was possible, forgetting my geography in the fog of jet lag. We drove together with colleagues Ben and Mary Fischer to Liége across the border from Aachen, a two-hour drive from Bonn. During the next two weeks, I traveled with Jon to turnover assets in countries where we had responsibilities. I knew immediately that I was in for a terrific experience.

My work required considerable travel throughout Germany, Austria, and Switzerland, hardship locations all. Speaking German greatly facilitated the logistics, but I found that my interlocutors quickly switched to English in diplomatic and professional circles. To gain confidence in

Im Steifel, "The Boot"

the language, I took additional lessons at the embassy from a very proper German woman from whom I learned a great deal about her postwar experiences. She described the terrible hunger her family had faced between 1945 and 1947 and the concern over food shipments from the US. The initial packages were labeled "*gift*," which means "poison" in German. But mainly, my German improved by talking to Germans whose English was less fluent than my German. The perfect place was a pub in downtown Bonn called Im Steifel, meaning "the boot," located three doors down from Beethoven's birthplace house. The crowded bar scene made it easy to strike up conversations.

On one of my early visits to Im Stiefel, a friendly but quite risible German fellow greeted me as Herr Botschafter, which means "ambassador" in German. He was not to be persuaded otherwise, and after that, when he spotted me, he would very loudly call out to me as Mr. Ambassador. Finally, we agreed that we must keep my identity a *Geheim*, or secret, and he took great pride in playing our little game going forward. It was not the last time I was mistaken for the US ambassador. It seemed that I arrived in Bonn at about the same time as the new US ambassador, Richard Burt. We were close enough alike in appearance to cause the confusion. He was popular with the German people and received good TV coverage, perhaps because he often played in a rock band. One evening during the annual pre-Lenten *Carnivale,* I celebrated the event at a popular and very crowded nightspot with some German friends. Shortly after we arrived, I was approached by a fellow who showed me his identification as a BKA officer, our FBI equivalent. He called me Herr Botschafter, and said I shouldn't be there without security. Despite my protestations, he decided to take it upon himself to provide for my security. I was able to enjoy the evening in safety thanks to my dual identity.

My work activities soon expanded into more clandestine assignments that were engaging and sometimes tinged with a bit of tensity as well as humor. I was handling a covert action agent with whom I met periodically. We met in a safe house located in a building that contained several offices and apartments. A wrought iron fence surrounded the building grounds that covered a square block. During one of our meetings, there was a loud banging on the door and shouts of, *"Polizei!"* All of the blood drained out my agent's face as I slowly opened the door. Two policemen in SWAT gear informed us that there was a bomb threat, and we were not to leave the room. After regaining our composure, we looked out the window to see that the entire block was cordoned off and a large bomb squad truck was approaching. We also spotted the culprit, a black bag with what appeared to be protruding wires hanging on the fence. We later learned that the panic had been caused by someone who had forgotten his briefcase.

The response by the *Polizei* was prompted by heightened concern in Germany over terrorist bombings that had taken place in Berlin. Some weeks before, Libyan terrorists had bombed a nightclub in Berlin, killing two American servicemen and injuring seventy-nine others. The German response increased vigilance and enhanced security at US facilities, in-

German airport: Going somewhere

cluding the embassy's residential complex in Plittersdorf. Entry to the area was barricaded, and German military police used mirrors to inspect the undersides of all vehicles waiting to enter. On one occasion, I was to meet with an asset who had arrived in Bonn from Egypt. It was snowing as he drove in a rental car near Bad Godesberg. He stopped to photograph the snowy scene for his children when he returned to Cairo. Suddenly, he was confronted and arrested by the German police. Despite his innocence, the police had a different take when seeing a bearded foreigner in a rental car taking suspicious photos of an embassy that just happened to be in the background of his snowy photo scenes.

The bombing episode in Berlin was one of many perpetrated by terrorists that initiated what became an almost universal war on terrorism. The Agency established its own Counterterrorism Center to deal with the growing threat. My friend and CT classmate Karl Ruyle was appointed Deputy Chief of the Center, where his analytic skills were crucial. A lot more can be said about this issue that consumed so many resources over the coming decades and unknowingly extended my career.

The Brandenburg Gate behind the Berlin Wall

On a trip to an Eastern European country, I was more than ready to get off the old Soviet Tupolev passenger plane with its noisy engines. We landed at night and disembarked on the tarmac. I kept looking out the window to get my bearings on the bus ride into the city, but it was totally dark. Then I remembered that there were no neon signs or other lights on in the stores and commercial buildings since everything was state-owned. The next morning, while doing a surveillance detection run, few people were on the streets except for some older women using brooms to sweep the detritus that crumbled from the sides of the aging buildings. I made my way after several hours to the meeting site. The meeting involved a carefully coordinated plan with high expectations. As sometimes happens with prearranged meetings, the target didn't show. There was nothing to do but enjoy the thermal waters of a nearby Turkish bath and ponder the next steps.

The starkest reminder of the Cold War was the Berlin Wall. Like most who visited the city before the wall came down in 1989, I climbed a view ladder to look across the no-man's-land that separated the divided city. I couldn't resist giving the finger to the guards in the tower on the other side, despite their display of rifles. The crosses lining the concrete barrier, dedicated to the East Germans who were killed trying to escape, made the experience even more poignant. Under pressure by the Soviets, the East German government built the concrete barrier in 1961 ostensibly to keep Fascist agitators from coming into Communist East Germany. The real reason was to stop East Germans from leaving after some 2.5 million people moved to West Germany. The city of Berlin ended up deep inside the Soviet sector following World War II when Germany was partitioned into four sections controlled by the US, France, the UK, and the USSR. However, the four powers also had joint control of respective sectors in the city of Berlin. This scenario made for many tense confrontations between the east and west sectors of the city over the next thirty years.

In early 1987 I requested and was granted an extension for a third year in my Bonn assignment. However, a few months later, I received a message from the newly appointed chief of the domestic division, Dale Zeimer. Dale was a highly regarded senior officer with a clear vision of his objectives for the division. He said that he had selected three of my division colleagues and me to help him run the division's headquarters. The wording left no room for protest, and it was hard to argue against a headquarters assignment after eighteen years in the field. I returned to Washington and joined Bill Wenger, Paul Ropp, and Earl Walker, all good friends, to start our new jobs. Departing Bonn meant many goodbyes and selling the BMW. I did, however, take advantage of a discount and ordered a 1988 Saab 9000 for delivery in the US.

A few weeks before leaving Bonn, one of my old friends and CT colleague Jon visited the station from his foreign posting. We met for breakfast at one of my favorite spots on the Rhine, a restaurant in the Rheinhotel Dreesen overlooking the river. The hotel had much history, a subject that both Jon and I enjoyed. Hitler had stayed at the hotel frequently when he was in Bonn, and he met there with the British Prime Minister Neville Chamberlain before their later infamous 1938 meeting in Munich. As World War II ended in 1945, General Eisenhower had his headquarters in the hotel. A fluent German speaker, Jon advised that he was leaving for a short stay in Washington before returning to head a project in Munich. When discussing my own return to headquarters, I lamented having to leave Germany so abruptly. Jon then planted the seed for a new opportunity with his request that I join him. After many bureaucratic entanglements and much negotiation, we were able to meet up back overseas a year and a half later.

Chapter 27

HEADQUARTERS

I joined my colleagues Earl, Bill, and Paul at the domestic division headquarters of the National Collection Division (NC) in DC in the fall of 1987. My responsibilities were to supervise NC offices in the northeast region of the US. A startling development occurred within weeks of my arrival, which was that our respected Division Chief, Dale Zeimer, was abruptly removed from his position by the Deputy Director of Operations. My introduction to organizational politics at a different level changed my thinking about my career path. Despite many efforts to introduce new management concepts to the Agency organization, the structure remained quite hierarchical. The new Division Chief was David Cohen, and his Deputy was Gust Avrakotos. Cohen was brilliant but could, at best, be described as rough-hewn, and both he and Avrakotos were given to using extreme profanity. Cohen had come from the analysis directorate and was unfamiliar with operations, so he deferred frequently to Avrakotos. Ultimately, however, Cohen succeeded in his own right and went on to become the Deputy Director of Operations.

Avrakotos was branded a rogue officer for flaunting rules, but he was also an effective (if controversial) player in the Afghan war of the 1980s. He was head of a task force that had been set up to assist the Afghan mujahideen in the fight against a Soviet military invasion. The Soviets were intent on setting up a Communist government in Afghanistan that many Afghan tribal groups opposed. Avrakotos developed a tight relationship with US Congressman Charlie Wilson, a strong advocate for supporting the Afghan guerillas. Wilson was able to channel federal funding and gain congressional approval for providing Stinger missiles to the mujahideen. The significant advantage of the Soviet forces in Afghanistan was air superiority, which allowed their helicopters to attack without opposition. The missiles supplied by the US enabled the guerrillas to force the Soviets to withdraw from Afghanistan. The conflict became known as Charlie Wilson's War. Later, a book and movie of the same name featured Wilson and Avrakotos. Nonetheless, Gust's bullying behavior led to his dismissal from the Agency after a year in the NC Division.

By the end of 1987, all three of my colleagues—Bill, Earl, and Paul, had had enough of the new division managers and found other positions in the directorate. They each went on to have exemplary careers. I was less nimble in plotting my escape, but it wasn't long before I called my friend Jon about the position we had discussed in Bonn. He began to lay the groundwork with his component in the Directorate of Science and Technology (DDS&T). Meanwhile, I soldiered on and learned a great deal about the complexities of managing operations. Part of my responsibility was to travel to the field stations in my jurisdiction. I was also in a position to get to know many of the senior officers in the Agency, and more importantly, assist in the careers of many of the junior officers in the division.

Finally, with the backing of Avrakotos, who somehow took a liking to me, I was able to leave the division after one year without burning any bridges. To prepare for the Munich assignment, I spent four months in the DDS&T offices situated in the new headquarters building. The new structure had just been completed a year earlier and connected to the original building. The combined facilities on the 250-acre campus

New headquarters building

were ever impressive to me. The extraordinary project in which I would have a role involved training at the National Security Agency's (NSA) headquarters at Fort Meade, Maryland. The NSA had responsibility for cryptographic and communications intelligence. This opened up a whole new world for me in the intelligence business. I also had time for additional courses in tradecraft, including advanced surveillance detection and self-defense. During my time in DC, I met my future wife, Elizabeth Buechler, and she subsequently joined me when I moved back overseas.

Chapter 28

IN EUROPE AGAIN

Jon W. met me at the Munich airport in early January 1989, and we drove to our project offices. Over the next three years, my work involved almost weekly travel to countries outside Germany. This meant traveling in alias and dealing with a dedicated network of agents supporting our mission. The project was financially intensive and involved frequent interactions with colleagues in DC. This assignment was one of my favorites, even if it was occasionally fraught. For this tour, my living accommodations were in the city.

The 1989 Fall of the Berlin Wall and the subsequent collapse of the Soviet Union in 1991 occurred during my tenure in Germany. The joy-

With Elizabeth at the House of Wittelsbach

The Brandenburg Gate after fall of the Berlin Wall

ful outpouring of people into the streets in Munich when the Wall fell was an exhilarating spectacle. Elizabeth and I tried without luck to fly to Berlin to witness the historical event that presaged the end of the Cold War. The West German government immediately set about the process of reunification. This included a 10 percent increase in income taxes to finance the cost of trying to update the neglected infrastructure of the eastern sector. It also set in motion the capital's move from Bonn back to its historic center in Berlin. When Eastern Europe followed East Germany's lead and broke loose from Soviet domination, the consequences were enormous. One was the pent-up demand in the east to travel to Western Europe. This was especially true for families previously separated when Germany was divided after World War II. One comic-turned-tragic event was East Germans driving west in their tiny three-cylinder-engine Trabants. The little cars trailing smoke were thought at first to be cute, but then the East German drivers, inexperienced with driving on the autobahns, couldn't get out of the way of faster Mercedes cars. The results were many fatal rear-end accidents and the ultimate decision to ban the polluting vehicles from the roadways.

In Vienna, Austria, I was on a weekend trip after the Eastern European borders opened to the West. I had taken the train and was in a cab going to my hotel, usually a fifteen-minute drive. It took almost two hours because the streets were choked by drivers who had crossed the border from Hungary and Czechoslovakia to shop for Western goods. The open borders allowed us to take an early trip to Prague, Czechoslovakia. Recovery had not yet started, so the city still had the run-down appearance resulting from a Soviet-enforced Communist economy. We nonetheless could sense the euphoria of the people. We visited the historic sites and enjoyed an excellent Czech pilsner for twenty-five cents.

In late summer 1991, I received a message from David Cohen, who was still head of the Agency's expanded domestic division renamed the National Resources Division (NR). He wanted me to return to the US and take a Chief of Station (COS) position in Dallas, Texas. I had planned to extend my tour until the summer of 1992, but the offer of a COS job was not to be turned down. Moreover, it was another opportunity to skip the bureaucracy in Washington. In December 1991, Elizabeth and I packed up after three glorious years in Deutschland.

Chapter 29

THE DECADE OF THE 1990S

We returned to the US to a changing world both internationally and at home. The seminal end of the Cold War officially came with the collapse of the USSR in 1991. The result was that fourteen new countries were created from the former Soviet republics, and the six Eastern European countries were now democracies. The relatively peaceful irredentism experienced by the former Soviet Union did not occur in Yugoslavia, where the independence movement of ethnic groups led to a years-long war. The new Balkan wars eventually led to the dissolution of Yugoslavia and the formation of seven new countries. The Cold War ended, and the world seemed at relative peace, so the US dramatically cut back on defense spending. The 25 percent reduction in the budget for intelligence came just as new security threats emerged. Terrorism as a burgeoning threat in the US was foreshadowed by the explosion of a bomb in the basement of the World Trade Center in Manhattan in 1991. The Middle East became increasingly problematic beyond the Israeli-Palestinian conflict, and the US was drawn in militarily by Iraq's invasion of Kuwait in the 1991 Gulf War. The proliferation of nuclear weapons was evident with a standoff between the new nuclear powers of India and

Pakistan and Pakistan's sale of the technology to Iran, Libya, and North Korea. On the other hand, Europe became a more powerful entity and ally with the formation of the European Union.

The CIA was tasked with dealing with new post-Cold War issues that included terrorism, drug trafficking, nuclear proliferation, and unresolved regional conflicts that surfaced when Soviet hegemony came to an end. As one DCI observed, we slew the dragon but opened a Pandora's box of snakes. The US was now the only superpower and was able to play an even more critical role on the international scene. A robust intelligence service was in many ways more important than ever for confronting these new challenges. Unfortunately, the so-called peace dividend took a tremendous toll on our capabilities. The impact on the agency resulted in staffing cutbacks that cost me an approved promotion. More importantly, the reductions meant a hiring freeze that extended for several years. Closing the personnel pipeline is not the way to run a railroad, let alone an intelligence service. Adding to the decline in Agency morale was the revelation of the perfidy of CIA officer Aldrich Ames and FBI agent Robert Hanson. Their spying for the Russians resulted in the assassinations of most of our valuable spies in Moscow. The seeming rapprochement with the Russians after the Soviet collapse belied a soon resurgent KGB and the subsequent ascension of former KGB officer Vladimir Putin. As our attention diverted to other issues, Putin's ambitions would later come to haunt us. Meanwhile, a succession of Agency directors occurred during the 1990s as five different appointees held the position. The turmoil made it all the more advantageous to be posted in the field.

The US underwent major economic growth during the 1990s after an early recession as the private sector overtook the Defense Department in developing new technologies. The combination of the Internet and personal computers revolutionized both personal and business communications. Later in the decade, the cell phone was on its way to becoming a universal necessity. Technology and the globalization of international trade increased the standard of living for most people and had a far-reaching impact on most aspects of society, from education and medicine to manufacturing and agriculture. The transfer of much of our manufacturing operations overseas led to cheaper consumer goods. The tragedy was no support for displaced workers, which led to greater wealth inequality and consequential political realignments. Democratic President Bill Clinton presided over most of the decade from 1993 until 2000.

Chapter 30

DALLAS

As Chief of Station, I had responsibility for a large territory and a resident office. My case officers were a talented group of young, primarily first-tour officers needing more guidance and support. From experience and observation, I practiced wandering around management to get to know them and encourage their professional development. Elizabeth and I hosted periodic gatherings for special occasions. Based on my experiences in previous assignments, I immediately started building relationships with the heads of other federal agencies, especially the FBI and the INS. I also arranged to meet with significant players in the private sector.

One of my longtime associates, Rex Latham, had a brother Will, an army general who had retired in Dallas. He was Director of the Dallas Council on Foreign Relations and was a helpful contact. I arranged to have DCI Bob Gates give a presentation to the members of the council. Unlike many other directors who traveled with an entourage and on the Agency plane, Bob came in on a commercial flight with a single security officer. Although I didn't know him personally, we had joined the Agency in the same year. His rise was as meteoric as mine was mundane. I drove him to our office for a private meeting before gathering with my staff. He gave his usual unvarnished assessment of the key intelligence issues extant in the immediate Cold War aftermath. Appointments to the DCI position had become more politicized, and Bob left the position shortly after his Dallas visit with the election of Bill Clinton in 1992. Clinton's first appointment to the DCI position was James Woolsey, followed by John Deutsch, both lesser lights in the annals of Agency leadership. In 1997 George Tenet became the director and served for seven years. He was generally very highly regarded and popular within the ranks.

The region has long been the center for oil production in the US, and oil is a leading industry in the state and the creator of numerous billionaires. A key question and lingering issue was peak oil, or the point at which oil production reaches a level where it begins to decline because of limited reserves. Oil as a national security concern became more and more acute for the US as domestic production did not keep up with demand, and we became more and more dependent on imported oil. By the mid-1990s, the US relied on foreign sources for half of our oil requirements. The primary region for imported oil was the Middle East, especially Saudi Arabia. Another factor in the national security equation was Russia's large reserves. Monitoring the world markets for oil was a continuing intelligence concern with our dependency and the volatility of foreign sources, making it a significant national security concern. Moreover, oil imports were still subject to the vagaries of military conflicts, just as they were during the Cold War. I met with many knowledgeable businesspeople in order to discuss trends and developments in the oil industry. I had more than usual interest in the industry with my earlier work experience at the bottom of the production ladder.

Ironically, the US ultimately became an oil exporter because of new technologies for extraction, which rendered moot the perceived problem of peak oil. A decline in oil production is anticipated not because of the supply side, but because demand will decrease with alternative energy sources. Oil, however, will still be a significant industry in the coming decades with intelligence implications. I was helped along the way by a friend who was well-connected. On occasion, he invited Elizabeth and me to watch the Dallas Cowboys football games from his company's box. Granted, it was during a lull in the prominence of America's team during the post-coach Landry era and before quarterback Troy Aikman took them once again to the Super Bowl, winning for three consecutive years.

Periodically, I would arrange a lunch meeting with three former chiefs of the station who had retired. They were a helpful and convivial bunch, but I was somewhat bemused that our lunch conversations started with an organ report, or a discussion of their health issues. Later in life, I had a more forbearing understanding of aging conversations. My friend and former CT classmate Earl Tomlinson had also retired, and like most Texans, came home where he was working as a consultant in Dallas. Earl had a ranch in West Texas, and we had many enjoyable weekends engaged in the Texas pastime of hunting doves and quail. I also learned a great deal about the region from Kip Rolland, who became a good and enduring friend. Kip was well positioned in the community and had repeated successful careers. A Vietnam veteran, Kip was a true patriot and philanthropist.

An interesting episode for me in Dallas was the opportunity to meet one of the Norwegian resistance fighters who had been a member of the team that sabotaged a heavy water facility in Norway during World War II. Heavy water was used in nuclear reactors and was potentially useful in the development of atomic weapons. The primary facility in the world at that time for heavy water production was a hydroelectric plant in Norway. When the Nazis occupied Norway, the Allies were concerned that heavy water from the plant would be used in the German effort to develop nuclear weapons. An operation to blow up the plant, called Operation Gunnerside, was organized with the Norwegian resistance based in England. Arne Kjelstrup was on a nine-member team of Norwegian saboteurs that parachuted into Norway to carry out the mission. I was invited to a small lunch gathering by an old colleague who had invited Sergeant Kjelstrup to Dallas. Arne then made a presentation on his role in the operation. The sergeant was a member of the sabotage team airdropped in the Norwegian mountains on a flight from England. Arriving in the area in midwinter 1943, the team skied at night to the location of the hydroelectric facility. Arne was part of the four-man squad that surreptitiously entered the plant. After the bombs were planted, he and his team evaded capture by the Nazis and made their way over 200 miles on cross-country skis to Sweden. Although the famous operation has been recounted in many books and films, Arne's account was more than riveting and of particular interest to me since I had written an academic paper on the Gunnerside operation.

After three and a half years as COS, I planned my retirement, having served for over twenty-five years. The CIA had a performance award program that gave line managers the prerogative of giving out awards to officers for outstanding work. In a turnabout that was a surprise for Agency management, my officers and staff to a person put together a four-page document that they secretly sent back to headquarters in which they proposed that I be given a significant award. Taken aback in DC by this bottoms-up proposal, I was given the Donovan Award for recognition as a mentor to young case officers.

Our retirement plans were to relocate to Colorado, a longtime dream. During a vacation trip to Colorado, an idea occurred to me that could facilitate the transition. The Agency had a program for assigning officers to college campuses as visiting faculty. I could teach at the Air Force Academy in Colorado Springs as an Agency officer. To set the plan in motion, I contacted the Chief of the National Resources Division, my friend Chuck Campbell. Chuck endorsed the idea, and I worked with the CIA's Center for the Study of Intelligence (CSI) which administered the Agency's Officer-in-Residence program. The program had been established a few years earlier to improve the CIA's relationship with the academic community and foster a better understanding of the role of intelligence in foreign policy and national security. The next step was visiting the Academy, where I met with the general who was Dean of the Faculty and then with the head of the Department of Political Science. After successful interviews, I received the appointment and made plans to start my new assignment for the fall semester in 1995.

Chapter 31

COLORADO SPRINGS

The CIA's Officer-in-Residence (OIR) program held a two-week training conference in DC for the seven Agency officers selected for university teaching assignments. We spent some time at the Farm, which would be my last visit to the place I had viewed so fondly after taking numerous tradecraft and management training classes there, beginning as a Career Trainee when I first joined the Agency. My fellow soon-to-be faculty members were going to different universities around the country, including some Ivy League schools. We received many of the Agency's unclassified materials and could access continuing support from the academic coordinator at the Center for the Study of Intelligence. I arrived at the US Air Force Academy (USAFA) in early August 1995 for a weeklong program informally called the "New Guys" school for new faculty. The new staff was made up primarily of air force officers, many of whom had attended the academy and had gone on to receive graduate degrees. The weeklong sessions provided an excellent introduction to the institution and its history, mission, and academic objectives. Although I had interacted with the military numerous times during my career and indeed had military officers assigned to me, it was much different now having this assignment. Although the academy was in part an academic institution, it operated as a military base with its attendant hierarchical command structure. The academy students, or more appropriately cadets, were training for careers as military officers with an additional curriculum for that purpose.

The Air Force Academy had been established in 1955, more recently than the much older army and naval academies. It occupies a 10,000-acre air force base bordering the northern city limits of Colorado Springs. Organizationally, the academy is headed by a superintendent who has the rank of lieutenant general. Reporting to him are three brigadier generals who lead each of the components for training the cadets. These are the Dean of Faculty, the Commandant of Cadets for military training, and the Director of Athletics. The cadets are organized into what is called the cadet wing and are assigned to squadrons. Each squadron has about one hundred members, with forty squadrons making up the student body of four thousand.

At the end of the New Guys" school, we met with the faculty in our academic departments. Each department was headed by a permanent professor with the rank of colonel, which was my equivalent rank. Permanent professors had tenure, as opposed to the military faculty members who were on rotational assignments. The academy was under congressional pressure to include more civilians on their faculty and have at least 10 percent nonmilitary. There was only one civilian professor in the Political Science Department, except for myself and a foreign service officer from the State Department. There were two additional instructors from the army and navy. We all soon melded with much camaraderie and numerous departmental social activities. All of the instructors were serious and dedicated teachers.

Two of my fellow "New Guy" teachers who were military officers became lifelong friends. David LaSalle was a career intelligence officer who had just completed a tour as a military advisor in the Balkan War. After his academy tour, he went on to subsequent deployments in Afghanistan

David LaSalle and his wife, Alex

and Iraq. Fluent in French and German, he organized a German-speaking seminar in the department for those who enjoyed the language.

Brad Gutierrez flew bombing raids as a B-52 pilot over Iraq in the 1991 Gulf War. He received a PhD in political science at the University of California San Diego and served as an air attaché and pilot at the US embassy in Budapest. Both were outstanding officers and good buddies. Elizabeth and I were happy to attend both of their weddings.

The lowly first-year cadets at the academy are ranked as fourth class and called doolies. Seniors are ranked first-class, or firsties. The doolies are subject to all kinds of pressures and indignities aside from their studies. In my experience, the students followed a predictable bell curve in their abilities but at a higher level of achievement. The top students were indeed a remarkable and talented group and a joy to teach. The washout rate occurring in the first two years at the academy was around 20 percent. When the academy was first established, all cadets had to meet pilot training standards, and most became pilots for many years after that. As air force requirements changed over the years with new disciplines, some years find only around 50 percent of the cadets entering pilot training

Brad and Beth Gutierrez

after graduation. Incidentally, all cadets graduated on time in four years at a cost in 1995 of $250,000. They earned their keep and have my utmost respect. I expect most university students have no idea about the difficulty and rigor facing their counterparts at the military academies.

It had been over thirty years since I had been engaged in academe, so I had my work cut out for not only developing a syllabus for my course on intelligence but also mastering the subject matter for the core classes. Unlike many of my Officer-in-Residence program counterparts who spent the first semester observing and developing their course syllabi, I immediately started my teaching duties. For the first two years at the academy, the cadets all took a broad selection of courses referred to as the core, which involved classes in most academic departments. There was an emphasis on space and engineering, where half of the cadets would select their majors. For their requirements in political science, the cadets took courses in American government and international relations. I taught both of these classes and my own course on the role of intelligence in foreign policy that I designed for seniors majoring in political science. Teaching American government came easily with my early training in

American history, but I most enjoyed the core course in international relations that included a history of the Cold War. In military fashion, my colleagues and I appointed a cadet on the first day of class to be the sergeant at arms. Their responsibility was to call the class to order and report that they were ready for instruction. There were no skipped classes, tardiness, or disciplinary issues. Instructors were available for consultation by email or in person and maintained daily office hours. I was enjoined from recruiting cadets for the CIA, but several came to me asking about opportunities. I was encouraging but told them to apply after completing their military obligations.

One of my responsibilities at the academy was serving as faculty advisor to the Academy assembly. The assembly is an annual conference focusing on foreign affairs. Each year, 150 select university students from around the country are invited to the academy to participate in a topic of current significance. It is an honor for students to receive an invitation, and they are divided into groups of ten for roundtable discussions. Distinguished experts from the government and from universities serve as moderators at each table. The topic during my tenure was the role of the US in the United Nations. A key feature of the assembly is that cadets organize all aspects of the function. The cadet in charge was an outstanding young man, and it was a pleasure working with him. The keynote speaker for the conference was the US ambassador to the United Nations, Madeleine Albright. She spoke to the entire cadet wing in the academy's Arnold Hall auditorium, where a cadet made her introduction. Shortly after her appearance at the academy, President Clinton appointed her to be Secretary of State, the first woman to hold the position.

One of the contributions I made to my students and the academy was arranging for guest speakers from the Agency. On a trip back to CIA headquarters, I met with my friend Lloyd Salvetti, who at this time had returned from Europe and was serving on the vaunted seventh floor as

Chief of Staff for the Directorate of Operations. He introduced me to some of his colleagues, including the CIA General Counsel Jeff Smith. Jeff was eager to visit the academy. He was a West Point graduate and was currently serving on the Board of Governors for that military academy. A prominent Washington lawyer, Jeff was involved in many political and national security issues before and after his appointment at the CIA. He and Lloyd were later engaged with the 9-11 Commission assessing that terrorism catastrophe. I arranged for him to speak to my classes and meet with the USAFA Superintendent. In addition to Lloyd and other speakers, former Acting DCI John Blake accepted my invitation.

When my two-year tour at the academy ended after the spring semester of 1997, I was looking forward to retiring when the National Resources Division Chief asked me to extend through the summer as interim Chief of Station covering the great plains. I took the thoroughly enjoyable job, and it gave me greater familiarity with the region. I also served on a terrorism task force set up for the Summit of the Eight meeting in Denver during June 1997. The summits, meetings of the seven world powers referred to as the Group of Seven (G7), were an annual gathering of heads of state from Canada, Japan, Britain, France, Germany, Italy, and the United States. The Denver meeting was called the G8 in deference to Boris Yeltsin, the first elected president of Russia, who was invited to attend. The security arrangements behind the scenes for protecting this venerable group were enormous and required extraordinary coordination. Parenthetically, there was a significant intelligence and counterintelligence dimension to these conferences apart from security considerations.

Finally, the end time had come for my career, and I entered the Agency's transition program for retirees. This ninety-day period started with a series of briefings and paperwork in Agency headquarters. Coincidentally, I was in DC when the Agency celebrated its fiftieth anniversary with a week of special events in September 1997. I was in the unusual position of attending as both an employee and a retiree. Speakers at the conclave included then-President Bill Clinton and former President George H. W. Bush, who had earlier served as DCI. I joined other retirees at a special gathering in a tent that had been set up in front of the headquarters building that featured all living directors. Richard Helms, George W. Bush, Stansfield Turner, William Webster, Bob Gates, James Woolsey, and John Deutsch were seated on the stage. The recently appointed DCI, George Tenet, served as the master of ceremonies. He did a magnificent job introducing the august lineup. Humorous, and at times perhaps embarrassing, moments occurred following the introduction of each of the directors. The applause line following each director clearly indicated their esteem among the old guard. Helms and Bush received standing ovations, but Turner and Deutsch were met with a polite but faint tribute. A repeat of this occasion would undoubtedly bring an ovation for Tenet. My reflection on the experience was that my time encompassed thirty of those fifty years, and that the CIA was only twenty years old when I came on board.

Although I retired in November 1997 after thirty years of service, it turned out that my time with the agency was not over. On September 11, 2001, Islamic terrorists hijacked passenger aircraft and used them as missiles to bomb the World Trade Center's Twin Towers in New York City and the Pentagon in DC. These attacks put tremendous pressure on the CIA to deal with the perpetrators but, more importantly, to determine whether additional threats were imminent. Congress approved major resources to counter terrorism, and the agency brought back a large cadre of retirees to assist in this effort. I spent another five years during a quite different time from the Cold War era. The Trade Center bombing that took the lives of three thousand people represented a colossal intelligence failure. However, the real issue was why our intelligence apparatus had failed to predict the attack or interdict the attackers. The answer is quite simple. The cutbacks in budget and personnel during the 1990s had emasculated the agency's ability to monitor, penetrate, and assess these terrorist groups properly and deal simultaneously with many other national security concerns. The consequence was a prolonged war on terrorism with the additional loss of thousands of lives and a cost of over $2 trillion. Ten years later, the 9-11 ringleader Osama bin Laden, who founded the terrorist group al-Qaeda, was finally tracked down and terminated. However, the ongoing issue is whether a bitter lesson has been learned or whether the vagaries of our political system would once again cause us to forget.

In another retrospective, the extreme focus on dealing with the terrorist crisis had unintended consequences. We let our guard down yet again by not keeping pace with the ongoing aggressive actions of the Chinese and Russian intelligence services. Chinese ambitions of becoming the world's leading power led them to exploit the US advantage in technology by using commercial agreements and their intelligence services to steal intellectual property for both military and commercial objectives. Putin's spy services had a more nefarious objective for boosting Russia's diminished standing as a world power. Both the SVR (former KGB) and the GRU orchestrated a campaign to discredit democratic institutions in the US. Using cyber tactics and traditional espionage methods, they interfered in our elections and successfully sowed disinformation that fostered a dangerous political divide in our country.

After Trump was elected in 2016, he ignored the advice of his intelligence services and dismissed the accusations of Russian interference in our election. He inexplicably said that he believed Russian interference did not occur following a personal meeting with Putin, who denied the allegations. At this point, the consequences of the president's denial of Russia's aggressive cyber active measures against the US are yet to be revealed. During his administration, the CIA reached its worst nadir since the Carter and Clinton years. The Trump tenure adds to the three low points in the CIA's history after the post-Nixon era: the Turner (Clinton) Trough, the Deutsch (Clinton) Ditch, and the Trump Tumble.

Post-Retirements Events

During our vacation at a resort in the Rocky Mountains in the summer of 1997, Lloyd Salvetti confided that he was considering a position as Director of the CIA's Center for the Study of Intelligence (CSI). He later took the job and extended his career to 2001 when he retired. One of his responsibilities at CSI involved a project to declassify documents on key events in the Agency's history. A few of these studies resulted in conferences where experts, historians, and intelligence officials gave presentations on the subject. One of these was the CIA's Corona Project that launched the country's first spy satellite. Lloyd invited Elizabeth and me to attend a conference in Berlin, Germany, in early September 1999 that involved an extraordinary gathering of 150 invited guests. Senior government officials, authors, journalists, and academics attended, but more importantly, aging spies who participated in the events revealed by the project were also there. Intelligence officials from the four allied powers in occupied Berlin were on the program. The conference was called Berlin: The Intelligence War, 1945–1961.

The location of the conclave at the Teufelsberg in Berlin, Germany, could not have been more propitious. The Teufelsberg is a large hill built from the rubble resulting from the bombing of Berlin during World War II. It is the highest point in the city and was used by US intelligence during the Cold War for the field station in Berlin. Its mission was to serve as a listening post for monitoring communications in the east. Lloyd organized the assemblage with the cooperation of the Allied Museum in Berlin. Keynote speakers included Germany's Minister of Internal

Affairs and the US ambassador. I especially enjoyed the address given by Vernon Walters at the concluding dinner. Walters, who had completed his fifty-year government career as the US ambassador to Germany a few years earlier, gave his expected humorous and insightful observations. Lloyd moderated the two-day conference with a lineup of fascinating presentations and panels that dealt with Berlin's role as the center of espionage confrontations between the CIA and the KGB from the Berlin Airlift in 1949 until the construction of the Berlin Wall in 1961. The Berlin Wall closed off opportunities for our case officers to interacted with Soviet and East German citizens who might have had access to information of intelligence value.

With Lloyd in Berlin

The conference highlights were presentations by the intelligence officers from all sides. Leading spymasters from the US were Hugh Montgomery, Burton Gerber, and David Murphy, who served in Berlin during the 1950s. Fittingly, David Murphy had just published his acclaimed book on the conference topic entitled *Battleground Berlin: CIA vs. KGB in the Cold War*. Conspicuously absent at the gathering were representatives from the former East German spy agency, the Ministry for State Security (Stasi). With the abrupt end of their power just ten years earlier, the feelings of this group were apparently still a bit raw.

One of the conference events that Elizabeth and I most enjoyed was a tour of the intelligence sites of Berlin. At a visit to the former Stasi head-

Herdes taking over Mielke's desk

quarters recently converted to a museum, my CIA associates and I were not deterred by the velvet rope blocking the entrance to the ruthless Stasi spy chief Erich Mielke's office. We took one another's photos rotating in his chair while eyeing the telephone with its red alarm button and a death mask of Lenin (since removed).

In addition to many stops, including the former KGB headquarters in Karlshorst and Checkpoint Charlie, we walked out on the Glienicke Bridge, the site of spy exchanges between the Soviets and the US. One of the most notable exchanges occurred in 1961 and involved Gary Powers, the CIA pilot shot down over the USSR in the famed U-2 spy plane. Powers was exchanged for Rudolf Abel, a Russian spy who had been caught and imprisoned in the US. I took an ironic photograph of Powers's son Gary Powers, Jr.; Oleg Kalugin, a KGB general attending the conference; and a CIA officer who escorted Rudolf Abel under military cover to the bridge during the actual exchange. The Powers/Abel exchange was later dramatized in the excellent film *Bridge of Spies* featuring Tom Hanks.

Traveling to the conference, Elizabeth and I flew in and out of our beloved city of Munich. We rented a car in Munich to drive through the former East Germany on our way to Berlin. En route, we went to the cities we had missed during the Cold War desolation, including Leipzig, Dresden, and Weimar. Although Weimar is a famous and beautiful small city, in its shadow are the remnants of Buchenwald, one of the notorious and the largest of the Nazi concentration camps. While visiting this site with all its horrors, we took a path through a forested area that led to a memorial to German military officers. It seemed that the Soviets used Buchenwald as an internment camp for captured German military officers when the war ended. Though paling compared to the Nazi atrocities, over eight thousand German officers were starved to death by the Russians during the period from 1945 to 1950. The Russian cruelty underscored why so many German soldiers fled from the eastern front to be imprisoned by the US Army forces advancing from the west.

While in the former East Germany, we also visited the town of Wernigerode, located on the eastern edge of the Harz Mountains. The Herdes family seal was registered in this town in 1496. The archivist for the city located centuries-old files for us to view references to the Herdes namesake. The town landmark is a prominent medieval castle built as a hunting lodge for Prussian emperors, but there is, unfortunately, no linkage of the castle to the Herdes heritage. There is more evidence that the Herdes clan was made up of either sheepherders or horse thieves.

As a follow-on to the Berlin conference, Lloyd organized a CSI conference in November 1999 at the George H. W. Bush Presidential Library and School of Government on the campus of Texas A&M University. Called US Intelligence and the End of the Cold War, the conference featured an illustrious group of government officials who presided over national security policy from 1989 to 1991 as the Cold War concluded. Key participants were President George H. W. Bush, Secretary of Defense Richard Cheney, National Security Advisor General Brent Scowcroft, and CIA Director Robert Gates. Former CIA Directors William Webster, Richard Helms, and James Woolsey attended, as did the current DCI George Tenet. Several undersecretaries and intelligence officials who composed the national security team were also there. I was privileged once again to be invited to the conference that included journalists, academicians, and former government specialists engaged in foreign policy and national security. One of the themes highlighted during the two-day session by various speakers and panels was refuting the contention by some observers that the CIA failed to predict the collapse of the USSR.

I drove to the conference from Colorado Springs and stopped in West Texas to pick up my friend and CT classmate, Earl Tomlinson. I arranged with Lloyd to get him an invitation so we both could enjoy the conference and hobnob with the participants. One evening at the conference hotel bar, I witnessed a small and unusual collection of jovial attendees laughing and reminiscing about the old days. On a couple of barstools, refighting the intelligence war, was Paul Redmond, the CIA officer who was chief of counterintelligence, and Oleg Kalugin, the ubiquitous KGB general. One of the attendees was Floyd Paseman, who was a fellow Officer-in-Residence. He, Earl, and I were old CT classmates, and we all engaged in the merriment. Current DCI George Tenant put a white towel over his arm and served drinks to former DCI Ricard Helms, who was sitting on a couch, as well as to me and Earl—a nod to Tenet's youngster days when he and his twin brother waited tables in his family's Greek restaurant.

It was fitting that President Bush kicked off the conference as it was Tenet giving the closing remarks. The highlight of the weekend, however, was the ceremony conveying the Distinguished Intelligence Medal to Ryszard J. Kukliński, the first foreign recipient of the agency's highest award. Kukliński was a Polish colonel who had spied for the CIA during the period from 1972 to 1981. He provided invaluable information on Soviet weapons systems and Warsaw Pact military capabilities. Also of great interest to Western allies was the intelligence he provided on Soviet intentions regarding the Solidarity dissident movement in Poland. Kukliński was exfiltrated by the Agency when he came under suspicion by the KGB and Polish authorities. Later he was tried in absentia by the Polish military government and sentenced to death for treason. He and his family were resettled in the US under new identities, an operation in which I was directly involved. The ceremony was skillfully arranged with the Texas A&M Corps of Cadets in dress uniform and swords raised, lining the pathway for the procession to the podium. President Bush and George Tenet gave moving tributes, as did David Fordham, the CIA case officer who handled the relationship with the revered Kukliński in Warsaw. His life is portrayed in an excellent biography, *A Secret Life*, and in a film called *Jack Strong*. I felt a moment of satisfaction from my tiny window on his achievements.

Life in the CIA gave me an enormous exposure to people, events, and places; and like the iconic broadcaster Walter Cronkite used to say, they made and illuminated my time. Among the many lessons I learned was the value of maintaining long-term friendships over time and distance. It sometimes meant overcoming differences in outlooks, lifestyles, and politics while highly regarding what is truly important in relationships. Unlike some who leave jobs with bitterness, I left my career with a tremendous sense of pride and gratitude that I could serve the country as an intelligence officer in the CIA. My colleagues and I always felt that we were joined in a mission much more significant than ourselves. It fulfilled my early dreams in a way I didn't comprehend when contemplating the right career path. I am forever grateful that an index card, posted on a University of Illinois bulletin board with the phone number of a CIA recruiter, caught my attention.

Part Four

2000–202?

THE GOLDEN YEARS

The conventional wisdom when approaching retirement is to have a plan about how to spend the coming years. My career and overseas assignments limited my time to stay in touch with people who were important to me, so a major priority for me was to strengthen my relationships with family and friends. The advent of email and cell phones made this task a lot easier than when letter writing and expensive long-distance telephone calls were the primary means of communication. My daughters were entering new phases in their lives, and following their journeys would be of great interest, especially with grandchildren on the horizon.

Other priorities were reconnecting to my roots in southern Illinois, renewing connections to the church, and staying somewhat current with the rapid changes in technology. Important for both Elizabeth and me was exploring more of the world through trips abroad. In this regard, we eventually were able to visit sixty countries and six continents. I also realized that it was necessary at the outset to engage in those activities and sports that required some vigor. Another interest was to try my hand at writing family histories

Chapter 32

PERSPECTIVE ON THE DECADES FROM 2000 TO 2020

The first decade of the twenty-first century was shaped by a range of domestic and international challenges. On the political front, the election of 2000 continued the alternating pattern of one political party succeeding the other in the Oval Office. Republican George W. Bush replaced Bill Clinton and started his presidency in January 2001. President Bush's legacy was shaped in part by the terrorist attacks on September 11, 2001. This 9-11 tragedy was the cause of my return to the CIA, along with many of my former colleagues. My five-year career extension brought new experiences under much different circumstances than my previous assignments. The subsequent war in Afghanistan to remove the threat of the al-Qaeda terrorist organization that carried out the attacks resulted in a protracted twenty-year engagement. A second war commenced two years later when the US invaded Iraq to eliminate what proved to be nonexistent nuclear weapons. This war was followed by a new round of crises in the Middle East as the region remained a chessboard of ethnic, religious, and political conflicts.

Meanwhile, China experienced dramatic economic growth and became the second largest economy in the world. In addition, China increased its geopolitical influence, often in conflict with US interests. In Russia, Putin consolidated his power as an authoritarian kleptocrat and challenged Western democracies with his belligerence and efforts to expand Russia's sphere of influence.

Barack Obama was elected to the presidency in 2008 as a Democrat and was later elected to a second term in 2012. Foreign policy issues during his time in office remained pretty much the same. He inherited a significant economic recession when he took office, which had been brought about by an accumulation of financial mismanagement problems in both the public and private sectors. His primary policy achievement was controversial legislation that brought about broader access to health care.

A long-simmering issue politically was a sense among many blue-collar workers that their interests were being ignored. Corporate money and lobbying efforts in the late 1980s and early 1990s started the movement of US manufacturing operations offshore. Unemployment and wage stagnation contributed to a dramatic increase in wealth inequality and a distrust of government and elitism. In the election of 2016, television celebrity Donald Trump exploited the prevailing alienation and was elected president with bombast and iconoclasm. The election was marred by the disinformation campaign orchestrated by Russian President Vladimir Putin. Social media became the vehicle for misinformation and other societal abuses.

During Trump's term in office, the major event was the worst world pandemic in over a hundred years. The coronavirus, labeled COVID-19, caused a devastating health crisis and the loss of a million lives in the US, more than in any country. After a tumultuous four years and two impeachments, Trump was defeated for reelection in 2020 by Democrat

Joe Biden. Trump's refusal to accept the election's outcome led to an insurrection on January 6, 2021, when a mob stormed the US Capitol. This date ranked among the four worst days in the US during my lifetime, along with the 1963 assassination of President John Kennedy, the 1968 riots following the assassinations of Martin Luther King and Robert Kennedy, and the terrorist attacks of September 11, 2001.

The cloud of political division that dominated the media and public discourse continued as we entered the century's third decade. Unfortunately, the divide inhibited efforts to deal with many of the nation's pressing issues, including climate change, immigration, education, health care, income inequality, and poverty. Cultural issues regarding race, identity, and religion dominated much of the political discussion. A potential bright spot was new technologies that continued to be transformative. Smartphones, the dominance of the Internet in business and commerce, the growth of electric vehicles, medical breakthroughs, and new adventures in space contributed to advances in almost all fields of endeavor. The downside on the international front was Vladimir Putin's orchestration of Russia's second invasion of Ukraine in 2022. Branded an international pariah, Putin's war disrupted a relatively stable global order that had prevailed since the end of the Cold War in 1991.

Chapter 33

FAMILY

Elizabeth and I settled into life in our neighborhood in Colorado Springs as I retired and she started a new career. After sitting for the bar exam in Colorado, Elizabeth was faced with choices for her future. Moving away from the software field of her two previous jobs, she developed her expertise in a new industry to later become a leading expert on natural gas transportation and safety. During her seventeen years working for the El Paso Corporation, Elizabeth developed a unique skill set around energy pipeline safety, integrity, and management. A larger company purchased El Paso in 2012, so Elizabeth decided to take a severance and considered retirement. Her network of contacts convinced her otherwise, and she launched her own consulting firm. Over the next decade she contracted with a number of clients to provide her expertise on issues of concern to the pipeline industry. Her clients ranged from large utility and energy companies to state governments and Native American tribes. As she traveled throughout the United States, she established a network with energy experts and other consultants. She received recognition in her field and received numerous invitations for speaking engagements. In addition to enjoying her work, her own company gave her a rewarding and lucrative extension of her career.

Jackie and Shawn, 2000

Daughters

One of my greatest pleasures in retirement was seeing my daughters become capable young women as they pursued their careers, marriages, and family. Jackie was the first to get married, and she and Shawn held their wedding on the shores of Lake Geneva, Wisconsin, in 2000. It was a grand affair at a venue on the lakeshore, and over 150 guests attended. They returned to their jobs in Denver, where they purchased a small condo.

O'Shea family, 2017

One of Jackie's early jobs was serving as the director of a Montessori school in Denver. Shawn worked for a start-up company called eCollege, a firm that helped colleges put courses on the Internet. Shawn developed his computer skills at this firm, but he had other ambitions and decided to pursue a graduate degree at the University of New South Wales in Sydney, Australia. Jackie was not that thrilled with what she was doing and eagerly supported the move to Australia; it followed, of course, that Elizabeth and I visited them in the summer of 2001.

Back in Denver in 2002, Shawn launched a new career in sports clothing, starting with Pearl Izumi. He later took a job with Under Armour, and he and Jackie moved to Baltimore, Maryland, for a four-year period. His big break came in 2009 when Zoot Sports hired him in Carlsbad, California, as a director for operations. A few years later, he and a partner took over ownership of the company.

Front: Maple, Jackie, and Sydney
Back: Stella and Piper
2020

Jackie left the workforce in Denver and became a full-time mother, starting with the birth of Sydney Lynn in 2006. Elizabeth and I made it to the hospital just in time for the occasion. Shortly thereafter, the little family moved to Baltimore for a four-year period. During that time, Sydney was blessed with two sisters. Piper Ray was born on October 14, 2007, and on March 5, 2010, Stella Roy arrived. The family moved to California in 2010, and some time passed before another sister joined the family. Maple June was born on June 28, 2016, and rounded out the family with four sisters. All came with blond hair, so they looked right at home in southern California. They all became excellent swimmers, following in their athletic parents' footsteps. The girls were also competitive gymnasts. The location of their house, which was within walking distance to the beach, was not a coincidence since Shawn had this in mind long before their relocation from Maryland.

Christy and Joe, 2005

Christy was a career professional who had various jobs when she returned to Minneapolis after her graduation from the University of Virginia. While working full-time, she received her MBA from the University of Minnesota. With credentials in hand, she moved to New York City in 1999 to experience life in Manhattan's fast lane. When we visited her there in 2000, she took us on a tour to include the view from the top of the World Trade Center. On a visit a few years later we visited the memorial to those who died when terrorists destroyed the World Trade Center's Twin Towers. Christy returned to Minneapolis in 2001 and

Joe, Christy, Esme, Finley, and Avery in Munich, 2019

gave birth to Avery Linden born June 26, 2001. Avery's dad is Christy's longtime friend Paul Linden, a dedicated and caring co-parent.

In 2005 Christy married Joe Carlson, a high school teacher who taught history and economics. Joe is also a gifted athlete and played hockey at his alma mater, St. John's University. He later studied in Russia and received his MA at St. Thomas University. True to his Swedish heritage, he loved winter sports. Also, in Swedish tradition, Joe and his three brothers bought a cabin on a lake in nearby northern Wisconsin that became a family gathering place. Meanwhile, Christy left a position as a project manager at a division of the British firm Pierson to join United Health, the largest health insurance company in the US, headquartered in Minneapolis. Her career advanced rapidly as she became a vice president for product development at United Health.

Joe and Christy bought a home in Minneapolis in 2006, and soon they had a baby brother for Avery. Finley Burke was born in 2006, not long after his cousin Sydney. His birthday on June 4 made it possible for him to celebrate each year with his granddad. Avery and Finley were joined by a baby sister, Esme Mary, on August 19, 2009. To accommodate the growing family, the three sibling's mom and dad bought a beautiful home near Lake Harriet on the south side of Minneapolis. Not surprisingly, the boys excelled in winter sports, and Avery was on his high school ski team. Later, when he was in high school, Finn joined the cross-country ski team and made the varsity as a freshman. Esme was a shining light in a different way. She was also athletic, but she developed her musical talent as a violinist and played in a youth orchestra. She also became an accomplished equestrian and swimmer.

Elizabeth and I were no different from most grandparents in that we figured our job was to spoil our grandchildren at every turn. Watching them grow up as they went through the various stages of their development was a delight, especially since we didn't have day-to-day responsibilities. Birthdays were celebratory times for marking the growth of our grandchildren. We went to Minnesota to celebrate June birthdays with grandsons Avery and Finley. Birthdays for the California granddaughters always featured a shopping day with Grams, as the grandchildren called Elizabeth. In addition, she adopted a tradition of taking each granddaughter on a trip of their choosing when they reached thirteen years old.

Clay City

After my brother died in 1998, the mainstay for Elizabeth and me in Clay County was our continuing relationship with Garold's wife, Glenda. We worked together on renting and caring for our adjoining farmland, but our friendship was a lasting one. One of my great joys was later officiating her marriage to Steve Iffert. Steve blended right in, and we enjoyed many outings together. Glenda fostered a continuing relation-

Glenda and Steve, 2017

ship for Elizabeth and me with her two daughters and their families, who were so important to my brother.

The farmland allowed me to reengage with farming without doing the actual work. We leased the land to a neighboring farmer with good results over the years. To further my understanding of the ever changing trends in agriculture, I attended seminars and took extension courses in

Piper, Sydney, Esme, Maple, Stella, and Finley, 2019

Esme, Finley, and Avery, 2011

Top: Elizabeth at our Clay City house, 2001
Bottom: Tractor house

farm management from the University of Illinois College of Agriculture. I learned enough to know how little I knew.

Garold's son Greg and I wanted to ensure we retained our ties with one another and our families and farms in Clay County. Greg and I purchased a house in 2000 from one of our Stanley cousins that gave us a permanent place to stay during our visits to Clay City. The house had attractive Bedford stone siding and was located on a corner lot across the

Top: Waiting for the parade
Bottom: Parade Hit; Elizabeth with King Sprocket in chariot

street from where Garold and I had gone to grade school. Glenda had oversight of the house and took great pains to see that it was properly maintained and cared for in our absence. Over the years, we remodeled the house and added a new shed for a tractor collection.

One of the joint projects that Greg and I undertook was adding old John Deere tractors to the collection that Garold and I had started. Garold and I had found the Model B John Deere that had belonged to our dad and that both of us had driven during our growing-up days. Garold was restoring this tractor when he died. Over the coming years, we acquired a 1947 Model H, a 1958 Model 430, a 1960 Model 530, and the

Scott, Greg, Pat, and Kim

Model 60 that had also belonged to our dad. I also had the 1974 Model 110 John Deere garden tractor that I had purchased forty years earlier in Indianapolis. We had it restored to join the collection.

Clay City's annual fall festival each September was a tradition for many small towns in southern Illinois. The event was the occasion for us to host family and friends for a traditional BBQ picnic. The gathering preceded the festival parade, and our tractors were lined up in the front yard. Elizabeth, however, headlined the show. She drove the garden tractor, pulling a trailer with our Australian Shepherd proudly looking like a king dog.

In 2017, my nephew Greg married his companion, Pat, in a grand affair in Las Vegas. His sister Kim and her husband, Scott, made sure that

Greg and Pat, Kim and Scott, and Aunt and Uncle attending Greg's daughter Rachel's wedding, 2019

Greg was there to follow through on his commitment. I was privileged to walk her down the aisle. Pat was accompanied by a gorgeous array of her Thai friends.

We enjoyed very special times with my niece Kim and nephew Greg. Elizabeth and I enjoyed traveling with Kim and her husband, Scott, who lived in Florida. Our travels took us to New York City and excursions on the West Coast. It was always fun when we were joined by my nephew Greg and his wife, Pat, as Greg and Scott were always entertaining with their antics.

Chapter 34

NEIGHBORHOODS

Colorado Springs

The backyard of our house on Wittenberg Court adjoined 800 acres of open space with hiking trails, bluffs, rock formations, and wildlife, including an occasional bear passing through our backyard. Best of all was the view of Pikes Peak from our deck. The sun and cloud formations gave us changing and often spectacular scenes each day. Since our house was the first to be built, we could welcome new neighbors as their homes were

Elizabeth with Jane and Brien Whittington

built. The cul-de-sac made it a quiet location, and our neighbors developed a close connection. We had regular dinner parties and almost daily chats. Our gatherings included three doctors, two engineers, two lawyers, two entrepreneurs, and a rocket scientist.

Our time in Colorado Springs gave us many opportunities for local adventures, travel, and time with friends. We were especially pleased to have time with my cousin Jerry Stanley's son Bart and his wife, Kim, who moved to Colorado Springs.

Right: Kim and Bart Stanley
Bottom left: Tom and Joyce
Bottom right: David Kukul and Gayle Gilroy

We had many occasions to get together with friends, and it was a plus that we lived in a tourist destination.

Right: Chick and Jan Mckormick
Bottom: Dining out with
Gayle and Paul Ropp

Top left: Talking basketball with Donn Hammer
Top right: With Gene and Dottie Lewis, master martini makers
Bottom left: Fishing trip with Chuck Coskran
Bottom right: Cousin Jerry Stanley, my farm consultant

Top left: Hiking with Paul Silverman and Lou Mehrer
Top right: Bob (Rupert) Hill at EIU for our fiftieth graduation anniversary
Bottom: Hiking with Brad Guterrez

Our convoy headed to California

California

Our time in Colorado extended to twenty-two years, the longest that Elizabeth and I had ever lived in one location. Our grandchildren in Minneapolis benefited from having grandparents nearby, but Jackie's daughters were growing up in California without as much grandparenting. In 2017, when the girls reached the ages of one, seven, nine, and eleven, Elizabeth and I decided to pull up roots in our beloved Colorado and move to California to be nearby. It was difficult to decide whether to live the next phase of our retirements in the cold of Minnesota or in sunny southern California. In 2017, however, we moved to Carlsbad, California, in San Diego County.

We purchased a home in a neighborhood close to Jackie and Shawn that was two blocks from the ocean, so there was some compensation for leaving our mountain view. Moreover, driving a convertible on the coastal highway in a sunny climate was Californian dreaming. To enhance this experience and meet new friends, we joined a Corvette club in San Diego. To keep our minds from entering atrophy, we joined the Osher Lifelong Learning Institute at the University of California San Diego. The range of semester lectures and programs was outstanding.

Above: Our California house
Right: Audrey, Bev, Carol, and Elizabeth

Our California location fulfilled our hopes of connecting to the granddaughters. Elizabeth was very comfortable with southern California, as we were less than two hours from her hometown and the colleges she'd attended. Best of all, she and her law school comrades were in the same state with more opportunities for fun get-togethers.

Chapter 35

REUNIONS AND BIRTHDAYS

Stanley Reunions

The last of my mother's twelve siblings, Aunt Mary, died in 2005. It seemed appropriate that the next generation renew the family tradition of the Stanley reunion. The practice, which had lapsed years earli-

Stanley cousins, 2008

er, would be a way for my first cousins and their progeny to remain in touch. Starting in 2006, we organized our first annual cousins' reunion. Thus, a new tradition of the Stanley cousins reunions was underway. We decided to hold the event every two years, and on one occasion, 175 relatives attended the gathering. Two of our remaining aunts, Hazel (who was married to Uncle Nelson) and Uncle Delton's wife, Lucille, were the longest-lived of the first-generation children of Cyrus and Sally Stanley. Aunt Lucille was able to attend until she was 104 years old! When I reached the age of 81, nine of my older cousins were still in line ahead of me. After ten years of organizing, our generation was happy to turn the reunion organization over to the next to carry on the tradition. These occasions were an excellent way to retain relationships and pass on family lore.

The Herdes family also had gatherings, but they were on a much smaller scale. The favored tradition of the Herdes cousins was meeting for lunch at a local restaurant. We also developed our traditions for our immediate family and enjoyed very special times with my niece Kim and nephew Greg. Eventually, Greg and Pat moved to join his sister and Scott in Ocala. Florida was also the destination for many of our relatives and friends from Illinois, who preferred leaving the cold winters behind.

Elizabeth's Family

Following our move California in 2016, Elizabeth renewed her relationship with her two surviving siblings, sister, Chris Cook, and her brother, Jim Buechler. Jim hosted a family gathering at his home in San Diego that included members of the next generation.

Fraternity Reunions

When I retired from the Agency in 1997, I received a call from one of my favorite fraternity brothers, Lou Crane. He had seen my name

Standing: Elizabeth, nephew Adam, brother-in-law Jim, sister Chris, brother Jim, sister-in-law Julie
Seated: niece Jackie, sister-in-law Gayle, niece Atley

in a college alumni newsletter and gave me a call after several decades of lost contact. Elizabeth and I made arrangements to fly to Chicago to visit Lou and his wife, Carolyn. This led to an enlarged ensemble of our fraternity brothers, including Cal and Judy Stockman and Don and Barbara Tolliver. At one of our confabs on the eastern shore of Lake Michigan, where Lou and Cal had vacation homes, we decided to organize a reunion of fraternity brothers from the classes of 1957 to 1963, which were the first years of the fraternity's founding at Eastern Illinois University. We scheduled the reunions to occur during homecoming weekend on the campus. The turnout and program were met with enthusiasm and rekindled relationships among old friends. I was pleased to connect with some of my old classmates, and we went on to have reg-

Lou Crane, Cal Stockman, and Don Tolliver

ular get-togethers, often at our Clay City house and especially at festival time. Rupert and Barbara Hill, Donn and Kay Hammer, and Terry and Kim Fortman were in this group. We all were southern Illinois boys, so there was no lack of common interests and always jovial conversations usually instigated by Rupert.

High School

When possible, I enjoyed attending our high school class reunions, typically held every ten years. Inevitably, the numbers dwindled as we aged, but we had good times catching up and reminiscing about those good old days.

Birthdays

Elizabeth and I adopted the German tradition of having special celebrations when our birthdays fell on years ending in zero. Remembering

High school sixtieth reunion, 2018

our time celebrating my fiftieth in Salzburg, Austria, Elizabeth elected to return there for her fiftieth and sixtieth birthdays. The restaurant for birthday dinners was the Restaurant Schloss Mönchstein, which overlooked the city. The view was particularly enchanting when watching the city lights emerge at sunset. These trips started by flying to Munich to visit our favorite places before traveling to Austria.

Elizabeth organized rather lavish parties for my round-year events when I reached sixty, seventy, and eighty. The most over-the-top affair was for my seventieth when she arranged an event at the Garden of the Gods Club in Colorado Springs. Over seventy people joined us, and she organized a program that featured music, a film, jokes, speeches, and a grand banquet. One outcome of these gatherings was the opportunity to continue seeing old friends from different epochs. One such group included some of my close work colleagues. This connection started a tradition of future gatherings for travel and other celebrations. The celebra-

Elizabeth's birthday venue

tions of Lou and Andrea Mehrer were the most elaborate, and at one of Lou's round-year events, we met at the Luna Hotel on the island of Capri off the coast of Italy.

Chapter 36

ACTIVITIES

Church

The intent of moving to Colorado Springs was to have a permanent home. Indeed, we lived there for twenty-two years. One advantage was finding a church, and we joined the First United Methodist Church in downtown Colorado Springs. I volunteered at the church to become a Stephen minister. My mission after the training was to serve as a congregant caregiver. In addition, I chaired the church's parish committee. Elizabeth took on greater responsibilities. She chaired the Board of Trustees and served as chair of the church's foundation.

Dogs

Our location adjoining eighty acres of open space with hilly terrain and hiking trails made an ideal place to finally have a dog. We researched a variety of breeds and settled on an Australian shepherd. We acquired a dog from an excellent breeder, Laura Belveal, and we named the dog Rika. Rika had an aggressive temperament and could be difficult, but she was amazingly athletic and a great watchdog. She was with us for twelve years. After Rika, Laura sent us another Aussie named Sprocket. Sprock-

Top: Rika
Bottom: Sprocket

et was a retired show dog and thought of himself as quite handsome. He was well-trained and made an excellent companion.

New Horizons band

Music

Music was always a source of enjoyment. My favorite genres were barbershop and Southern gospel quartets, Dixieland jazz, big bands, bluegrass, and 1950s rock. I liked symphonic music, but it never became a mainstay. My primary instrument over the years was the guitar, and the harmonica to a lesser degree. My old sunburst Gibson from the 1950s logged many miles over the years, but it was no match for the new Taylor guitar I acquired in later years. Unfortunately, the new guitar didn't improve my below-mediocre play. Elizabeth and I also enjoyed going to jazz festivals, often with Warren and Mary Wildes, featuring traditional jazz from the 1920s and 1930s, especially Dixieland and big bands.

A late-in-life addition in the music arena was joining a concert band sixty years after laying the old baritone horn to rest during my college days. The New Horizons band network was the perfect organization for old musicians, and I fit in with the well-run concert band in Carlsbad.

1999 Chevy Silverado

Cars and Trucks

Trips to our Illinois farm and exploring old mining passes in the Colorado Rockies made it clear that we needed a pickup truck. My first truck was a 1999 Chevy Silverado with off-road upgrades. It was a fine vehicle, followed by another pickup I bought to keep at our place in Clay City. Three more Chevy pickups came at intervals in the following years. Two of these were Chevy Avalanche models I bought in 2004 and 2009. The last truck was a midsize model Chevy Colorado that I traded for in 2015.

The trucks all had crew cabs, so the hiking gang was happy that I could be the driver for carrying our gear up to mountain trailheads for our backpacking adventures. Our vigilant Australian shepherd, Rika, was not to be forgotten, and she enjoyed riding and looking out the window to make sure nothing escaped her attention. Elizabeth preferred to hang on to the cars she liked, and during this time, she drove two Saabs, a Lexus, and a Mercedes SUV. My legacy with her Lexus was an accident that

Top: 2017 Chevy Colorado
Right: 2022 Lexus, Christmas, 2021

totaled her car. I had no injuries except wounded pride for causing the wreck, but now she could get a Benz. This was later traded for another Lexus.

Our cars and trucks were practical vehicles. I had, however, a longtime fondness for Corvettes. My retired FBI friend and Corvette owner Ron Madd urged me on, and I bought a 2003 golden anniversary model in 2014. Of course, it was a convertible, and we had many enjoyable outings on mountain rides around Pikes Peak and beyond. I went to many car shows in Colorado with Ron and during trips back home to Illinois. Ron's car collection included several muscle cars, and he would frequently take home trophies from these shows. In 2017 I made a significant upgrade and traded for a new red Corvette convertible. As I discovered by taking a Corvette driving school course at a track

Ron Madd with Michelle

in Nevada, the technology incorporated in the new machines was simply amazing.

The 2017 Corvette was barely broken in when we moved to California. The dream drive was taking top-down runs on the Pacific Coast Highway along the southern California coastline. Elizabeth and I joined a Corvette club in San Diego that had many activities, including fun drives on winding roads in the nearby mountain ranges. Our club organized a caravan and joined four thousand other Corvettes that converged in Bowling Green, Kentucky, for the 25th anniversary of the National Corvette Museum in 2019. The club allowed Elizabeth and I to meet new friends: Chip and Vicki Fox and Brad and Marilee Thorp. To round out our engagement with cars (or maybe obsession), we bought a Jeep to replace the pickup on our Illinois farm. The Corvette passion continued, so I ordered a mid-engine model for 2023 delivery.

Top: 2003 fiftieth-anniversary Corvette
Bottom: 2017 Corvette

Chapter 37

SPORTS

Hiking and Backpacking

During lunch with David Barber in June 2000, he asked me to join him and his friend Mike Wallace for a backpacking trip. I had done a lot of hiking in Germany, including beautiful mountain hikes in the Alps, and I was happy to reengage in the activity. Backpacking, however, was not part of my experience, but I soon had the necessary equipment to join them. Our destination was a hike up to Willow Lake in the Sangre de Cristo Mountains, the southernmost range in the Rockies that extended from southern Colorado into New Mexico. The hike started at a trailhead near Crestone, Colorado, on the western side of the range. The trail is rated as difficult, and it was a five-mile hike with a steep three thousand feet of elevation gain. My forty-pound pack was not correctly balanced, and I wondered if I could make it. Fortunately, David's son Chris joined us. Chris was an Outward Bound instructor and an experienced mountaineer, so he soon balanced my pack. Willow Lake is in a glacial basin fed by a stream that drops into the lake from a beautiful waterfall. We hiked around the lake and climbed up to the top of the waterfall, where we set up camp at nine thousand feet.

Mike Wallace, David Barber, and student mountaineer

The big surprise for me came the next day when Chris persuaded us to join him and climb the nearby Challenger Point. Challenger Point was named in honor of the space shuttle Challenger that disastrously exploded on reentry in 1986. At 14,081 feet, Challenger Point is considered one of the difficult Colorado Fourteeners to ascend. I felt every foot of it as we climbed the 5,000-foot elevation from Willow Lake to the top on a nonexistent trail of rocks. But it was an exhilarating experience to stand at the top, breathing the thin air and looking across to the next mountain range in the distance. Chris left us and hiked across a saddle to climb Kit Carson, a slightly taller Fourteener. David and I picked our way slowly on the steep descent when a windstorm came up. I looked down at our campsite in time to see my tent come loose from its moorings and tumble toward the precipice overlooking Willow Lake. Once again, Chris saved the day as he caught up with us after his additional climb and ran down to grab my tent and pack in time to avoid a watery grave.

The Willow Lake hike was the first of many hikes and backpacking trips over the next decade. Our guru and trip planner for most of the

Left to right: Glen Alexander, Dave, Rod Podszus, Mike Wallace, and David Barber

undertakings was Mike Wallace. Mike had lived in Colorado for thirty years and was an avid hiker and fly-fisherman. Mike organized adventures for us in most of the major mountain ranges in Colorado. Our favorite backpacking destinations were trails in the Wasatch Range, a high mountain range that includes fifteen of Colorado's fifty-two peaks over fourteen thousand feet. The most famous of these are the Collegiate Peaks, named after some Ivy League colleges. On most of these hikes, we followed trails along drainages leading to high mountain lakes formed by receding glaciers and usually surrounded by high ridgelines on three sides. Indeed, the Continental Divide went through this range.

We set up camp near the lakes and then spent a couple of days hiking the ridges. Some of our hikes led to old gold mines that were testimony to the often disappointing efforts by the thousands of young men from the East and Midwest seeking their fortunes during the Pikes Peak gold rush. To be assured of having trout for dinner, we relied on Mike to catch rainbow or brook trout in the lakes or nearby streams. We carried water purifiers to hydrate safely, and each of us was responsible for an evening

With Jackie and Shawn, Mount Bierstadt

meal. After my comrades soon tired of my old-time harmonica tunes, we swapped stories during evenings around a campfire.

The hiking group grew as two additional guys joined us, Glenn Alexander and Rod Podszus. We coalesced into a gang of friends, and our gatherings soon included dinners and outings with our wives. Rod had a keen interest in the history of the Santa Fe Trail and introduced us to another dimension of hiking and camping in the southeastern part of the state. In addition to our hiking and fishing trips around the state of Colorado, we ventured to Montana to join John A. for fishing on the Madison River and rivers in nearby Yellowstone Park. Another memorable trip was to the Big Horn Mountains in northeastern Wyoming, where we hiked ten miles to a lake for camping, hiking, and fishing. Our burden getting to the site was eased by having a wrangler carry our gear in with his horses. When mountain snows prevented high-elevation backpack trips, we often did day hikes on the many hiking trails near Colorado Springs. Our appetite for these undertakings—or more appropriately, our stamina diminished as we entered our seventies, so we abandoned our more strenuous undertakings. Our first loss was the death of Glenn Alexander, and by the time we reached our late seventies, all of us had moved away from Colorado Springs.

One of my favorite hikes was climbing a Fourteener, Mount Bierstadt, with Jackie and Shawn. They kindly slowed their pace so I could keep up.

Fly-Fishing

My cousin Bill Stanley moved to Colorado Springs from California shortly after we had settled there. Bill and I got together regularly for coffee, and he joined me in taking fly-fishing lessons. Learning how to tie knots and cast, and learning about the intricacies of aquatic life was a far cry from bobber fishing with a sapling pole on the dredge ditch. Fly-fishing never became a strong passion, but I enjoyed the sport and seeing many beautiful locations along the mountain streams in Colorado. Most important was the opportunity to fish with my hiking friends and John A. in Montana. I joined John at his beloved log home on the Madison River for over twenty summers. In addition to fishing, John and I took camping trips to explore the Lewis & Clark National Historic Trail in Montana. We took a float trip on the Missouri River, starting at historic Fort Benton, to see the Missouri Breaks and the white cliffs that Lewis described in his journals. In Idaho, we camped on the Lolo trail traversed

Left: Cousin Bill with Rita
Right: Fly-fishing on the South Platte, Colorado

by the Lewis and Clark expedition and used by the Nez Perce tribe to reach their buffalo hunting grounds in Montana. John was a good friend and an interesting interlocutor from whom I learned a lot about navigating the outdoors, Montana, and his CIA experience as a Russian specialist. Elizabeth also tried the sport, and we used our developing skills during our travels in New Zealand and Alaska.

Golfing

I had planned to continue playing tennis as my primary retirement sport, but I decided to try golf after the Achilles injury. Colorado had a beautiful public course called Patty Jewett, which offered a perfect view of Pikes Peak looking down the eighteenth fairway from the clubhouse. Despite lessons at this club, I never reached even a mediocre level of play. But I enjoyed the game and played with tolerant friends. I played regularly with Karl Ruyle, my Agency colleague and career training classmate, who also retired in Colorado Springs. We had to give up our efforts at the

Dan Bradley

game when his health failed him. David Barber and my cousin Bill were frequent partners, but my favorite outings were with Dan Bradley, a retired FBI agent. He organized a weekly foursome and a guaranteed good time. I had met Dan through work before we retired, and we continued our friendship. Dan was a good athlete, an avid sports fan, and a loyal Air Force Academy sports fan. He was especially proud when his son became an AF Academy graduate. When I reached my mid-seventies, the old back injury from the Nürburgring ski accident caused lumbar arthritis and a ruptured disc. After back surgery, I had to give up golf.

Biking

Randy Schlack, my friend from working in Yellowstone Park during our college days, was an avid biker. He once biked across the United States from Oregon to the East Coast. In 2001 he invited me to join him and his friend David Gillespie on a bike trip in Europe. The three of us flew to Zurich, Switzerland, to start our adventure; that was where Randy retrieved euros to finance the trip. His Dad, who had died a few years earlier, had left funds for him in a Swiss bank account.

Swiss Alps, biking with Randy Schlack
(left) and David Gellispie (right)

We planned to watch the Tour de France as it went through the Alsace region in France, so we drove there in a van with our bikes attached to the rear. After biking in the foothills of the Vosges Mountains, we found a small village through which the tour passed. The road through the town had a right-hand turn where a pub was conveniently located. We sat at an outside table to see the preliminary parade and then watched Lance Armstrong, the ultimate winner, lead the peloton as they rounded the corner in front of us. The next day we drove to the town of Colmar on the Rhine River and joined the huge crowd gathered to watch the bikers conclude that day of their ride. After the Tour de France, we returned to Switzerland to ride our bikes in some picturesque valleys. One of the villages where we stayed was Gruyére, where we feasted on their brand of cheese in a large pot of fondue. The high point of the trip was a visit to the town of Zermatt at the foot of the Matterhorn, one of the tallest peaks in the Alps.

The trip with Randy was the first of two more biking trips in Europe that we took together in 2003 and 2005. On these trips we spent time in Austria and southern Germany, as well as Switzerland. However, my favorite overseas biking adventure was a trip Elizabeth and I took to Ireland in 2006. We joined a tour group organized by a former bike racer who ran a dairy farm as his primary business. We flew into Galway and took a bus to his small village, where our ride started. The first day turned out to be a real test, as we rode forty miles on small winding roads in the rain. Our guide, who had the advantage of his motorcycle, would monitor our progress as we rode among the stragglers. If the introduction was a bit unpleasant, the rest of the trip was magnificent. The beauty of the Irish countryside was followed by seeing the rugged coastline. We rode through the Burren, a coastal region with a moonscape-like surface made of limestone. Along the shoreline were the spectacular Cliffs of Moher. A highlight each day was a pub lunch, usually accompanied by a Guinness fresh from the tap. We usually were able to find a pub each evening to hear very entertaining Celtic music. After riding around Galway Bay, we enjoyed our stay at a spa hotel. We encountered and had an enjoyable conversation with the American actress Kathy Bates, who was in Galway for a film festival.

Basketball

Although I never played organized ball, basketball remained my favorite sport. Elizabeth and I started attending the NCAA regional tournaments that soon became known as March Madness. I enjoyed returning to Illinois to watch the Fighting Illini during the season, but it also allowed me to see Glenda's three grandchildren play basketball. Allison,

Kay and Donn Hammer

Landon, and Lanie all excelled on the court at their Flora, Illinois, high school. A major factor in returning to Illinois for basketball was my old friend and fraternity brother Donn Hammer. Donn and his wife, Kay, were huge fans, and his son Ryan was a standout player at Southern Illinois University. Donn was elected to the Illinois Basketball Hall of Fame for his support and engagement with the sport.

Hunting

My hunting experience was mainly limited to hunting squirrels during my high school days. However, when we lived in Texas, I continued to follow the tradition of "when in Rome, do as the Romans," and I took up bird hunting with my old friend and colleague Earl Tomlinson. We usually hunted dove and quail on his West Texas ranch. I liked hunting the elusive quail, although my shooting prowess meant they were not endangered. Later, on trips back to Illinois, I joined my cousin Dale Stanley and other friends to hunt on familiar farms. Lance Kauble and Craig Carder, my brother's sons-in-law, introduced me to hunting the eastern

With ace hunting guide, Lance Kauble

wild turkey found in southern Illinois. Thanks to their guidance, I managed to bag one. I was never interested in hunting big game, but I enjoyed skeet and trap shooting, especially during our time in Colorado.

Chapter 38

TRAVEL

Foreign Travel

Elizabeth and I knew that traveling to other countries would be important from the very beginning of our relationship. Over the years, we tried to take a trip abroad each year. We planned most of these trips ourselves. The advent of the Internet made these undertakings much more manageable than relying on letters and expensive overseas phone calls required in earlier times. By the end of the first decade of my retirement, we began to take planned tours on cruise lines. The logistics were far easier to manage, and we expanded our reach to more exotic places than our favorite European venues. After our previous tours to Israel and the Middle

Pyramid at Giza, Egypt

Saint Basil's Cathedral, Red Square, Moscow

East, we discovered an Italian cruise line called Silversea that was very much to our liking.

Our initial outing with Silversea was a tour that took us around the Baltic Sea to many countries we had not visited. This trip took us to St. Petersburg in Russia, where we booked a side trip to Moscow. I never thought that I would ever set foot in this capital city where Soviet military and espionage operations had been planned, a significant focus during my working days. There were no untoward incidents as we marched around Red Square and walked inside the Kremlin walls. Most

From the deck of the Marina Bay Sands, Singapore

of the older historic Kremlin buildings, including the landmark Saint Basil's Cathedral, have been well preserved. Other treasures, however, were destroyed and replaced by Khrushchev's monstrosity called the Grand Kremlin Palace. It was disappointing that Vladimir Putin didn't come out of his office to greet us.

Our next Silversea cruise was our first-time visit to Asia in the summer of 2016. Starting in Singapore, we went around the west side of the former Indochina with stops in Malaysia, Thailand, and Burma before crossing the Indian Ocean to Sri Lanka and India, then westward to Dubai. In Burma, or more appropriately Myanmar, we traveled to the interior city of Bagan for an unforgettable visit to the valley of two thousand temples.

Myanmar, as a whole, was in stark contrast to our later visit to the most modern city in the world, Dubai. The trip challenged my Eurocentric view of the world and prompted a vow to return.

Two years later, we went to China. After a few days in Shanghai, we flew to China's most notable tourist destinations, including a boat trip on the Yangtze to see the Three Gorges Dam. After a hike on the Great

Big Buddha, Phuket, Thailand

Wall, we walked around Tiananmen Square and other sites in Beijing. After marveling at the terra-cotta soldiers in Xian, we completed our tour in Hong Kong. Fortunately, all of this occurred before the COVID-19 pandemic and the stiffening political and military relationship between China and the US, complicated by Chinese President Xi Jinping anointing himself as the permanent leader.

Top: Bagan temples, Mandalay, Myanmar
Bottom: Shwedagon Pagoda, Yangon, Myanmar

Top: Piazza San Marco, Venice, Italy
Bottom: Great Wall, China

Above: Tiananmen Square, Beijing
Right: Brandenburg Gate, Berlin

And we always enjoyed returning to Europe over the years to visit old and new places of interest.

We were lucky in early 2020 to take another Silversea voyage to Latin America before the COVID-19 pandemic brought travel to a halt. One of our long-term objectives was to traverse the Panama Canal and see the Machu Picchu ruins in the Peruvian Andes. Both the ancient-world wonder and the industrial-age wonder were marvels indeed.

Top: Panama Canal
Bottom: Machu Picchu, Peru

With the Carlsons, Arc de Triomphe, Paris

In the summer of 2019, we took the Carlson family to spend a week each in the cities of Munich and Paris. Munich was somewhat obligatory as we wanted to share with the grandchildren a bit of what our lives were like when we had lived there long ago. The second week in Paris was quite in contrast to the immersion in Germanic culture. Still, the adventure was equally rewarding to see how the young people responded to the experience.

Chapter 39

OMEGA

The downside of longevity is dealing with the ultimate challenge of loved ones dying. Often, like my brother, they died too soon. Too many important friends managed to precede my knocking at the pearly gate. One of the first to take that path was Jerry Greer. Among others of my vintage who followed were colleagues and good friends Lloyd Salvetti, John Aalto, Karl Ruyle, Earl Walker, David Duberman, and Jon Wilson. Equally important to me were the losses of old friends Barry Guinagh, Lou Crane, Lou Schmitt, Jim Long, and many cousins.

Lou Crane and Carolyn

Top: John Aalto
Bottom: Lloyd Salvetti

Top: Karl and Karen Ruyle (standing)
Bottom: Barry Guinagh and Becky

Top: Earl Walker
Bottom: Jim Long

Top: David Duberman and Inger
Bottom: Butch Swanstrom and Judy

Epilogue

On June 5, 2023, my birthday will mark fourscore and three years that have given me the privilege to live the American Dream. Any pearls of wisdom I have were evident, I hope, within the context of this story. I can repeat in some form lessons that bear consideration. Family and friendships are our most valuable assets. Honor tradition, and accept that learning is a lifetime proposition. Physical activity, including sports and exercise, and developing all corners of the brain should be paramount. Even if it doesn't come naturally, curiosity is a trait to be nurtured. Music ought to be a daily engagement, if only in the listening. Although we live in a secular society, the spiritual dimension should in some way be incorporated. Last, but not least, a happy marriage may be the best of all. While striving for perfection, accept that we have limitations and that the human condition is such that the same applies to both society and nations.

The Smith Cemetery on a lonely Clay County hill in Illinois is where four generations of the Herdes clan are buried, including my dad, mom, and brother. The Long Gravel Road, still graveled, will end at this place, only a mile from the farm where I was born.

Our family 2022